INDIVIDUALISM AND PUBLIC LIFE

Individualism and Public Life

— *A Modern Dilemma* —

RALPH KETCHAM

Basil Blackwell

Copyright © Ralph Ketcham 1987

First published 1987

Basil Blackwell Inc.
432 Park Avenue South, Suite 1503
New York, NY 10016, USA

Basil Blackwell Ltd
108 Cowley Road, Oxford, OX4 1JF, UK

Library of Congress Cataloging in Publication Data

Ketcham, Ralph Louis, 1927–
   Individualism and public life.

   Includes index.
    1. United States——Politics and government——1945–
2. Individualism.   3. Self-interest.   I. Title.
JK261.K47   1987   320.5′12   87-20944
ISBN 0-631-15773-5

British Library Cataloguing in Publication Data

   Ketcham, Ralph
   Individualism and public life : a modern
   dilemma.
   1. Social role —— United States
   2. Individualism —— United States
   I. Title
   302.5′0973   HN59.2

   ISBN 0-631-15773-5

Typeset in 11/13pt Baskerville by
System 4 Associates, Gerrards Cross, Buckinghamshire
Printed in the USA

Contents

3 East Asian Counterpoint: The Shadow of Confucius

4 Individualism and the Public Interest in the 1980s

Preface

Ours is generally a non-political age. This is, ironically, in part because American public life, especially since World War II, has been a success of sorts. People have been able to direct their energies in other than political ways partly because dire public threats or crises have not much intruded. Americans have not been called to the barricades or felt the oppression of dictatorships or even been asked to pull together in serious or sacrificial ways to cope with common problems. We have been materially well-off, unthreatened from without, moderately governed, and untouched by the sort of traumas that have afflicted China, Iran, Poland, Korea, Argentina, Israel, Lebanon, Bangladesh, Cuba, Ethiopia, Spain, the Philippines, and so many other nations that have either been poorly or harshly governed, or perhaps simply had natural or geopolitical bad luck. This is a blessing, of course, for which we can be thankful. Indeed, more than that, it is a benefit we can properly, and pridefully, in part ascribe to our political institutions and to the fairness and good sense that have often characterized our public life. Because we have a political system that is in many ways admirable, and a reasonably responsive citizenry (including a useful, goading awareness of the nation's many flaws), we have gone along comparatively well, all things considered.

So much, in fact, have Americans experienced openness and variety that they tend often to be entirely preoccupied with private existences, and even to suppose their freedom and fulfillment to be directly proportional to the absence of government in their lives. Lack of contact with government bureaus or law enforcement agencies, minimal diversion of energy into citizen obligations, decline of political party support, and insistence that representatives be guardians of special interests, are all viewed positively in part because they allow widespread preoccupation with the non-political. Countless successful political campaigns pledge to "get Washington (or Albany, etc.) off the backs of the people." In his first campaign for the presidency, Ronald Reagan responded to a question about his conception of leadership with the answer that he would be "the voice of the people *against government.*" Once politics is defined negatively, that is, seen as a means merely for protecting or enhancing private interests, then explicit public concerns become secondary or even non-existent. Citizens of such a negatively defined entity, habituated to see even their own democratic government as a problem, will tend to blame it for troublesome intrusions, to see public-spirited initiatives as masks for self-interests, and to absolve themselves of any responsibility for the inadequacies, frustrations, and injustices of the nation's common life.

Thus Americans have tended to see their freedom and fulfillment as proportional to their relative lack of public burden and intrusion – and perhaps actually dependent on active leadership scornful of governing. We might even say that the United States has practiced government according to "the politics of privacy" – but without noting the possible irony or contradiction in the phrase. Can politics – the life of the *polis* or political community – really sustain itself amid determined insistence on the primacy of the private? Indeed, can individual personhood – the private individual – really be considered as complete and fulfilled in the absence of a public role, a willing acceptance of political obligation?

The central concern of this essay, then, is to see what has become of American public life, especially since 1945, under the deliberate, celebrated ideology of anti-politics, or at least minimal politics. (Even the justification for the vast *growth* of government since 1933 has been pragmatic; government programs are put in place *ad hoc* to restore or enlarge individual opportunity and are not, on the whole, justified by elaborate, polity-exalting ideology.) Since this anti-politics is part of the ideology of individualism, its origin and many-faceted development will be investigated through 2,500 years or more of western history. Then, to seek insight from a culture less emphasizing individualism, the ways of public life and attitudes toward self and society of the Confucian-based nations of East Asia are considered. With this comparison in mind, three basic concepts in democratic politics – citizenship, leadership, and decision-making – will be examined to seek improved or enriched understandings of them. Altogether, then, the intention is to discern a more profound and perhaps, in the last decades of the twentieth century, more propitious *public* philosophy than that entangled in the individualist ethos so long dominant in the West.

My use of the term "individualism" follows Tocqueville's understanding when he (and his English translators) coined the word in *Democracy in America* (1835–40). Distinguishing the word from egotism, or the plain selfishness more or less characteristic of human society and human nature in all times and places, Tocqueville saw individualism as a deliberate preference for being on one's own and for diminishing organic and sustained ties to society. Individualistic society, he wrote, "not only makes every man forget his ancestors, but...hides his descendants, and separates his contemporaries from him; throws him back forever upon himself alone." Dictionary definitions ever since have followed Tocqueville's lead. The *Oxford English Dictionary* defines individualism generally as "self-centred feeling or conduct as a principle; a mode of life in which the individual pursues his own ends or follows out his own ideas; free and independent individual action or thought;" while its definition in metaphysics is "the doctrine that the individual is a self-determined whole, and that any larger whole is merely an aggregate of individuals, which, if they act upon each other at all, do so only externally."

Tocqueville proceeds, though, in a view generally shared in this essay, with a critical assessment of the idea. Individualism, he observes, is an "erroneous judgment...originating...in deficiencies of the mind:" that is, a mistaken understanding or ethic of human life (see pages 138–41). The essence of individualism, then, is not an assumption about the excessive selfishness of people, or oppositely about potentialities for personal fulfillment, but rather is a judgment which celebrates and extols self-interest and self-achievement more or less to the neglect of explicit concern or capacity for benevolence, attention to the common good, or civic virtue. The crux is not what exists, but what is valued and encouraged. As Joseph Tussman has put it, "self-interest and competitiveness are ancient facts of life....But there is something novel and bold in seeing them not as tendencies to be curbed but as powers to be encouraged;...converted [from] ...political diseases into the model of proper political function, harnessing the power of private vice to the chariot of public virtue."

In common understanding, individualism takes the single person as the self-evident starting point for considering the nature and purposes of social life. Society is not thought of as having an organic life of its own that might make legitimate demands on individuals beyond those accepted voluntarily for the necessity and convenience of living in proximity to other human beings. (In the common example, we obey traffic rules because they are necessary and convenient – in our own enlightened self-interest.) Each person is preoccupied with individual survival, success, and satisfactions. Society and government are thus, we might say, the "creations" of individuals, subordinate to their private rights and significant and real only as the context for personal endeavors. People are assumed to have the capacity to take advantage of openness and opportunity, and society is thought to progress and even exist only in the aggregation of these individualities. The whole, then, is simply, and certainly no more than, the sum of the parts. This view arises from and is on the whole congenial to the thought of Hobbes, Locke, Adam Smith, and J. S. Mill – but would be dangerous nonsense to Aristotle and Confucius.

Though there is some over-simplification and even caricature in this definition of individualism, it is, I believe, a roughly accurate account of the assumptions contemporary Americans generally make in ethics, social understanding, and, especially, political or public philosophy. Countless books on the end or collapse of liberalism, and on the self-preoccupied, "protean", "narcissistic," "habits of the heart" of many Americans, all make the same point about an atomized, unsubstantial, vacuous social outlook common in the United States. My intent, then, is to look at the development and nature of individualism, and to understand especially its place in our political attitudes and processes since 1945. Though I hope some suggestions and implications for reform of particular political practices are evident (especially in chapter 4), I am most concerned to outline a revised approach to citizenship and government that might improve the depth and quality of our public life and revive the reality of the idea of a common good that might be pursued actively by the *polis*.

After watching Senate hearings on the federal budget in the summer of 1985, *New York Times* economics editor Leonard Silk noted that a "paralysis has seized the budgetary process, with politicians, private individuals, and interest groups unwilling or unable to find a way to sink their differences for the common good." He then wondered if perhaps this was "the price one pays for a free society based on the principle of self-interest, . . . [for] a capitalist [system] . . . that . . . receives a powerful thrust from the pursuit of self-interest and does not rely on public spirit." Citing A. O. Hirschman's observation that public spirit will atrophy if not used enough, Silk suggests that the United States in the 1980s might need to depend less on individuals and groups motivated by self-interest and more on "civic spirit, morality, benevolence, and a concern for the well-being of others" in its public life. I hope in this essay to lay out the origins and dimensions of the outlook Silk finds so problematic, to probe for comparative insights by looking at a culture that makes different assumptions about human relationships and public life, and then to suggest altered guidelines for concepts of citizenship, for leadership, and for making political decisions.

In writing the comparative chapter on East Asian culture, I have had especially to depend on the help and insight of scholars from that region. In Japan I have had the invaluable assistance of Professor Homma Nagayo of the University of Tokyo, Professors Sasaki Hajimu, Sato Shinichi, and Onishi of Tohoku University, Professors Ide Yoshimitsu and Ide Sachiko of Tsukuba National and Japan Women's Universities, and Professors Okuda Shinjo and Okuda Natsuko of Yokohama National and Japan Women's Universities. I have also benefited from the explanations and comments of many Japanese students and colleagues: Kume Teruyuki, Takamura Hiroko, Iino Masako, Shimada Noriko, Ito Hisako, Komei Sukeyuki and Komei Teruko, Ito Kazuko, Tsuruki Takako, Ohta Kazuko, Mayumi Atsuko, Kawasaki Akiko, Hiyoshi Kazuko, Omomo Toshiyuki, and Nara Noizumi.

President Hwang Byung-tai of Hankuk University of Foreign Studies, Professor Kim Dal-choon of Yonsei University, Dr Kim Yong-bock and the Reverend Kim Kwan-suk of the Christian Institute for the Study of Justice and Development, and especially Dr Chang-soo, Nyle, and Emily Kim, were helpful, hospitable, and insightful during a pleasant and enlightening visit to Korea.

I am enormously indebted to Professor Liu Zuo-chang of Shandong Teachers' University both for arranging for me to study and lecture in China, and for his wise and helpful comments on our common interest in the educational and political philosophies of Confucius and Thomas Jefferson. An Zuo-zhang, Professor of Chinese History at Shandong, Yang Sheng-mao, Professor of American History, and Liu Ze-hua and Chen Zhen-jiang, Professors of Chinese History, of Nankai University, and Professor Kwok Sui-tong of the Chinese University of Hong Kong, also made incisive comments and suggestions. Conversations, too, with many kind, patient, and interesting students and colleagues were very helpful; especially Song Hye-jeung, Paik Hae-jung, and Lee Jin-hwa in Korea, and Chen Hai-hong, Wang Wei-ping, Yang Ping, Li Tsiao-bai, Wang Fei, Fan Yun-ping, Li Cheng-kang, Xue Jie, Li Xue, and Song Jin-mei in China.

In presenting names and transliteration of Far Eastern languages, I have used the following system. The family name comes first in Chinese, Korean, and Japanese names, except for some instances in the source notes where an author's name is well-known in English-language publications using the Western convention with the family name last. Chinese names, places, and other words are generally transliterated in the new, official pinyin system of the People's Republic of China. The exceptions are when reference is to people or places well-known at an earlier date in the Wade Giles transliteration (such as Chiang Kai-shek and Chungking in 1943) or when deceased authors are better known (and in card catalogs) in Wade-Giles transliteration (such as Liang Chi-chao).

Colleagues and students at Syracuse University have also been most helpful. Todd Holden, Amanda Porterfield, Marie Provine, Joseph Julian, and Guthrie Birkead have, to my great benefit, read and responded to parts of the manuscript. At crucial stages Robert McClure, Jeff Stonecash, and Donald Meiklejohn read and criticized the entire work, and thus were able to make immensely valuable comments and suggestions. Klaus Heberle and Catherine Landis also made interesting and insightful observations. Colleagues at the Center for the Study of Citizenship at the Maxwell School – John Agnew, Fred Frohock, Thomas Green, Robert Daly, David Rosenbloom, Richard Schwartz, and especially its Director, Manfred Stanley – have provided support and friendly criticism. Judith Jablonski and June Dumas performed miracles in transferring my very rough manuscript to the marvelous flexibilities of a word processor. And, as usual, Julia Ketcham has been both a much-needed improver of style and a thoughtful critic, from the first surfacing of the idea for this book five years ago until the last revisions of yesterday. Also as usual, Ben and

Laura Lee have endured their father's preoccupation and mania with proper doses of patience, good nature, and amused derision.

Ralph Ketcham
The Maxwell School
Syracuse University

To nourishing and complementary antipodes:
The faculty and students of the Maxwell School,
on one hand,
and the friends of Rapha Community,
on the other

I

Paradoxes, 1945–85

OF ALLIED VICTORY AND THE AMERICAN CENTURY

In 1941, in *Life* magazine, Henry Luce heralded "An American Century." To Luce, the twentieth century "so big with promise for human progress and happiness," had, plagued by war and depression, proven to be "a profound and tragic disappointment, . . . baffling and difficult and paradoxical." To recover the great promise would require the projection into the world of American economic vitality: expand world trade, train huge numbers of engineers, scientists, artists, educators, and doctors to spread the benefits of American "technical and artistic skills," and become "the Good Samaritan to the entire world" by distributing the surplus food grown on American farms.

But these tangible goals would not be enough, Luce insisted, unless "great ideals" were also "spread throughout the world." Some of these, such as "a love of freedom, a feeling for equality of opportunity, a tradition of self-reliance and independence and also of cooperation," Luce thought were especially American. Others, though, "justice, the love of truth, the ideal of charity," were "the ideals of civilization."[1] Some Americans, to be sure, did not share Luce's internationalism (in fact he wrote explicitly to argue against isolationism), and others saw his idealism as a mask for American imperialism. He nonetheless epitomized a widespread aspiration that the United States might use its power to guide the world out of the nightmare of the first half of the twentieth century into the bright dreams of its second half.

A year later, after the United States had entered World War II, Vice-President Henry Wallace found Luce's "American Century" ideal too parochial and asked instead that the eventual Allied victory usher in nothing less than "the century of the common man." This meant to Wallace the spread of modern science, industry, education, better health and nutrition, and democracy. Wallace saw Axis slavery and aggression, corporate greed, and primordial ignorance and oppression being overwhelmed as great progressive movements gathered power, perhaps abetted and even led by the United States, but propelled more fundamentally by the rising expectations of common people everywhere.[2] Although some critics ridiculed Wallace's "unrealistic" hope to banish want and oppression, he, like Luce, bespoke a widespread conviction that American power and good intentions might coincide with worldwide aspirations to enable "the common man" to find a place in the sun.

The most significant and influential American statement of prognosis and aspiration for the second half of the twentieth century, however, was Wendell Willkie's *One World*, written after a globe-girdling trip to the Middle East, Russia, and China in the last months of 1942. After talks at El Alamein with General Montgomery, in Moscow with Marshal Stalin, and in Chungking with Chiang Kai-shek and Chou En-lai, and visits with hundreds of other people from Nigeria and Iraq to Yakutsk and Chengtu, Willkie was convinced that to "win the peace" three things were necessary. "First, we must plan now [1943] for peace on a world basis; second, the world must be free, politically and economically, for nations and for men; . . . third, America must play an active, constructive part in freeing it and keeping its peace." Willkie shared with Luce and Wallace the belief that since "geographic isolation no longer exists, . . . withdrawal [by the United States] from the problems and responsibilities of the world after this war would be sheer disaster." He acknowledged that while abundant natural resources, free political institutions, and "the character of our population" had contributed to American growth, "the greatest factor [had been the creation] . . . in America of the largest area in the world in which there were no barriers to the exchange of goods and ideas." Wilkie concluded by holding up to the American people "the most challenging opportunity of all history: an invitation which the peoples of the East have given us to join them in creating a new society of independent nations, free alike of the economic injustices of the West and the political malpractices of the East, . . . in which men and women the world around can live and grow invigorated by independence and freedom."

Willkie also applied his "one world" idealism to domestic matters by calling attention to "our imperialism at home." That one oriental nation, Japan, was an enslaving enemy, and another, China, was a courageous ally, and that even the super-racist Hitler had been compelled to make common cause "with those honorary Aryans, the Japanese," was evidence to Willkie that "it is not racial classifications or ethnological considerations which bind men together; it is shared concepts and kindred objectives." At home, Willkie declared, this required an end to "a smug racial superiority, to a willingness to exploit an unprotected people, . . . to a crawling insidious anti-Semitism, . . . to the flaring of mob law, . . . [and to] the revival under emotional strains of age-old racial and religious distrusts." The strength and glory of the United States, he added, derived from "two hundred years of re-invigorating immigration. . . of peoples possessing varied religious concepts, philosophies, and historical backgrounds, . . . which has brought us new blood, new experiences, new ideas." In an argument foreshadowing a generation of praise for the blessings of "a pluralistic society" and for a politics of many interest groups, Willkie made a virtue of American diversity and individual enterprise. To suppress any group or people in any way, he insisted, "would tend to freeze society and prevent progress, for the majority itself is stimulated by the existence of minority groups."[3] Thus for Willkie, as for Luce and Wallace, the victory of the United States and its allies in World War II entailed a comprehensive agenda for the worldwide spread of liberty, democracy, and a rising prosperity.

In fact, seldom in history had victory in war seemed so utterly to validate a national culture. Only Britain's triumph over Napoleon, won in the counting houses and factories of London and Manchester as well as on the playing fields of Eton, bears comparison. It, too, seemed to rest not only on military success but more fundamentally on superior values, national character, economic enterprise, and social organization. Total war required total effort at home as well as on the battlefield, testing every aspect of a nation's being. The aphorism that Americans had fought for "mom and apple pie" in a way made the point. The common decencies and affections of American life and the mouth-watering abundance of the widely-shared standard of living were as much a part of the triumphant crusade as were Atlantic charters, big power conferences, and global strategies.

The tides of war as they washed over the major belligerents, moreover, left the United States uniquely validated as well as uniquely powerful. The defeated nations were not only discredited and in ruins; they were seen as well, with considerable justification, to have been supremely evil. Japanese armed forces had "raped Nanking," tortured prisoners of war, and fought with a suicidal fanaticism that revealed an uncivilized contempt for human life. At home the militarists had imposed a regimentation and thought control utterly repugnant to ideals of freedom. Mussolini's Italian fascism was revealed to be a cowardly, bombastic farce, impotent and humiliated in war, and treacherous to the best in Italian culture. And Nazism emerged from the war as the most monstrous, diabolical conception in human history, committing and celebrating genocide, brutality, and cynical corruption on a scale both unmatched and unimaginable. Hitler so personified evil that his defeat and destruction seemed, even with all the slaughtering effectiveness of modern military technology, to have made the war worth it and to have left the victors heroic defenders of humankind's most cherished values. Unlike the ambiguity and ghastly stalemate of World War I, World War II had indeed been *won*.

Furthermore the major allies – Britain, China, France, and the USSR – not only were more ravished and exhausted by the war than the United States, but also were seen as somehow or other deeply flawed. Britain, though at home fully sharing American commitment to freedom and democracy, seemed compromised in the eyes of the non-western world for her too-reluctant dismantling of empire. Also, her vitality and power had so diminished that she was nearly inconsequential in world affairs. Though the China of Chiang Kai-shek had been upheld during the war as a valiant nation fighting for its life and on the road to freedom and democracy, it became increasingly clear that the nation was deeply divided, waiting only for the defeat of Japan to resume a civil war between rival leaderships perhaps equally tyrannical. France had been defeated largely, it was often argued, because of inner rot, lack of vigor and virtue. Even in defeat she had wallowed in a disgraceful native fascism and collaboration with the Nazi overlords. The intrepidity of free France under Charles de Gaulle and the growing effectiveness of the resistance movement in France restored some of the luster to "America's oldest ally," but nonetheless French character and capability could hardly shine as a beacon for the world.

The USSR was in an even more paradoxical position. Visiting

Russia in the fall of 1942, when her people had, despite fearful losses, survived the Nazi onslaught and her armies were beginning to push the Germans back, Wendell Willkie had been struck with the energy, pride, and patriotism of Russian soldiers, officials, and workers. He saw as well a society that worked, that had survival value, and that had in many ways improved the lives of tens of millions of chronically oppressed and backward people. It was, moreover, essential that Russia and the United States work together both to win the war and to establish a lasting peace. As Willkie travelled thousands of miles in the USSR, he also made many comparisons with the United States. The new cities in Siberia reminded him of stories his own grandfather had told of pioneer days in Indiana. The diversity of peoples seemed often another version of the American melting pot. He found the same "hardy, direct, energy" that for a century or more had made Tocqueville and other observers sense that Americans and Russians were kindred people, sure to have an enormous future impact.

But Wendell Willkie, embodiment of frontier individualism, self-made industrialist, and practitioner of democratic politics, had little use for communist ideology. The tight thought control, the severe punishments (slave labor camps and "liquidation") meted out to dissidents and failures, and the inefficiencies of a planned economy, evident even amid the zeal of wartime patriotism, were anathema to him. Yet, he admired what the communists had accomplished in some ways for a people who, as one farm manager put it, "were less than a hundred years from serfdom."

Willkie was even willing that Russia continue to be communist; he saw that as perhaps the best system for the time being for Russia, and certainly no threat to the United States. "Many among the democracies fear and mistrust Soviet Russia," Willkie observed, because they "dreaded the inroads of an economic order that would be destructive of their own." This fear was groundless, he thought, "unless our democratic institutions and our free economy become so frail through abuse and failure in practice as to make us soft and vulnerable. The best answer to Communism is a living, vibrant, fearless democracy – economic, social, and political. All we need to do is to stand up and perform according to our professed ideals. Then those ideals will be safe." "So deep is my faith in the fundamental rightness of our free economic and political institutions," Willkie concluded, "that I am convinced they will survive" working together with the Soviet Union in peace as well as in war.[4]

To Luce, Wallace, Willkie and a host of other Americans, then, the victory in World War II seemed at once to reveal the physical weakness and ideological flaws of America's allies as well as enemies, and to vindicate free enterprise economy, political democracy, pluralism, humanitarian generosity, and rugged individualism. These qualities had made the United States "the arsenal of democracy," the nursery of the world's "finest fighting men," and a "beacon of hope" for an otherwise exhausted, war-weary, and discouraged globe. Americans, or at least some of them, also knew that all was not quite as rosy as this picture displayed, and that the war itself had been won with the aid of temporary restraints on free enterprise and individualism. Yet, to a remarkable extent, at home and abroad the United States seemed to have demonstrated that its values and its way of life were overwhelmingly potent and irresistibly attractive.

This validation of American traditions came, however, in a way that gradually revealed profound ironies. The enthusiasm of Luce and Willkie, for example, required an attention to international relations that seemed to many "un-American." From the first English settlements in North America the sense of separation, of deliberate, necessary departure from the ways of the Old World, had been strong. Massachusetts and Pennsylvania, founded as havens from Old World persecution, harbored especially intense feelings of isolation and distinctiveness. The American Revolution, though in part a war of international rivalry and alliance, was also powerfully isolationist. The Great Seal of the United States proclaimed a *novus ordo seclorum*, a "new order of the ages", and "Common Sense" asked that the new nation be "an asylum for mankind" in search of liberty amid the tyranny that oppressed the rest of the world.

Circumstances after the Napoleonic wars conspired to heighten American isolation. The common Anglo-American interest in the end of European colonialism in Latin America, proclaimed in the Monroe Doctrine, acknowledged at once American separation from conventional European geopolitics and British enforcement of freedom of the seas in the Atlantic Ocean. The effect was more than a century of "free security" for the United States. That is, her need to bear heavy national defense expenditures, to worry seriously about attack from abroad, or even to concern herself intimately with the affairs of the rest of the world, largely disappeared. At the same time, the westward march of settlement and the building of an industrial nation by a flood of immigrants fleeing the Old World and anxious to begin life anew, turned American energies inward until well into the twentieth century. Interpreters of the frontier from Jefferson and Frederick Jackson Turner to Daniel Boorstin found the open lands of the west the source not only of wealth and prosperity but also of the very character of the American people and of the dynamic quality of democratic government. American creativity, Boorstin asserts, came largely from its "fertile verges" in the west. Why, then, court or even risk serious involvement with the rest of the world?

The immigrants, bringing foreign accents, customs, and attitudes to the United States, vastly enriched national diversity, but they, or their children, also sought or were pressured to assimilate. The descendants of the earlier immigrants met not foreigners eager and confident in their culture (and thus in a position to heighten American sensibilities about the rest of the world), but instead met only foreigners who wanted to become *Americans*. Thus both the frontier and the tide of immigrants, the unique and formative aspects of American history, increased feelings of isolation in the United States.

In a way, the very triumphs of the 125 inward-turned years that had followed one era of United States preoccupation with international affairs (1776–1815) unsuited the nation for the understandings and task of the next such era, which emerged dramatically that May morning in 1940 when Americans awoke to learn Hitler's armies had broken the Anglo-French front to appear on the English Channel at Abbeville. Instead of the quarrels of Europe any longer being something the United States could safely shun, both national defense and the protection of all that Americans claimed to value seemed to require involvement in world affairs. Senator Arthur Vandenberg revealed the tension of his famous "conversion from isolationism to internationalism" in 1945. He confessed his long-standing faith in American self-reliance, but concluded nonetheless that the real self-interest of the United States would henceforth reside in promoting "a new dignity and a new authority for international law." He also urged "maximum American cooperation" to make the contemplated United Nations Organization succeed. "I do not believe," Vandenberg told the Senate, "that any nation hereafter can immunize itself by its own exclusive action."[5]

The paradox was apparent: the long-celebrated attitudes arising from the aspirations of the immigrants to the New World, the sense of being a unique city upon a hill, the rugged individualism encouraged on the frontier, and the lack of involvement in the problems of the rest of the world, seemed after 1940–5 no more to be valuable hallmarks of national policy and character. Indeed, in many ways one can hardly imagine a *poorer* preparation for the responsibilities Senator Vandenberg asked the United States to shoulder than the experience, intentions, and preoccupations of its recent past. This ambiguous legacy shaped opinions of both Americans who in 1945 faced the internationalist future with foreboding (some of whom would even reassert a "fortress America" strategy a few years later), and foreigners who feared and scorned American inexperience and naivety in world affairs.

However much, that is, American ingenuity, enterprise, and even goodwill were seen in the world as crucial to recovery from the ravages of war and to the building of a lasting peace (in 1945 such diverse figures as Ho Chi Minh, Winston Churchill, Jawaharlal Nehru, and Yoshida Shigura looked forward to such leadership), equally widespread was a concern about dangerous qualities that seemed just as characteristically American. The frequent caricature of the American as a boisterous, impulsive cowboy inclined toward simplistic showdown solutions, suggested a people unmindful of the subtle and complex needs and ways of others. Though the frontier spirit, rugged individualism, and a candid preoccupation with a higher standard of living were in many ways admired and even aspired to, it seemed increasingly, as years stretched into decades after World War II, that these traits were a mixed blessing. Indeed, as thoughtful observers pondered the events and trends of the post-war world, it seemed not only that the effects of American values and mass culture were problematic, but also that perhaps the very idea of individualism itself might be flawed. Could the notions that all values, duties, and purposes originate in individuals, and not in society as a whole, and that, as J. S. Mill put it, "human beings in society have no properties but those which are derived from, and may be resolved into, the laws of individual men" (see pages 60–4), be impoverished conceptions? Might individualism itself, that is, somehow be a less profound and less humanly satisfying outlook than its advocates could concede or even understand? Could it be that the individualism Americans had long sought – and achieved to a remarkable degree – was ill-suited, in many ways, both to human nature and to an interdependent world?

OF SUBURBIA AND THE AMERICAN WAY OF LIFE

The most visibly significant post-war trend, the spread of Americans out into vast suburbs of single-family homes, embodied long-standing American aspirations: to own a home of one's own, to have a place of maximum openness and sociability for child-centered families, to have good schools and many churches, to be surrounded by landscaped yards. In short, Americans sought to be in charge of one's life in a place allowing maximum fulfillment for all members of the family. Yet, more than any other setting, the suburb put people on their own in a way that contrasted sharply with traditional understandings of community. Except for the neighborliness required by cooperative care of yards, pets, and children, the emphasis was overwhelmingly on separations. Unlike older agricultural, mining, and industrial communities or neighborhoods, the wage and salary earners of suburbia worked at disparate jobs in different places. A sense of common task or common interest arising from occupation was virtually non-existent. Nor did the multitude of churches that sprang up during the 1950s do much to draw neighbors together. In fact, the very diversity of faiths among the new suburbanites resulted ordinarily in families driving considerable distances to go to the church of their choice. The community connotations of parish (in American cities often ethnically oriented) or village church or even ghetto synagogue largely disappeared as Americans took part in the widely heralded religious revival of the Eisenhower era.

As relatively distant shopping centers replaced neighborhood groceries, corner drugstores, and local tradesmen, other sources of community camaraderie disappeared. Inevitably, the natural bonds of doing everyday tasks and activities together, with those living nearby, atrophied as people took advantage of the mobility offered by the automobile to go where they pleased when they pleased. Working, worshipping, and shopping became not grounds for community association but rather further demonstrations of independence, free choice, and mobility – all desirable in and of themselves as people sought release from the kinds of nettlesome restraints Carol Kennicott had found so stultifying in Gopher Prairie. But as long-range and unintended results accumulated, the ambiguity and irony of "suburban community" heightened.

Even such local institutions and enterprises as remained in suburban neighborhoods – local government, public schools, and a welter of voluntary activities from little leagues to cancer fund drives – were often oddly discordant. Local politics often gave neighbors common concerns, but the patchwork of jurisdictions typical of American suburbs had the overall effect of setting group against group as people worked for often incompatible goals through overlapping and unco-ordinated public authorities. The sense of *polis* and a public good was not nurtured in Levittown or Shawnee Mission or Orange County, however much well-intended individuals sought to be good citizens. Indeed it seemed that local politics became not so much an exercise in shared concern for community affairs as exercises in organized divisiveness as various special interests competed for privilege or advantage.

OF EDUCATION

Schools, especially the elementary school, provided the most signifi-cant community bonds. As rising birthrates yielded a swelling tide of school age youngsters, suburban districts built schools on a vast scale. Bond issues were almost invariably approved by district voters, and parents, teachers, and school officials took great pride in the high-quality education provided for the new generation. Though centralized junior high and high schools were often miles away from many homes in sprawling suburbs, and busing became a normal part of life of many students, a considerable community spirit still gathered around school activities, especially athletics. Highly visible school superintendents and principals, together with popular teachers and especially coaches, served as community leaders as their opinions were sought and listened to, and as they became role-models for the young people under their guidance.

At every level, from pre-school through graduate study, sheer growth was staggering, not only in numbers being educated but also in quality and specialization of studies. Initially modest audio-visual aids to education programs exploded until often they were centers rather than auxiliaries in teaching. Spurred by the space race, schools spent billions of dollars to improve and accelerate the teaching of science and mathematics. Large, well-equipped, diversified high schools in rural and small town areas, especially in the south and west, brought more sophisticated education to students long disadvantaged compared to their metropolitan counterparts. Advanced placement and other specialized courses enabled many high schools to offer college level instruction. The number of young Americans receiving two to four years of post-secondary education reached 50 percent of the age cohort, a proportion hitherto unheard of anywhere in the world. The expansion of graduate and professional studies of all kinds kept pace; by 1970 four times as many MAs and PhDs were being awarded by American universities as in 1955.

Yet, along with this astonishing growth, paradoxical forces were at work. The sheer magnitude of the educational enterprise, and the beguiling benefits of consolidation, increasingly distanced what had been traditionally the closest and most intimate of public institutions. Though the shibboleths of "local control" and "neighborhood school" retained nearly universal appeal, actual circumstances, especially intrusive state control and, increasingly, federal guidelines as federal support grew, emptied them of content. Perhaps more than any other institution, the American public school in the middle of the twentieth century seemed to mock the individual and social goals that were the reason for its being. The popular book *Up the Down Staircase* (1964), satirizing public school bureaucracy, mindlessness, and dehumanization, evoked all the perversions and paradoxes.

At the same time the substance and methods of instruction both heightened individuality and subtly cast young people loose from any sense of overarching purpose or meaning. The more sophisticated level of education, together with ever-intensifying specialization, steadily diminished the proportion of studies shared by students. Electives and various kinds of diplomas became increasingly common in high schools, made possible in part by the economies of size that went along with consolidation. In colleges the immediate post-war emphasis on general education soon gave way to pressure that students be allowed both to pursue their own interests and to take advantage of the explosion in the number of specialized courses offered at rapidly growing institutions. The results were huge numbers of graduates at all levels much more highly skilled and trained than ever before, but with a subtle yet fateful difference. The emphasis by the 1960s was almost entirely on the usefulness of the education for the fulfillment and prosperity of the individual. Only in a kind of "invisible hand" way that supposed the general good was served automatically as a result of individual efforts was there any attention to the public role of the educated specialist or to the common purposes of society as a whole. Again paradox surfaced: as large numbers of people achieved their goals of individual learning and success, it became increasingly doubtful that sociable, purposeful human fulfillment was growing in anything like a proportionate way. In fact, an inverse relationship seemed in many ways to develop: the very attainment of the individual goals seemed at the same time to hinder both full human satisfaction and bonding social institutions.

The paradox was apparent in the circumstances surrounding the publication of Clark Kerr's *The Uses of the University* in 1964. Kerr intended his work to be a celebration of what the University of California (under his presidency) and other great universities had become by the 1960s: centers of research and teaching where thousands of specialists (faculty and students alike) expanded knowledge and applied it to the growing number of uses society had for "the knowledge industry" which, in a calculation cited by Kerr, accounted for 29 percent of the GNP in 1962. To capture the essence of this new institution Kerr coined the term "multiversity," to concede frankly that the modern university was no longer "a single community [having] a central animating principle." Though Kerr admitted some regret at this development, he hurried along both to declare it an inevitability that all should at least understand, and to point out its advantages.

"The knowledge industry," Kerr speculated, might be to the second half of this century what the railroads were to the latter half of the nineteenth century and the automobile was to the first part of the present one: "the focal point for national growth." And since the university was "at the center of the knowledge process," it would, Kerr thought, be required increasingly to be a "service institution" to society. "The total system" would then be "extraordinarily flexible, decentralized, competitive – and productive." Expressing approval of these developments, Kerr declared that in 1963 "pluralism in higher education matches the pluralistic American Society. The multiversity, in particular, is the child of middle-class pluralism; it relates to so much of the variety of the surrounding society and is thus so varied internally."[6] Kerr was well aware of the contrast, ironic in many ways, between his idea of a multiversity and Cardinal Newman's "idea of a university" as a cloistered place where a community of scholars might seek the enlarging, unifying, purposeful visions without which, as the proverb declared, "the people perish."

His conception was in many ways splendid. Indeed, it embodied all the liberal, pluralistic, individualized values of the western and particularly the American world-view. Though some faculty, especially from the humanities, grumbled and lamented the demise of the ivory tower and of the liberal arts, the enthusiasm for useful knowledge (which Cardinal Newman had declared a "deal of trash") was widespread and certainly more influential. This view saw the multiversity as the culmination of a progress in higher education begun in the United States a century earlier at Johns Hopkins, Cornell, and Harvard. Finally American universities really had become places where "any person could study any subject," as Ezra Cornell had hoped for his new university in 1865. The burgeoning of state university systems in the 1960s, and the continuing vitality of private colleges and universities, like the impressive growth of elementary and secondary schools, seemed embodiments of the grand ideal of maximum individual fulfillment in a pluralistic society. Far from suffering from a sense of failure or misdirection, that is, American universities saw themselves as the vanguard to adapt American habits and values to modern needs.

That the student radicals of the late 1960s regarded Kerr's book not as a cause for celebration but as a self-indictment was merely the most dramatic evidence of the profound ambiguity and insufficiency in the idea of the multiversity. To the radicals, its technological triumphs, its contribution to the knowledge industry, and its social service were marks not of its success but of its terrible malfeasance. Though much of their direct fire focused on the "complicity" of the universities in the Vietnam war and other enterprises of the "military-industrial complex," with equal intensity the students rebelled against the educational institution itself. Beneath such surface issues as "governance," *in loco parentis*, and racial/sexual discrimination, there boiled a deep discontent with the philosophy and practice of education as the students experienced it. The crux was dehumanization. Whether taught in huge lecture sections by distinguished professors often more intent on their publications and travels than on their teaching, or by graduate assistants intent on *their* research rather than on the learning experiences of their charges, students sensed inattention, disarray, alienation, and incoherence. Accumulated learning, marvelous libraries and laboratories, and world-famous scholars seemed somehow not to be serving human needs.

Most revealing, the discontent was strongest at precisely those institutions that were most celebrated as multiversities. With some plausibility Kerr and others asserted that Harvard, Columbia, North Carolina, Wisconsin, Yale, Cornell, Michigan, and California were the premier universities in the whole world. (Indeed, the thousands of students and faculty who came to them from abroad seemed to validate that claim.) But even the finest of scholarship, expertise, and facilities, it seemed, were not substitutes for certain human qualities. More precisely, it was often the very excellences upon which the universities and their faculties most prided themselves – intense specialization, sophisticated methodology, and elaborate objectivity – that were most offensive to the human beings in the classrooms and lecture halls. The stunned confusion among the faculty, who thought they had been doing very well what their profession and their deans expected of them, heightened the irony of the whole spectacle. How could it be that so great a success story as that of higher education in the 1960s was answered with the scorn and violence of Harvard Yard, Telegraph Avenue, and Morningside Heights?

The questons had to surface. Was it that the values and conceptions and objectives pursued so enthusiastically by Kerr and his colleagues were themselves flawed? Did their very success largely *cause* the discontent and disarray? Was the trouble not that goals had been missed but rather that there was something amiss with goals? If the answer to these questions was in any substantial way "yes," then the antidote needed by the educational system went beyond institutional reform or more funding or even disengagement from some of its service functions. Rather, the difficulty may have arisen from the uncritical acceptance by the universities of the very values on which Americans had prided themselves for centuries.

OF AFFLUENCE

The same irony surrounded the achievement in the 1950s and 1960s of "the affluent society." Though there was still clear need in 1964 for

Lyndon Johnson to declare a "war on poverty," though in the 1970s there was still an "underclass" of 10–25 percent of the American population, and though the percentage of Americans "below the poverty line" had increased under Ronald Reagan, at least poverty had become a minority rather than a majority problem. It seemed to John Kenneth Galbraith and others that the conventional wisdom of "an economics of scarcity" had become obsolete. Relative affluence was possible for everybody and was in fact nearly a reality in the "post-industrial" nations of North America, western Europe, and Japan. Some even thought a radical change in values about work, leisure, consumption, and personal security was in order. Despite concern over growth in population, social injustice imposed by totalitarian regimes, and depletion of resources, it seemed possible that even the "less developed world" might in time share the affluence.

The spread of affluence had a special impact in the United States. It had led the way and had most unashamedly asserted the validity and importance of the quest for material abundance. This, after all, was a crucial component of the American dream, the traditional goal of the pioneer and the immigrant alike: to achieve a higher standard of living that would bestow on individuals and families greater opportunity, comfort, and fulfillment. In the flush of a victory in World War II that seemed so to validate American ways and attitudes, to find as well a peacetime way of life surrounded by well-being on an unprecedented scale seemed a kind of epiphany. Again, the sense was powerful that the nation was on the verge of achieving what had long been sought; success and fulfillment was at hand.

Noting the peculiar congruence between this widespread affluence and a long-cherished American outlook on life, David Potter declared that the distinguishing feature of Americans was that they were a "people of plenty." In an extension of Frederick Jackson Turner's thesis that derived such American traits as "individualism, economic equality, freedom to rise, and democracy"[7] from the frontier experience, Potter argued that the culture and habits associated with the geographic frontier also gave Americans "an aptitude for exploiting new industrial potentialities." There was, then, a prospect of more "new frontiers" as Americans applied these traits to ever-changing environments and opportunities – space, cybernetics, alternate energy sources, re-industrialization, and so on. Nor was the significance of the pursuit of abundance confined to the United States. The geographic frontier as well as later symbolic frontiers, Potter suggests, "stimulated [American] technology and entire productive system in such a way that . . . developed an unparalleled aptitude for converting many previously inconvertible materials and sources of power into forms that also constituted wealth." Hence, though the geographic frontier may have been a unique and lucky American asset, the "application of technological skill" was a transferable trait. Americans were therefore "qualified to show other countries the path that may lead them to a plenty like our own."[8] Many nations of the world, with American blessing and often assistance, learned these lessons well enough after 1945 to equal and even surpass the United States in material abundance and productivity. This seemed to many Americans further evidence that the pursuit of affluence had been a stunning success story: after all, wasn't the whole world eager to follow suit?

But was it really so complete a success? Ancient religious and ethical warnings about the immorality and insufficiency of a single-minded pursuit of wealth were accepted, verbally at least, by many Americans. Was it really as difficult for a rich person to enter the kingdom of righteousness as it was for a camel to pass through the eye of a needle? More specific concerns and anomalies emerged as the nation became affluent virtually *en masse*. Could productivity, and the habits sustaining it, remain strong even as the nation became a consumer society? Could expanded leisure time be used in truly satisfying ways? Would the relative wealth of most of the population, combined with majority rule, leave the still-poor minority even more helpless and oppressed? (Many thought that was the lesson of Ronald Reagan's presidency.) Would the material well-being of millions of individual Americans weaken concern for shared problems and diminish the vigor and competence of their public life? Indeed, did the celebration of ever more dazzling private prospects somehow atrophy effective attention to public needs? Did economic abundance, then, really make Americans a "people of plenty" in anything like the full range of human needs and potential?

The paradoxes surrounding affluence revealed most especially, though, the ambiguous fruits of the idea of individualism itself. Millions of people, increasingly relieved of hard labor and grinding poverty, gave instinctive assent to W. C. Field's famous words: "I've been rich, and I've been poor, and believe me, rich is best." Whether the ideology was that of the *laissez-faire* capitalist in the 1890s declaring that the growth of industry and the fabulous benefits of new inventions would improve life for everyone, or that of Franklin Roosevelt in the 1930s proclaiming "freedom from want" as a birthright of mankind, the assumption was the same: material well-being undergirded meaningful concepts of individual dignity and fulfillment. Yet, at least after the focusing of energy and purpose required to achieve relative affluence, the condition itself seemed engulfed in irony. Far from feeling dignified, fulfilled, or even satisfied, the improvement of individual or family standards of living seemed often to breed ennui, loneliness, dissatisfaction, and alienation. Hobbes had observed in 1650 that human life was "solitary, poor, nasty, brutish, and short;" in three centuries, had man only succeeded in elevating his condition to one that was solitary, *rich*, nasty, brutish, and *long*?

Phrases from the titles of books of a host of social critics and novelists revealed the dark side of the affluence-based, supposedly individualist culture of the 1950s and 1960s. Instead of encouraging a self-reliant individualism, had post-war American society produced "other-directed" masses milling about in "lonely crowds"? Were there shatter-prone "cracks in the picture windows" of idyllic suburbia? Were American cities "unheavenly" places with streets and neighborhoods near "death" because "eyes" of human concern and decency and social order had disappeared? Had would-be entrepreneurs become mere "organization men"? Was "the man in the grey flannel suit" a frightening admonition, not a positive role-model? Rather than individuals having control over their lives, did a "power elite" dominate the United States? Had the paradox of a "radical right" become an ominous fact in the heyday and aftermath of McCarthyism? Did the "hidden persuaders" of advertisers and media manipulators make a mockery of ideals of consumer choice and individual autonomy? Were Americans "hollow men", "one-dimensional" "status seekers"? Was the society one of a nauseous "surfeit of honey"? Again and again critics made the same point: the peculiar American variety of affluence that characterized the post-war decades, instead of being a culture of genuine fulfillment, seemed empty and misguided. That is, the problem was not that Americans were generally unable in an immediate material sense to get what they wanted, but rather that what they wanted was somehow individually unsatisfying – and perhaps socially pathological.

OF PLURALISTIC POLITICS

The sense of insufficiency and disarray in the decades after World War II seemed less at first in politics and public life, but in fact the conventional wisdom there was also breeding a discontent that would thunder down on the corporate state and on liberalism itself in the next generation. For a time the success of American political institutions and practices, first in coping with the depression under the New Deal and then in winning the war, provoked waves of almost venerating analysis. Admiring the style and accomplishments of Franklin Roosevelt, commentators emphasized the open, pragmatic, reformist quality of American politics. "Dr New Deal" could become "Dr Win the War" because flexible institutions and an undogmatic ideology allowed easy movement from one concern to another as the needs of the nation shifted and evolved. One reason for this was that "the vital center" of American public life was so strong. It included all but small fringes of the two major parties and a few insignificant minor parties devoted to dogma or single issues. Missing were strong parties on either the right or left (fascist or communist), and even the doctrinaire parties working within the democratic process in many other nations. Widely applauded works celebrating "the genius of American politics," "the democratic way of life," and "the liberal tradition of America" all made the same point. American public life in mid twentieth century had discovered a blend of democracy, freedom and diversity providing millions of people with maximum individual fulfillment.

The argument of Karl Popper's *The Open Society and its Enemies* (1948) received wide endorsement. The enemies of freedom were systematic theorists, most notably Plato, Hegel, Marx, and *laissez-faire* dogmatists, who in deductive fashion offered final, absolute answers to political questions. The ideal republic, the state as "God working in history," the classless society, and the doctrine of the minimal state were equally enemies of freedom because each shut off social evolution and "engineering" by insisting on final, perfect, and therefore "closed" patterns. Popper argued oppositely that open societies, those emphasizing change, democratic process, and evolving goals, were most likely to enhance freedom, social progress, and individual fulfillment. The instructive political philosophers in this view were Aristotle, Locke,

J. S. Mill, Dewey, and the Fabian socialists. Though Popper was in one sense merely recasting an ancient tension in political thought, he so nicely suited the stance of a free world, hostile alike to fascism and communism, that his phrase "the open society" became the revealing shibboleth for a generation of political analysts.

David Truman, E. P. Herring, John Fischer, and other American political scientists fashioned Popper's argument into a "conflict of interest" theory of how American politics did and should work. Its crucial dynamic was a multitude of interests and intentions spawned by freedom contesting with each other to reach the compromises necessary in a pluralistic society. The conflict of interest theorists discovered a blessing from the founding fathers in Madison's *Federalist* no. 10. They hearkened as well to Calhoun's notion of "concurrent majorities" and to Justice Holmes's interpretation of the constitution as "an experiment" made for "people of fundamentally differing views." Ultimate virtue, they argued, resided in a political system adept at accommodating and counterpoising a wide variety of interests and purposes. American political history is thus seen as a shifting series of balances and alignments that, while not resulting in utopia, have at least allowed countless group and individual fulfillments. The guiding "principle," perhaps ironically, becomes compromise – denying anyone all of what he wants in order to preserve for everyone something of what he wants. Moreover, Madison's insight, that a large country would contain enough factions to prevent the dominance of any one and thus preserve the freedom of all, seemed even more valid in the large, heterogeneous nation the United States had become in mid twentieth century. The notion of countervailing powers, picturing big business, big labor, and big government checking and controlling each other, was the updated form of the conception suited to the modern corporate state.

Madison, however, supposed that the competing factions would neutralize each other and then rational deliberation might discern and act upon "the permanent and aggregate interests of the community." The conflict of interest theory held, rather, that the only acceptable definition of public policy was simply the resultant of the competing forces. This arena of conflict included not only legislatures, but also pressures that could be brought to bear on executive departments, bureaucracies, regulatory agencies, and even courts. The most profound justification for this model held that it allowed the citizens of a pluralistic nation to seek their own diverse goals, their own self-defined purposes, rather than having national goals or purposes forced on them. One could celebrate, without any sense of irony or contradiction, "the politics of privacy." The key operational requirements were that no groups or individuals be denied access to the arena, and that all levels and agencies of government be responsive to citizen concerns. Democracy, in fact, meant zealous attention to these requirements.

Implicit in conflict of interest politics was the assumption, contrary to Madison's, that there were no "permanent and aggregate interests of the community." Rather there were only resultants of competing forces. The only "permanent interests of the community" were equal access to the political process, the ready responsiveness of the system, and the definition of "public good" as the "output" of this procedure. Even in a conception of "strong democracy," repudiating conflict of interest theory and emphasizing community and active citizenship, the argument is still made "to give each individual's convictions and beliefs an equal starting place," and make them "earn legitimacy by forcing them to run the gauntlet of public deliberation and public judgment." There is no reason, in a logic following John Dewey's, to posit "independent grounds," or higher law, or natural rights, because democracy is simply the result of this process of public deliberation.[9] Democracy, in short, is whatever can be done democratically in a pluralistic society (see pages 187–95).

This understanding dominated American public life for a generation or more after 1945, and still has a powerful hold both as conventional wisdom and as a rough approximation of how the system works. In the late 1960s and 1970s, however, such a chorus of criticism arose that by the 1980s commentators spoke often of the collapse or end or fall or bankruptcy of this conception of democracy and even of the whole liberal, pluralistic world-view undergirding it. Though some critics emphasize the many ways access and responsiveness are incomplete, more profound challenges assert that not failure in its intentions but *success* foreshadowed "the end of liberalism." In part, that is, questioning arose not because liberal or democratic or pluralistic values had been repudiated or thwarted but because their application had become so widespread.

For some years in the late 1960s, for example, Lyndon Johnson was president of the United States, Nelson Rockefeller was governor of New York State, Robert Kennedy and Jacob Javits were the state's senators, and John Lindsay was mayor of New York City – men who together bestrode the full width of mainstream liberalism. Indeed, each in some way epitomized what was most admired in pluralistic politics. Johnson managed and cajoled interest groups to garner support for civil rights legislation, the war on poverty, and other liberal programs. Rockefeller practiced coalition politics in New York State to win elections in order to build a massive system of higher education, to put in place an advanced social welfare apparatus, and altogether to establish a model corporate state of the sort admired by liberals since the days of the New Deal. Kennedy and Javits, each representing the liberal apex of his political party, were in office partly because access to politics was easy for the state's diverse population, and because each responded to the various needs. And John Lindsay, walking New York City streets, dealing with its well-organized municipal workers, and expanding social services for its varied inhabitants, performed a mayorial virtuoso in the art of pluralistic, conflict of interest politics. Though there were claims that politicians were not listening and appeals for more effective participatory democracy, their grounds were not the formal injustice of the political system (the five leaders here mentioned, in fact, took leading roles in easing access to the ballot box and in improving mechanisms for hearing from the public), but rather that something was amiss with how the whole system worked out. Individual fulfillment, community harmony, and political effectiveness were not notable in New York City in 1967. The politics of those on the other side of "the vital center," moreover – Richard Nixon, Robert Dole and Ronald Reagan, for example – has been no more successful in improving the quality of our public life, as Watergate, ballooning budget deficits, and an escalating arms race reveal.

How could it be that such highly successful political careers, so fully embodying post-war conventional wisdom about democratic politics, were so soon to lose their luster? Even where electoral victories continued, the sense of confidence and of being on the right track eroded. Though assassination, an unpopular war, and fiscal crisis imposed from outside accounted for some of the damaged careers, it seemed clear as well that what these men had assumed and sought was also somehow flawed. Could it be that a whole approach to public life had at last been revealed in its insufficiency? Was the conception of polity as simply the aggregation of wants, mechanistic, impoverished, and perhaps finally absurd and tragic? Was there some connection between the disarray of American politics in the 1970s and 1980s and the growing sense that perhaps the whole liberal, pluralistic outlook contained within itself serious shortcomings?

OF WORLD POWER

The ironies of the "success" of conflict of interest politics were most fully revealed in the exercise of the unprecedented power, at home and abroad, accumulated by the liberal corporate state that came into being between the Great Depression and Watergate. Perhaps the crux of the problem, and a foreshadowing of paradoxes to come, inhered in Franklin Roosevelt's comment that he pursued Jeffersonian ends with Hamiltonian means. That is, he sought, in Jefferson's spirit, wider democracy and the welfare of the common people, but to get there he intended to use such Hamiltonian devices as a broad interpretation of the constitution, an enlarged role for the federal government, and centralized guidance of the economy. Theorists of this redefined liberalism argued that it was suited to an advanced industrial economy and would allow full, positive use of democratic government to serve the public. The need, Roosevelt insisted, was to be pragmatic: the government would respond to such specific problems as unemployment, agricultural over-production, and labor–management strife, doing what it could to improve conditions but eschewing both *laissez-faire* and socialist dogma.

As Roosevelt's own skill in coalition politics exemplified, the new liberalism seemed especially attuned to an enlarging sense of American diversity. But a crucial change had been introduced into the old pluralism. Under it, as Crèvecoeur and Benjamin Franklin had pointed out 150 years earlier, the American, "the new Man" amalgamated from the diverse people crossing the oceans, would simply flower forth in the open society of the New World. All that was required was to give free rein to the energies of the millions of individuals eager to take advantage of the beckoning opportunities. By the 1930s, however, when "the problem of social organization was most urgent," the dictum that progress would result willy-nilly from "the happy intuition of individual minds" was simply outmoded. Rather, John Dewey insisted, it was necessary to give direction to human affairs through a "conception of intelligence integrated with social movements."[10] Thus, as American polity under Roosevelt's leadership moved toward a pragmatic state activism somewhere in between rugged individualism and socialism, pluralism came to be understood not so much individually as in terms of groups, blocs, and organizations.

But to manage and guide such a complex society required the exercise of power on a scale not easily accommodated to conventional liberal ideas of the scope of government – a paradox Roosevelt recognized in saying he sought Jeffersonian ends by Hamiltonian means. Was it inevitable that the means, eventually at least, would absorb or dominate the ends? Was there something incongruous, even contradictory, about Roosevelt's intention? The success of the New Deal and the war against fascism, and even the progress and general social accord of the first two post-war decades, seemed to answer "no" to these questions; but others pushed to the fore. Did the flaw in both classical, individualized liberalism and modern corporate liberalism, the preoccupation with the parts rather than the whole, appear more and more evident as the scope of power enlarged? In such perspectives would skillful brokering rather than coherent purpose be dominant? (LBJ and Nixon come to mind.) Were the critical and challenging qualities of the liberal temper, so useful in combatting ancient dogmas and tyrannies and so suited to the expansive phases of Anglo-American entrepreneurship, somehow peculiarly unsuited, in the last quarter of the twentieth century, to a wise exercise of public power? If the answer to these questions was in any degree "yes", then once again the ironies of success would seem to be permeating American public life.

The paradoxes were even more apparent in the expanded American role in world affairs that Luce, Willkie, Vandenberg, and others had heralded so confidently in the 1940s. Some ambiguity and even hypocrisy arose, of course, from the mingling of greedy and imperial motives with professions of good intentions. More profound, though, was the disarray inherent in the exercise of such vast power by a nation whose individualist ideology was uncongenial to the larger, long-range, public perspective required in world affairs. In the hazardous, complicated arena of world politics, Walter Lippmann has observed, governments must make "hard decisions. They must assert a public interest against private inclination and against what is easy and popular. If they are to do their duty, they must often swim against the tides of private feeling" (see pages 215–19).

Furthermore, it has often seemed that ideas and practices valued by Americans had problematic effects when projected abroad. Free private enterprise seemed less attuned to economic progress in many parts of the world than it had been in the United States. Technological and engineering skill, generally assumed by Americans to be all-sufficing, often exacerbated social and ecological problems in foreign lands. Person-to-person goodwill, though amazingly effective in some cases, also often failed to accomplish anything like what Americans habitually assumed was possible on that basis. In a way, the individualist ideology seemed inadequate idealistically as well as geopolitically. It injected an often unhelpful self-assertiveness into cooperative ventures, and it both heightened doctrinal dispute with the USSR and hindered a realistic understanding of the modes and dimensions of Soviet world power. In fact, people from other cultures were often puzzled and even appalled at the assertive individualism that Americans both took great pride in and expected could solve all problems.

That for two decades or so after World War II American government, corporations, and individuals possessed material resources on a scale unimaginable and often daunting to others made the exercise of world power an especially revealing test of the values that went with the power. The exposure of American power abroad gave to individualist values, that is, a trial largely absent within the United States. Indeed, the incessant contrast with very different cultures frequently afforded vivid counterpoint. Nakane Chie points out, for example, that the idea of democracy in Japan came to connote a system of hierarchical, personal relationships where consideration is nonetheless given to those weaker and lower, where voting and majority decision-making are avoided, where harmony and consensus are achieved, and thus where "there is neither wish for opposition nor realization of the function of opposition"[11] (see pages 105–7). Clearly, such an understanding questions both the universal validity of western ideas of liberal individualism and the dependence of vital democratic government on incessant, confronting opposition. The acquisition of enormous power, by the federal government at home and by American economic and military presence around the world, then, seemed as often to baffle and challenge traditional individualistic values as to validate them.

OF THERAPY AND HUMANISTIC PSYCHOLOGY

Perhaps no manifestation of post-war American culture more poignantly reveals the ambiguities of individualism than the increasing interest in humanistic psychology. The movement seeks, using various thera-peutic techniques or spiritual disciplines from many different religious traditions, to release people from personal, psychological bondages or "hang-ups" and to strengthen one's "depth self," thus heightening individual fulfillment. Much of the therapy and psychic repair work is group-oriented, but the gatherings themselves, whether sensitivity sessions or encounter groups or support groups or communal medita-tions, seldom exist for a larger purpose than the strengthening of the parts. Instead of meeting to work for peace or improve the schools or fight vice or aid refugees or whatever, thus providing a common purpose within which close personal ties, self-understanding, and emotional commitment might flourish implicitly, the groups attend largely to themselves, explicitly – and perhaps self-defeatingly.

Thus, though the approach often embodies, indeed insists upon, togetherness of the most intimate sort, and recognizes the social aspects of human existence, the more profound implications of Aristotle's dictum that "man is by nature a political [social] animal" are unacknowledged. The groups, in so far as they turn in on themselves in order to meet personal psychic needs, a worthy goal in itself, also strengthen the already marked tendency in western culture to con-centrate on the parts – individuals. That sustains the assumption of individualism, which in fact may itself be unwarranted and hence in need not of validation but of challenge. At its worst, to attempt to cure psychic disorder by heightened preoccupation with self might be like pouring poison into wounds to heal them, a modern instance of what Luther had warned against in noting the ill effects of "the heart curved inward upon itself," the malaise of those outside the community of faith. In what sometimes seem bizarre or even perverse ways, then, the individualism of humanistic psychology affirms social-ness but at the same time often ignores the usual grounds for human association – a shared purpose in some degree transcending the individual parts.

Especially revealing, though, of the ironic and sometimes even grotesque dimensions of the movements for "self-actualization" is the emphasis on individual assertiveness. People are counselled to "discharge" their anger and hatred, to learn to "fight fair in love and marriage," to be "open" in marriage and "creative" in divorce, to "look out for number one," to insist on the "OKness" of themselves as well as of others, and to protect "private space." As an antidote to certain guilt and inferiority complexes these exhortations and techniques may have some value, but in another perspective they seem to mark a peculiarly graphic dead-end. "The trouble with the consciousness movement," Christopher Lasch has observed, "is not that it addresses trivial or unreal issues but that it provides self-defeating solutions. Arising out of a pervasive dissatisfaction with the quality of personal relations, it advises people not to make too large an investment in love and friendship, to avoid excessive dependence on others, and to live for the moment – the very conditions that created the crisis of personal relations in the first place."[12]

Like many other manifestations of American individualism, that is, the drive for self-assertion, apparently so in tune with long-sought goals to enlarge human potential – a psychological version, perhaps, of earlier efforts at individual economic or political fulfillment – turns out to be paradoxical. Again, it is not that direct intentions to be "whole," or to have "self-esteem," are in themselves ignoble goals. Surely on the face of it, being "whole" rather than "a worm" is as much preferable as being rich is to being poor or as being effective politically is to being denied political participation. One can even argue persuasively that inner esteem and strength is a prerequisite for effective participation in outer causes, or even for any balanced perception of the outer world at all. But there remains something peculiarly shallow and perverse about the explicit, self-centered pursuit of individual fulfillment.

The flaw is evident in the insubstantial conception of "values" that often undergirds therapeutic language and the therapeutic model of life. Individuality is sometimes understood as the ability to choose one's own values; at least any imposing or even inheriting of values is seen as an infringement of private rights and fulfillment. But if one asks what the individual values rest on, the answer does not reflect some objective criteria, but rather depends on personal wants, inner impulses, or what makes one feel good or enhances self-esteem. In an immensely popular book entitled *Passages*, emphasizing the protean quality of life, Gail Sheehy asserts that "midlife" is a time to "Let go. Let it happen to you. Let it happen to your partner. Let the feelings, let the changes [come]. . . . You are moving away. Away from institutional claims and other people's agenda. Away from external valuations and accreditations, in search of inner validation. You are moving out of roles and into the self. . . . Whatever counterfeit safety we hold from overinvestments in people and institutions must be given up. . . . It is for each of us to find a course that is valid by our own reckoning."[13] The assumption is the common therapeutic one that the unfettered, provisional self, unencumbered by tradition or institutions or social obligations or roles or objective criteria (generally scorned as "laid on"), is the source of ultimate, unjudgable value (being "judgmental" is also scorned). As Robert Bellah and his associates have pointed out, however, this idea of the "unencumbered" self "reveals nothing of the shape moral character should take, the limits it should respect, and the community it should serve" – and, it might be added, of the political obligation of a citizen in a self-governing society. Thus, the concept of values as arising from or implicit in one's own inner feelings and psychic needs, though attractively pluralistic, open-minded, and releasing, is also in the end vacuous and asocial in a way that impoverishes rather than fulfills the human potential for moral and political life.

Reinhold Niebuhr has pointed out the flaws in a "theory of family life" that accepts the individualist assumptions of the social contract idea of government. This theory supposes that a man and a woman might establish a life partnership and at the same time "preserve as much liberty as possible for each partner." But the organic, generations-connected quality of marriage contradicts this individual emphasis. "The deeply social nature of human life," Niebuhr notes, "certainly refutes the. . . conception of a free individual who must preserve his freedom even in the most organic forms of togetherness, and must be intent upon the perpetual possibility of reclaiming the absolute freedom which was 'compromised' in the marriage relationship."[14] In effect, that is, the very idea of marriage, or of family, in their rich, human meanings are themselves diminished, or compromised or even betrayed, when conducted in the calculating, contractual language of some therapy. Separate and equal selves, assertive individuals, in marriage or parental relationships, are often counselled to ask "Are they getting what they want? Are they getting as much as they are giving? As much as they could get elsewhere?" If not, the advice might well be to look elsewhere for "fulfillment."[15] But such determined, inward-curving of the mind and heart, so blatantly contractual in its outlook, may corrupt and prevent the very richness of sustained relationship that has long been essential to the role (accepted willingly, unreservedly, *whole*-heartedly) of wife, husband, parent, or child.

The point, insists Niebuhr, is that man "is bound to seek the realization of his true nature; and to his true nature belongs his fulfillment in the lives of others. . . . [But, since] the highest form of self-realization is the consequence of self-giving, [it]. . . cannot be the intended consequence without being prematurely limited. Thus the will to live is finally transmuted into its opposite in the sense that only in self-giving can the self be fulfilled."[16] Niebuhr is endorsing the Biblical paradox: "He that findeth his life shall lose it; and he that loseth his life for my sake shall find it."[17] The challenge of this ancient and often honored idea is implicit, of course, in the critical designations given to certain varieties of self-emphasis – "possessive individualism," "brittle individualism," and "rugged individualism," for example – but somehow its point has been largely lost on much of the self-awareness movement. And it may be symptomatic that in the United States, with its long-present, much-celebrated, and (luckily) generally un-damaging (until recently?) tradition of individualism, this movement has been especially influential. Is there, then, something to be learned from the circumstance that a widely attractive, sometimes useful, but basically flawed movement reaches a pinnacle of influence in a nation that has long harbored the paradox of individualism – and at a time when that paradox seems to stand exhibited with peculiar poignancy and perhaps pathology?

The trouble again is that the assumptions and language of many of the therapy/humanistic-psychology models are simply too thin and morally impoverished to nourish even minimal social concern. Other models, of course, especially those grounded in religious traditions attentive to social justice, encourage deep understanding and effective public responsibility. The flaws can be seen, however, when therapists counsel clients to seek out "caring networks, an interconnected system of family, friends, intimates, and community. . . needed to restore and sustain those now-absent feelings of belonging." "Get on a team, get on a political organization, join a church, go back to school, even if you don't want to learn anything," some therapists urge, all in order to find the relationships and "community" that will rescue one from personal psychic malaise. But the purpose of the joining and relating is for the satisfaction of *individual* needs. Hence, for example, organizations such as "Parents without Partners" are usually joined and abandoned as particular, personal needs and circumstances change.[18] One is compelled to ask, what sort of community can exist on such grounds? Is the direct seeking of community for selfish ends (at least that is the thrust of the language) likely to be deeply satisfying? Is real community, satisfaction in human relationships, and responsible engagement with social concerns likely to result from self-oriented, explicitly unstable, and insubstantial associations? And the therapeutic language and perspective are especially enervating in the most complexly social and morally ambiguous of all human activities, the citizen participating in governing the *polis*. Far from condoning the abandonment of role and institutional claims, and from downgrading the importance of the agendas and evaluations of others, public life requires all of those things – and at its best nourishes them in individuals in ways that enhance rather than interfere with or stifle self-esteem and self-fulfillment. Again one wonders whether the assumption and language of individualism, imbedded in deeply needed therapeutic programs, have created serious disproportions in American purposes and self-conceptions.

OF AMERICA AS A CIVILIZATION

In 1957, in an elaborate work entitled *America as a Civilization*, Max Lerner revealed the multiple tensions and paradoxes both in the individualist tradition itself and in its enthusiastic endorsement in the United States during the post-war decades. As a radical intellectual during the 1930s, Lerner largely accepted Marxist and "new liberal" critiques of Hoover-style rugged individualism and of American capitalism. As with Niebuhr and others who had feared for the survival of democracy, though, the great Allied triumph over fascism in World War II not only revived Lerner's faith in western liberalism but drew him into an almost awed fascination with American power and vitality. What sort of a people and culture was it, Lerner asked, that could have overwhelmed Hitler and his Axis cohorts? What sort of civilization existed in the American homeland after the great triumph? Indeed, Lerner's very presumption in speaking of "America as a civilization" measured the elevation the nation had achieved in his eyes and in those of much of the rest of the world.

Lerner searched high and low, probing the past and ransacking the present, for essentials. At one point he summarized that "the expanse of space, the mixture of race, the pluralism of region and religion, the fresh start, the release of energies, the access to opportunity, the optimism and pragmatism of a society in motion, the passion for equality were the crucial shaping forces of the American heritage." At another point, aware of the opening, separating, even atomizing aspects of these "shaping forces," Lerner worried about what might be the "cement" of American society. He concluded, with only a hint of irony, that an individualism uncongenial to a "valueless and normless. . . mass culture, . . . plus the impersonality of a market society, plus the insulation and later the integration of conflict groups, plus the effects of participation on the job and in the market, plus the ideal of equality before the law, plus finally the symbols and hero figures of folk belief – these have somehow added up to the cement of American society." [19]

The result, then, was that America was a "civilization" held together not by "feudal hierarchy, caste, aristocracy, monarchy, state church, religious or revolutionary mystique" as had been the case at other times and places. Rather it was a society that held together somehow, largely, it seemed, because it "worked" for the individuals composing it. Substantiating Locke, recognized as the foundational philosopher for the United States, Lerner argued that more than three centuries of life in Anglo-America had validated the idea of a social compact resting on convenience, individual rights, and enlightened self-interest. Put another way, Lerner held that America was a civilization because it *succeeded*, through freedom and mobility, in attracting millions of people from all over the world who created a culture of opportunity and a higher standard of living. But what sort of cement is that?

Lerner's interpretation, then, is filled with exactly the paradoxes permeating many other discussions and critiques of post-war American culture. The very cementing elements he sees as counteracting the atomizing tendencies turn out to be problematic restatements of the separating themes. How, really, can individualism, however useful as an antidote to mass culture, be itself a source of cohesion? How can the intricate interplay of market forces, however preferable to guild monopoly or social conflict, be itself a ground of genuine community?

How can the melting pot, however kaleidoscopic and sustaining of tolerance, be more than the sum of its parts? How can working together on jobs, however conducive to practical cooperation, furnish deeper spiritual bonds? How does equality before the law, however corrosive of formal hierarchy and privilege, get beyond the adversarial style of the courtroom to social harmony and the equivalent of what Quakers call "the sense of the meeting?" And what if the folk heroes themselves, like Daniel Boone, Davy Crockett, and the Lone Ranger, symbolize not sociability and concern for the *polis* but lonely self-reliance and combative independence? With such cement, one is tempted to ask, who needs emphasis on liberty and individualism? Does Lerner's analysis, that is, suggest a resolution of the ancient tension of the one and the many, or does it assume that the one, lacking substantial meaning in its own right, is simply implicit in the vitality of the many? And is this, finally, a resolution or an intensification of the problem?

One could argue, of course, that neither post-war United States nor any other existing nation enough embodies the liberal, individualist virtues to provide a satisfactory test for them, and hence that the first need is for their fuller, less compromised realization. This need certainly validates the emphasis on liberal values in countries under authoritarian governments (Korea, for example; see pages 75, 165), and it is doubtless still enough the case in the United States to warrant continued concern for liberal values here, too. Lerner's exposition, though, resting as it does on his own keen sense of an unfinished liberal agenda, takes that need into account. He scorns racism, monopolies, thought control, unrepresentative legislatures, and other "flaws" in America's democratic civilization. That the elimination of these flaws would perhaps heighten rather than diminish centrifugal forces in the society reveals, however, that the difficulty is not first with unfulfillment but more profoundly in the argument on behalf of the virtues themselves.

Lerner faces the problem when he admits that, resting on the "atomistic philosophy" of Locke, Bentham, and others, "liberalism built a trap for itself. . . which strengthened the hold of jungle individualism on the American mind." Lerner further concedes that the "alliance" of this mode of thought with pragmatism (often designated as characteristically or indigenously American) sometimes causes "the open mind. . . [to] become a drafty cave of winds" without definite goals or standards. Finally, Lerner sees that the common liberal emphasis on the supremacy of reason, far from itself creating a substantial natural law that might be a cementing ideal, manifested a failure to recognize "the irrationalism of the human mind and the limits of willed human action."[20] Though recognizing these "vulnerabilities," Lerner nonetheless accepts the liberal tradition in its emphatically individualistic form as the proper and valid "angle of vision" for understanding American society.

But what if the vulnerabilities are more serious than Lerner supposes? What if upon continued serious pursuit and more widespread realization, more rather than less serious liabilities assert themselves? Could not one argue that that is precisely what has happened in the decades since Lerner's 1957 celebration of America as a civilization? Could it be that the malaise and disarray and disillusion, words that in the 1980s more often dominate studies of American culture than the positive vocabulary of Lerner's analysis, arise more fundamentally from shortcomings in the goals and values themselves, rather than from any failure to achieve them? And if this is so, then it might be helpful to both understand what the tradition of individualism has been in western culture and to see if there are in other cultures useful counterpoint perspectives. Finally, then, it might be possible to suggest some improved ways to think about citizenship, leadership, and decision-making in democratic government.

2

Individualism in Western Culture

GREEK SOCIAL INDIVIDUALISM

Though Greek thought and culture from the Homeric sagas onward had a strong sense of *polis* and man's place in society, of what Alasdair MacIntyre calls "the self as...a social creation, not an individual one," emphasis on the individual steadily emerged.[1] As scientist-philosophers, beginning at least with Thales, more and more comprehended, rationally and mundanely, how the physical universe worked, one effect was to exalt the human "knower," to find significance and dignity in the being whose reason and ingenuity discovered the natural order of things. As discoveries in art, literature, technology, commerce, philosophy, government, and war, as well as in science, became ever more magnificent (and, in some ways, dreadful), and increasingly distinguished Greeks from "rude and ignorant barbarians," the earthly creators seemed worthy of study and understanding themselves. In the emergence from the darkness of ignorance and superstition, light focused on the "seer" as well as on what was newly seen.

At least as early as the scene from Aeschylus where Antigone and her uncle, the ruler Creon, argue out the conscientious understanding of the state versus the compelling needs of those in authority, Greek thought clarified, and dramatized, the standing of the individual. In the teaching methods of Socrates and the sophists, the critical intelligence of the individual mind took precedence. Both the Socratic dialogue and the Delphic injunction to "know thyself" dignified the human person. The growth and sophistication of ethics, the study of proper individual behavior (however social the context), from Aristotle through the Stoics and the Epicureans to the Roman moralists, insisted that each person take responsibility for his own life by learning to make correct choices. Both the assumption that it was valid for individuals to make such choices, and the emphasis on the personal responsibility for their correctness, moved human-kind away from the immemorial restraints of custom and toward the sense of individuality increasingly evident in Classical statuary and literature.

The point is not that by modern standards Classical thought was notably "individualistic" (of course it was not), but rather that the Greeks made profound and creative departures from ancient custom wherein "most primitive peoples had little consciousness of themselves as individuals apart from the tribe."[2] Under the Socratic dictum that "the unexamined life is not worth living" (*Apology*), individuals were enjoined not to accept traditional authority uncritically. They should instead obey only "the reasoning which seems to me best when I draw my conclusions" (*Crito*). Within such a philosophy (by no means dominant even in Athens, as Socrates' ultimately fatal conflicts with the authorities show), individuals were encouraged to think, act, and create according to their own talents and genius, and to leave their stamp on the world in the form of unique achievement in art, literature, sports, philosophy, government, and science. Especially in looking back from other ages of less brilliance, and perhaps often neglecting the full meaning of Greek political community (Socrates, for example, defied the authorities not on individual grounds, but in the name of the state, and ultimately refused to defy and leave the state), the legacy of Greek civilization has been to exalt and inspire the critical, creative, individual. Other ancient cultures, of course, in some ways matched the Greeks in great achievement and left accounts of remarkable individuals. But, at least as far as records and artifacts survive, the accomplishments, and especially the critical, questing style of Athens opened a unique chapter in human history of vast significance to its successor cultures.

Gilbert Murray, defending the British Liberal Party and its traditional ideals in the years after World War II, declared flatly that "liberalism is an essential part of civilization, the great Hellenic or Christian tradition on which the civilization of Europe is based." Defining the Latin word *liberalis* as meaning "with the qualities of a free man," Murray pointed out that in this sense freedom meant to abhor mean, stupid, cowardly, selfish ways that in fact enslaved people who were possessed by them. Human beings, then, had an individual moral responsibility to prepare themselves for this freedom. Murray also thought it "worth noting that the idealization of freedom is somewhat peculiar to the Hellenic or European tradition. You do not find much about it," he observed, "in the Hebrew or Egyptian or Chinese tradition."[3] Reflecting both the richness of his own scholarship in Greek culture and an earnest commitment to the free politics of a Britain that had just triumphed in the life-and-death battle with Nazism, Murray saw key elements of the western tradition coming from the peculiar Greek idea of the freeman: dignified, creative, and responsible in ways that made an indelible impression on all peoples who share the Greek heritage.

The Greek idea of *polis*, though, is also rich in its connotations of community, of active membership, and of the *public* good. Aristotle's famous dicta encapsulate the idea: that "man is a political animal," that "the purpose of the state is not merely for life, but for the good life," and that the *polis* is the "highest and most encompassing of human associations." For the Greeks, man could achieve his *telos*, or purpose, develop his highest nature, only as an active member of a body politic that was itself in active quest of the good life for the whole community. In Pericles's phrase, the Athenians regarded "a man who takes no interest in public affairs not as harmless, but as a useless character."[4] The Greeks simply had no concept of being fully human apart from the *polis*. To be good, to be ethical, was equated with the idea of responsible citizenship, just as to be tyrannical was equated with the suppression or denial of that idea.

Furthermore, the notion of the political was encompassing and all-absorbing, including within its scope religion, ethics, science, and esthetics. These were not categories to which one might escape from politics, or which one might protect from politics, but rather were aspects of life that were as much integral to the public good, and of as much concern to the state, as office-holding or diplomacy or acts of war. The modern ideas of the state existing to protect the sacredness of the individual, or of art for art's sake, or even of privacy itself, were not so much denied in Athens's Golden Age as simply unconceived. Within this view, it would be impossible to suppose that political participation might mean pursuit of selfish ambitions, or even the protection of personal privileges as emphasized in a bill of rights. Indeed, the granting of liberty to enable active participation in public life was virtually the *only* grounds for cultivating the ideal of the freeman in Greek thought of the era of Plato and Aristotle. Though the Greeks saw the philosophic life as in a way transcending the *polis*, that life itself was thought of as seeking universal (and hence public) truth, rather than an "individualized" truth. This precluded, made corrupt and nonsensical, the idea that liberty might be used exclusively or even mainly for private purposes. To so act betrayed not only the commonwealth but even human nature itself. It was only in the Hellenistic and imperial Roman eras, when politics became so large and complex administratively, that the Stoic and Epicurean schools of thought opened the way to a radical individualism by arguing that "man's fate was solely a personal matter."[5] This represented a sharp departure from the spirit of Plato's Academy, and foreshadowed important elements of Christian moral philosophy, but it by no means supplanted the public emphasis in Classical political thought.

To a modern sensibility there is much that is admirable and perhaps, as we shall consider later, even instructive in emphases on citizen obligation and on the public good, but there are also dangers. Incessant summonses to the public forum, and the large scope of the political, seem both totalitarian and anti-individual. How can a person find outlet for restless impulses, for creative idiosyncrasies, for private meditation, and for all the other uniquenesses in (modern conceptions of) human nature when the public demands so much energy and attention? And what scope is left for free, voluntary, pluralistic organizations and stimulating diversities when the *polis* (the word "state" is inadequate) is thought of as so encompassing?

There are profound ways, then, in which Greek political culture is very distant indeed from that of the modern West – and especially from the bundle of values that taken together constitute American individualism. As Mark Roelofs put it a generation ago in studying the tensions of citizenship, "the modern [American] citizen is a restless agent, a man of energy, with problems, ambitions and a vocation of his own," preoccupied quite properly, he thinks, with these private concerns. To carry such a burden of individual willing and acting, Roelofs notes, "the Greek sense of personality is simply too weak."[6] However much Greek emphasis on human wisdom and creativity exalted the individual, Greek culture nonetheless lacked (indeed repudiated) any model of the *autonomous* (independent, socially disconnected, self-willed) individual.

JUDEO-CHRISTIAN AUTONOMOUS INDIVIDUALISM

To understand the sources of the intense, active, personally willful sense of the individual one must turn in western culture to the Judeo-Christian tradition, the modes of Hebraic thought, faith, and practice that nurtured Jacob, Elijah, and Isaiah as well as Jesus of Nazareth and Paul of the Damascus Road (and the prophet Mohammed too, of course). In the Hebraic mind, implicit throughout the Old and New Testaments, is a conception of the human being as a uniquely valued soul, a private will, and an actor compelled to find a place not so much in a harmonious political society as in the divine, unfolding, design of history. From the Exodus to Paul's Letters to the Corinthians the Judeo-Christian sense of tribe, nation, community, and church contains strong connotations of membership and belonging to be sure, but the emphasis is on the individual's conscious acts of faith, loyalty, and allegiance to the whole. God's purpose, or Christ's kingdom, would reach fulfillment through the commitment and deeds of the faithful; that is, the individuals who were chosen, or made themselves, instruments of the divine will. Stories of zealous individuals, exertions by the faithful, heroic acts of will, emphasis on the name and genealogy of particular persons characterize the Bible. It is thus not a Greek-style philosophic treatise but a *record* of the deeds of men and women. Greek and Roman storytellers from Homer to Plutarch and from Livy to Suetonius evoked vivid heroes, villains, and odysseys, but without the Hebraic exaltation of the faithful individual.

The Christian version of the Hebraic world-view departed more radically from Classical understandings of human nature and of political obligation. Emphasizing moral and especially spiritual values, the Christian gospel declared the unique and inviolable worth of every person in the sight of God. The greatest good, indeed, the only good of real moment, was the salvation of the individual soul, an essentially inner experience of the grace of God through the mediation of Christ, the personal savior. Piety, trusting faith, love of God and neighbor, humility, purity, and a pervading other-worldliness became the cherished qualities. They were the pathways to the only thing that mattered – immortality through acquiescence in the will and purpose of God as revealed in the life and teaching and sacrifice of Jesus. Though the dominant institutional Church, with its hierarchical and parish organization, continued to embody important Classical social concepts, intentions always focused, whatever the ritual or dogma, on the salvation of the individual soul.

The Classical (especially Stoic) and Hebraic-Christian virtues in some respects overlapped, of course, but the difference in emphasis between Aristotle's *Ethics* and the Sermon on the Mount was large and important. Jesus's question, "What is a man advantaged, if he gain the whole world, and lose himself, or be cast away?"[7] would not so much have been answered differently by Aristotle, as simply unasked. The separation of the self from the world, the implication that somehow purpose and fulfillment required such distinction, or that there was something ultimately precious or sacred in the individual as over against worldly or public concerns, would have made little sense to Pericles or Augustus or in some ways even to Epicurus or Zeno the Stoic. Then, when Jesus made the distinction more explicit by declaring that man should "render therefore unto Caesar the things which are Caesar's, and unto God the things that are God's,[8] the contrast between the Judeo-Christian and the Greco-Roman outlook becomes stark indeed. The difference was between Aristotle's ideal, good life of rational contemplation, the Golden Mean, and concern for the *polis*, and Jesus's injunction that "except a man be born again, he cannot see the kingdom of God."[9]

In Christian doctrine, being "born again" was an individual experience that certainly had no necessary connection with public, political life, and in fact carried strong implications of separation from and even hostility to it. Like the prophets of Israel, Jesus of Nazareth insisted on individual soul-searching and righteousness that was not only distinct from politics, but was pre-eminent to it and thus provided the guidelines, set the standards and goals, for public life. This introduced a limitation and tension in the shared (political) life of every righteous and faithful person: to "render unto God" what was His, meant, necessarily, defining Caesar's sphere in terms of the requirements of the supreme standard, divine will and law. Thus, as the conception of man's *essential* nature became less political and more spiritual, so too did the place of temporal citizenship and ultimate purpose in life change radically. Neither for Christian nor for Jew (nor for Muslim) could the tyrant or oligarch exercise legitimate authority contrary to the "higher law." The will of God, as recorded in Scripture and revealed by His servants, was a command to be obeyed by all on earth, the few and the many, and even by Caesar himself.

The shift in understanding essential human nature, and in the definition of what it meant to fulfill one's potential or destiny, also influenced every other aspect of human life. For example, if matters of faith and spirit were central, then the crucial institution and the vital community would be not so much public and rational and decision-making as it would be spirit-nourishing and faith-sustaining; that is, a congregation or a parish or a monastery rather than a senate or a forum or a council. Moreover, in their essence, such communities and institutions of faith and piety could not be political and public as the Greeks understood, but rather had to be private and in some way volitional and inward-turning. The Christian ideal simply provided no room for the full dimensions of a Greek (or Roman) *polis*. When pagan critics of the early Christian Church, anticipating Gibbon in a way, charged that the new religion was destroying imperial Rome, they were correct in at least one sense: Christianity (no more than Judaism, as Pompey, Titus, and other Roman rulers discovered) left little space for, and offered little succor to, the sort of encompassing mundaneness, political preoccupation, and pride in earthly grandeur that the Greco-Romans took for granted. The emperor Hadrian, for example (in Marguerite Yourcenar's re-creation of his *Memoirs*), scorned the Jews as a people with "a god isolated from human kind."[10]

To Augustine, though, even the Athens of Pericles or the Rome of Augustus were no more than stupendous edifices of man's worldliness, grand monuments of misguided purpose and false principle, and thus of no real worth in the eyes of God. Indeed, even the best political systems, in part precisely because they so engaged and focused human energies, were, to Jews and Christians, dangerously and sinfully distracting. In "this temporal life," Augustine enjoined, Christians were to seek "the everlasting blessings that are promised for the future, using like one in a strange land any earthly and temporal things, not letting them entrap him or divert him from the path that leads to God." "Two cities have been formed by two loves," he added, "the earthly by the

love of self, even to the contempt of God; the heavenly by the love
of God even to the contempt of self. . . . In the one, the princes and
the nations it subdues are ruled for the love of ruling; in the other,
the princes and subjects serve one another in love."[11] Both of
Augustine's kinds of love, *caritas* (of the heavenly city) and *cupiditas*
(of the earthly city), furthermore, are personal and individual, rather
than social or public. Within such a conception of the world (and
entirely apart from the fairness or accuracy of Augustine's reading
of Greco-Roman history), the *polis* is substantially, perhaps fatally,
weakened, the idea of essential community transformed, and the
understanding of the human person altered qualitatively.

Though as early as the Letters of Paul, and especially in the writings
of theologians from Augustine to Thomas Aquinas, Classical thought
had enormous influence of Christianity, the vital priority established
in the Gospels remained. Paul released Christianity from the confines
of Jewish parochialism and even assimilated to it a kind of Platonic
idealism, but he was as clear as his Master on the new orientation
and purpose of life on earth. He emphasized repeatedly, often as if in
dialogue with both his Classical teachers and his Jewish rabbis, that
neither the rituals of Judaism nor the preoccupation with abstractions
and the *logos* so important for the Greeks were at the center of
Christianity. As Augustine put it in his *Soliloquies*, "god and the soul,
that is what I desire to know. Nothing more? Nothing whatever." He
also declared to God, "Thou hast formed us for thyself, and our hearts
are restless until they find rest in thee."[12] Augustine's *Confessions*
depict the dramatic struggle of a strenuous, willful individual to
overcome evil in his life and find salvation, eventually the free gift
of God to the questing soul. All the assumptions and intentions are
profoundly unclassical. The twelfth-century mystic, Hugo of St Victor,
encapsulated the essential Christian subordination of the mundane:
"The spirit was created for God's sake, the body for the spirit's
sake, and the whole world for the body's sake, so that the spirit
might be subject to God, the body to the spirit, and the world to
the body."[13]

With being and energy thus channeled between man and his
creator-savior, Christian political philosophy was given its basic
foundation. Augustine envisioned two cities: one heavenly and eternal,
of God and not of this world, where humankind might find love, bliss,
peace, and salvation; and another, earthly, where humans sojourned

amid selfishness, tyranny, sin, and idolatry. Affairs in the earthly city were supposed, first, to nurture as much as possible the transcendently important quest of salvation, and second, to provide such order, justice, and goodwill among people as was possible in a temporary, imperfect world. Within these precepts the Church, possessing the keys to Christ's kingdom, became pre-eminent to the state, obliging temporal rules to succor and sustain the Church as much as possible in its divine mission. And within this hierarchy, citizens (the term hardly seems appropriate in the altered role and status connoted) were obliged, practically, to obey the state as long as it played its part in the large design of salvation, but the state existed as a subordinate means rather than an encompassing end as it had been in the Ancient World. And even this limited, though essential role for the state, to say nothing of the persecutions and social conformity of some "Christian" regimes, rested uneasily in the most devout Christian consciences, as the repudiation of it by both Catholic mystics and Reformation zealots repeatedly showed.

A TENSION IN CITIZENSHIP

By requiring that ideas of citizenship and public purpose submit to the needs of a radically exalted spirituality, Christianity strengthened a tension already marked in Judaism. Individuals must judge all earthly matters according to the will and law of God. The social context, the nation, the *polis* in all its rich Greek meaning, had been downgraded, and concern shifted instead to the state of one's soul. Within this shift, human beings gained ultimate grounds for placing the inherently individual quest for salvation above any injunctions or requirements of the earthly city. The sense of individuality was strengthened both by shrinking the sphere of the state and by enlarging personal moral and spiritual responsibility apart from – perhaps in conflict with – any social or political obligations. The *separation* of the moral and spiritual from the social and political, evident in Augustine's fateful distinction between the heavenly and earthly cities, imposed on Christian ideas of citizenship a tension simply absent from the Classical model.

The Judeo-Christian outlook, that is, evoked an insistent idea of individuality that again and again exalted the conscientious and faithful actor upholding God's will: Abraham willing to sacrifice Isaac, Nathan challenging King David, Jeremiah chastising the monarchs of Judea, Christ driving the money-changers from the temple, Peter and Paul defying the power of Rome, and Francis of Assisi returning his worldly inheritances and even his clothing to his father, yet sanctified above either pope ·or emperor. These deeds, moreover, accepted a friction between the individual fulfilling his highest calling to serve God's purpose, and the laws and ways of the earthly city. Even more radically individual, especially in the Christian tradition, the exaltation of the human spirit seeking the love and law of God assumed a human nature powerfully resistant to public demands and instead emphasized the personal, the private, the volitional, the individual will and spirit.

The tension between the Classical and the Judeo-Christian versions of individualism is basic and at some level probably irreconcilable, especially in the political sphere (evident in the different definition each version gives to that sphere). In a more general, cultural sense, however, each version is an important part of the idea of individualism present in contemporary western ethos. Americans believe, in the spirit of Thomas Jefferson and John Dewey, that skillful, effective participation in public life is integral to the dignity of the individual. But we also believe, in the spirit of Henry David Thoreau and Martin Luther King, that the private life and the upholding of individual rights against cultural conformity and public injustice is integral. Furthermore, an impressive and talented array of writers and artists, as well as prophets and mystics, have assumed or proclaimed that their individual acts of creativity and inspiration best revealed and fulfilled human nature – and they have, at least implicitly, relegated the political and the public to a lesser, auxiliary role. Engulfed by this radical, spiritual individualism, the Classical, more socially-based exaltation of the human person was in part obscured from the Christian view, but it also remained as a counterpoint sense of obligation to the body politic that never entirely receded from western consciousness. And Americans, 2,000 years later and heir to both traditions, still face the tasks of understanding this unresolved tension, and of seeing where and how any of these deep-rooted conceptions might speak to an age where, in an immediate, physical sense at least, the fate of the earth is in human hands. The question is not whether the private, individual or the public, social ideal is the more conscientious or humane (in its own terms each is intensely so), but rather which ideal might need emphasis and cultivation in the present circumstances of American culture and public life.

THE RENAISSANCE, THE REFORMATION, AND PURITANISM

From this rich, many-sided legacy of emphasis on the individual, in the 400 years between the fall of Constantinople and the publication of J. S. Mill's *On Liberty*, western thought moved steadily toward an even more autonomous and candidly self-centered idea of human nature. The Renaissance, the Reformation, capitalism, modern science, the Enlightenment, romanticism, and evolutionary thought spawned sweeping and audacious ideas of individuality, culminating in the nineteenth-century ideology of liberalism. The founding of American nationhood and the maturing of a distinctive American character, moreover, occurring at this culmination, left the United States heir to this individualist ideology in a peculiarly forceful and unalloyed way. When Edmund Burke wrote of Englishmen in 1790 that "we fear God; we look up with awe to kings; with affection to parliaments; with duty to magistrates; with reverence to priests; and with respect to nobility,"[14] he had in mind entities and emotions that connected Britain with a medieval past. Only superficially and incompletely were they present in her newly-independent colonies. America was a New World, then, not only in the sense of its recent discovery by Europeans, but also in the vulnerable openness with which it felt the formative post-medieval forces.

As a rebirth of Classical learning, the Renaissance found its essential inspiration in the counter-perspective the Greeks and Romans afforded to Christian orthodoxy. Full exercise of human powers instead of self-denying asceticism, freedom of individual responsibility instead of obedience to God's will, and in place of faith the fearless quest of the intellect, defined the profound re-envisioning of human life that excited Shakespeare and Rabelais, Erasmus and Leonardo. In Florence, Pico della Mirandola celebrated Plato's birthday and wrote in his famous *Oration on the Dignity of Man* (1486) that "the Supreme Maker...took man, made in his own individual image,...and placed him in the center of the world [where],...restrained by no narrow bonds, according to [his] own free will...[he] shalt define [his] nature for [himself]." Man thus was his "own free maker and molder" with power either to "decline unto the lower or brute creatures...or be reborn unto the higher, or divine."[15]

Reinhold Niebuhr has pointed out ambiguities, however. In the first place, he notes that the idea of "the autonomous individual... [is a] very un-Christian concept and reality." Furthermore, though Renaissance thought is ostensibly a revival of classicism, "yet classic thought has no such passion for the individual as the Renaissance betrays. The fact is that the Renaissance uses an idea which could only have grown on the soil of Christianity. It transplants this idea to the soil of classic rationalism to produce a new concept of individual autonomy, which is known in neither classicism nor Christianity."[16] Thus the Renaissance was heir to two ancient traditions, but so used them as to create an idea of individuality which, whatever its ancient roots, was as well the essential beginning of modernity. Though the language was still theological, and habit or prudence kept most Renaissance discourse within a Christian framework, the scholars who refurnished men's minds with Plato, Livy, Cicero, and Plutarch nonetheless recaptured a sense of the potential for human life on this earth. A few even asserted openly, as Machiavelli did, that the civic influences of Christianity were pathological because they "assigned as man's highest good humility, abnegation and contempt for mundane things." Good government was unlikely, he added, when religion "glorified humble and contemplative men."[17] Machiavelli, then, appears as the first true modern because he is at once anti-Christian and more than Classical.

This modern view, as it gradually transformed attitudes toward the state, and the role of the individual in it, led first to an understanding called, retrospectively, "civic humanism." Espoused initially in the expansive, spasmodically republican politics of fifteenth- and sixteenth-century Venice and Florence, civic humanism sought, simply and self-consciously, to make contemporary (but thus, necessarily, Christian) application of the Athenian and Ciceronian ideals of citizenship and statecraft rediscovered in the ancient texts. Indeed, the relearning of the histories of Greece and Rome was a vast civics lesson that again focused attention on the polity, on the art of governing, and on public life for its own sake in ways the western world had neglected for more than a millennium. "Any attempt to excavate the foundations of modern political thought," it has been asserted, "needs to begin with the recovery and translation of Aristotle's *Politics*, and the consequent re-emergence of the idea that political philosophy constitutes an independent discipline worthy of study in its own right."[18] After that, there radiated out from Tuscany and Lombardy a "Machiavellian moment" when "the Athenian assertion that man was...by nature a citizen was revived in a paradoxical...relation with the Christian assertion that man was...formed to live in a transcendent and eternal communion."[19]

The civic humanists thus revived the idea that *public* obligation was an essential, inspiring aspect of human life and that to be a free individual meant, at least in some degree, to take part responsibly in politics. In the Florence of the Medicis an undergirding of Christian thought made conceptions of citizenship importantly different from those of Periclean Athens, but there was as well an exciting sense of new potential both for politics generally and for individual participation in them that came with the rediscovered ancient models and prescriptions. The ancient ideal of the publicly significant and fulfilled individual had been restored to the consciousness of the western mind (whatever the lapses in practice), ready to take its place in the flowering of political thought that followed Machiavelli's seminal work.

This ideal was especially important as efforts to limit monarchy and to found governments of consent spread in western Europe, particularly England, in the sixteenth and seventeenth centuries. Thomas Hobbes, James Harrington, Algernon Sidney, and John Locke were thus furnished with a perspective that encouraged a revival of the Classic, publicly-oriented ideal of individuality so weakly articulated in the Hebraic mind and so strongly pushed aside by Augustine and the medieval world-view. With Pericles and Cicero restored as "public saints," that is, at least the model of the uniquely fulfilled political individual was there both as a counterweight to the holy saint and as an inspiration to those engaged in statecraft. Though this view might restrain Christian spiritual individualism by reasserting the priority of the political, by also placing man "in the center of the world," as Pico put it, it opened up momentous opportunities for further projections of individualistic thought likely to be different from both the spiritual and the civic models. As Benjamin Barber has noted, "the largely pejorative meaning that the classical and early Christian periods gave to such terms as *individual* and *privacy* was transformed during the Renaissance in a fashion that eventually produced the Protestant Reformation and the ethics of commercial society."[20]

The Reformation, in spirit Hebraic but also confined within many of the assumptions of medieval thought, contributed in another way to the growing emphasis on the individual. The repudiation of the all-inclusive claims of the Church of Rome and with it the indispensable dependence on the sacraments offered by its priests, allowed a general release from hegemony and from submission to institutional authority. Most important, the sense of the individual standing alone and responsible before God was heightened. Luther, declaring before the Diet of Worms, "here I stand, I can do no other," defied all authority in the name of faith. Calvin insisted in Geneva on no law other than that which faith and intellect found in the Bible, and John Knox thundered against monarchs, lords, and bishops alike if they thwarted men living according to Christ's law reduced to seven words, "love God and thy neighbor as thyself." Each provided a graphic lesson in individual responsibility. Though Reformation doctrines and practices were often as authoritarian, intolerant, and other-wordly as the Roman Catholicism they opposed, the renewed emphasis on the Biblical word of God, and on the personal obligation to understand and follow His will, enhanced the power of the individual against all earthly authority. By loosening or at least dividing the ties of human to religious institutions, by challenging ecclesiastical hierarchy, and by emphasizing personal faith at the expense of the sufficiency of sacraments dispensed by religious officers, the Reformation released vast energies, transforming Great Britain, and especially her New World colonies.

One configuration of Reformation doctrine and practice, Puritanism, was particularly important in the shaping of American individualism. Articulated and espoused by a host of powerful writers and preachers from Knox and Christopher Goodman to Milton and Bunyan, Puritanism in Britain loosened ties to traditional institutions (for a decade even eliminating the monarchy itself) and released diverging streams of religious and moral energy. By insisting on the sainthood of all believers (eventually *masses* of believers), and on active membership in society as well as in churches, the Puritans and other Calvinists intensified citizenship and, potentially, vastly broadened it.[21] Intent on the primacy of conscience, devoted to the individual study of the Scriptures, tending toward congregational rather than episcopal church government, keen on the disciplines of work and devotion to calling, and quick to challenge secular authority, the Puritans became the premier ideologues of individualism in seventeenth-century Anglo-America.

The thought and career of John Winthrop reveals both the medieval anchors of the Reformation and the wide openings toward modernity that, by the time of the founding of the American colonies between 1607 and 1682, characterized the English culture brought to the New World. Earnest in his own faith and piety, Winthrop was quite willing to uproot himself from a comfortable life as an English gentleman for the sake of conscience. He also had a searing experience of intolerant and persecuting English secular and ecclesiastical officers. Thus deeply and authentically protestant, his migration with a community of believers to a "New Canaan" fulfilled the Hebraic pilgrimage of the faithful individual seeking to live according to God's will. In Massachusetts Bay, Winthrop and his colleagues were without a hereditary aristocracy (and fundamentally opposed to such, as John Cotton explained to English lords seeking privileged posts in the colony), an ecclesiastical hierarchy, and, for a time at least, effective control from London. They thus had an opportunity to found a biblical commonwealth unencumbered by many of the traditional bonds and political restraints that usually characterize human society.

But Winthrop was also in many ways as authoritarian in his political philosophy as the Tudor and Stuart monarchs from whom he fled, and as ancient in his habits of mind and in his assumption of social conformity as Thomas Aquinas or John Calvin. Winthrop revealed the profoundly unmodern aspect of the Reformation and of Puritanism in asserting that though as a faithful magistrate he would "hearken to good advice" from the people, a Christian understanding of "civil and lawful liberties" required that the people "quietly and cheerfully submit unto that authority which is set over you...for your good." Liberty, he insisted, was not the right of man "to do what he lists, ...to [do] evil as well as to [do] good," but rather "to do only that which is good, just, and honest" as prescribed in God's law. Despite his faithfulness to his own convictions and his willingness to defy authority in response to them, Winthrop still thought within a closed system of finally revealed truth, of a society controlled by its requirements, and of an individuality expressed through conformity to the good of the whole. "Since the end is to improve our lives to do more service to the Lord," he had told his shipmates on the voyage to Massachusetts in 1630, "the care of the publique must oversway all private respects, . . . [and] particular estates cannot subsist in the ruine of the publique."[22]

But Winthrop's Aristotelian emphasis on the usefulness of politics in pursuing the good life was challenged by his perhaps more radically Puritan colleague, Roger Williams. His fervent pietism led him to insist that the state had no legitimate place in matters of faith and religion. Williams utterly separated the individual from society in questions of religion. Salvation rested on an individual's relation to God through Christ, a matter in which state and even Church (as ecclesia) could play no useful role.

Later pietist and evangelical Christians, exalting religious and mystical experience, sustained and strengthened Williams's insistence that any person, individually through faith, could reach God. Though medieval and Catholic Christianity would not have disagreed theoretically with this primacy given to faith, the radically heightened emphasis and altered institutional framework in the varieties of protestantism most widespread in America dramatized the agency of the *individual*. If personal quest and religious experience rather than priestly ministrations were critically important, if congregations of the faithful rather than bishops or synods made decisions, and if governments were thought to do more harm than good by supporting religion, then much had been loosened up and opened both for "communions of saints" and for individuals in matters of ultimate concern. Roger Williams, that is, rather than Winthrop, would become an American hero because Williams more faithfully manifested a Puritan theology that would prove particularly compatible with other elements of the emerging American creed of individualism.

THE COMMERCIAL SPIRIT

As Max Weber, R. H. Tawney, and others have explained, there were strong connections between these religious loosenings and openings for individual zeal, and the spread in Europe of capitalism and private economic enterprise. In fact, many of the values – diligence, thrift, hard work, personal responsibility, and so on – so much overlapped that it often seemed capitalism spawned or "caused" protestantism, or perhaps it was the reverse. In any case, the linkage between the two, both in values and in historical fact, is patent. "The business man," Niebuhr observes, "developed a form of economic power which depends on individual initiative and resourcefulness rather than upon hereditary advantages; and which creates dynamic rather than static social relationships. It naturally sees human history as a realm of human decisions rather than of inexorable destiny."[23] Thus a parallel individualism emerges, and is often thought of as a single, inseparable ideology, whether one emphasizes the primacy of the religious or the economic motivation. And in America, where many traditional restraints were absent, it seemed that the logic and implications of capitalism and protestantism were starkly apparent – and especially bound together.

Beyond the emphasis on thrift, hard work, and personal responsibility, the new thought associated with a market economy articulated two startling innovations in how people viewed themselves and their place in society. First, it shifted attention away from both the medieval emphasis on the need for the state to support religion, and the classical obligation for government to "nourish the good life." It focused instead on advancing the economic well-being, the wealth, of the nation. Whether under mercantilism through guidance of the economy or under *laissez-faire* through the abandonment of controls, the intention was the same: to make increase in wealth the primary purpose of government, which would in turn assure the growth and power of the nation as a whole. Adam Smith thus opposed the mercantilists not in ends, but only in means; he argued that the *absence* of government regulation, rather than its presence, however skillful, would result in the greatest individual and therefore accumulated national wealth. In either case, both the comprehensive Classical ideal of the positive purpose of government and the Christian ideal of government as an auxiliary to religious life were abandoned.

Second, and more fundamental for the ideology of individualism, was the increasingly explicit validation of *self-interest* as a motivation in human affairs. As individual diligence and productivity appeared more and more to result both in the material well-being of the individual and in the economic growth of the nation, it seemed plausible as well to celebrate the motivation that yielded those gratifying results: self-interest. In Mandeville's terse dictum, "private vices [selfishness], public benefits [national wealth and power]."

Indignant, eloquent voices, however, protested this view. Alexander Pope complained that for commercially-oriented eighteenth-century England,

> In soldier, churchman, patriot, man in power,
> 'Tis avarice all, ambition is no more,

while John Dryden inveighed against London where

> Tides of wealth o'erflow the fatten'd land;
> Yet monsters from thy large increase we find,
> Engender'd on the slime they leav'st behind.[24]

Thus resisted, the moral shift came slowly, often covertly, but a momentous change was nonetheless under way. To the "still highly Aristotelian" critics of the commercial ethic and its political implications, "it was far from clear how any group intent upon its private interest could have any sense of the common good at all, and if it had not it would be no more than a faction, driving its members to further and further excesses of greed and frenzy."[25]

At first economic theorists merely pointed out the increased trade and growth of capital that came with the exaltation of the (individual) profit motive and the protection of private property. Then Pierre Bayle, Daniel Defoe, Bernard Mandeville and others elaborated and even began to approve the argument that greed and private ambition was the most effective stimulus to national greatness. More and more "enlightened" self-interest became the watchword. This resulted in astonishing growth in material well-being for tradesmen, merchants, and stockholders, and in the availability of less expensive goods and services of all kinds. Even more wonderful, in the famous argument of Adam Smith, it also led to "the wealth of nations" as competition engendered specialization of labor, efficient production, beneficial exchange, diversity of goods, and increased accumulation of capital for further investment.

The ethical revolution came when individuals were told it was not only necessary but morally correct to engage unashamedly in their own aggrandizement. The economic theorists did not, of course, *discover* self-interest and competition as human motivations, or even necessarily suppose them more widespread than other thinkers. What was novel was rather their *celebration* of them, their claim that they were virtues to be encouraged rather than impulses to be morally restrained. As a result, in the seventeenth century the competitive or adversarial stance came increasingly to dominate both human relationships and public affairs as self-interest more and more gained *approval* as a motivation.[26] Following this line of thought, by 1977 a leading economist could assert, proudly, in a book entitled *The Public Use of Private Interest*, that "harnessing the 'base' motive of material self-interest to promote the common good is perhaps the most important social invention mankind has achieved." These "market-like arrangements," furthermore, "reduced the need for compassion, patriotism, [and] brotherly love" in human society.[27]

Some blunt, new questions were coming forward. Could selfishness, even if one added caveats about it being enlightened or long range, really be regarded as a proper ethical principle? Furthermore, was there really an "invisible hand" that in a competitive economy led the whole toward maximized production and material well-being? Was this a plausible rather than a wildly utopian supposition? And did this mean that the whole was only the sum of the parts; indeed, that comprehensive, planned attention to the general welfare, and subordination of individual pursuits to it, was worse than futile because it rested on misguided conceptions of human nature and human society? Was it possible, really, to suppose that explicit concern for the welfare of the whole, and for the well-being of others beyond a small circle of family and co-workers, was neither materially nor morally necessary? Even the whole idea of the political as an essential, constructive part of human society receded. Was government at best a necessary evil? If the answer to these questions was "yes," then yet another powerful impulse toward a stark, self-sufficing individualism (one thinks of Ayn Rand's *The Virtue of Selfishness*) had been implanted or at least much strengthened in the western world.

When capitalism and the commercial spirit meshed with the also flourishing pietist, evangelical protestantism, moreover, a further, radicalized individualism resulted. The ego, the self-preoccupation with one's own keenest concern, was as central to Luther and Calvin as it was to Hobbes, Locke, and Adam Smith. Thus, whatever was cause or effect, the western world experienced a mixing of material and spiritual energies that resulted in the sort of many-faceted individualism seen in the English pair of Daniel Defoe and John Wesley, and in the American pair of Benjamin Franklin and Jonathan Edwards. Wesley and Edwards were quintessential protestants, filled with an evangelical zeal to save (individual) souls. Each had an individual, transforming experience of the Almighty. Defoe and Franklin were just as zealous for personal betterment. Both also had as rich a sense of life as a purposeful pilgrimage as their clerical counterparts. The spirit of modern individualism, that is, breathed in all of them.

The overlap of protestant and commercial energies was especially potent in English North America. There, as Crèvecoeur, Tocqueville, and other observers would notice, the liberal and individualistic impulses spawned in Europe were more readily fulfilled. As the steady secularization of American life made clear, though, the materialist or possessive individualism of the commercial spirit has a way of overawing the pietist variety. However much the United States has been a moral or religious nation guided by (individual) impulses of spirit and conscience, it has also seen repeated mergers, or confusions, of religious and material intentions. One would be hard-pressed to argue that the moral and spiritual energies have very often been able effectively to restrain (as their principles require) the lust for material gain of individuals or their corporate agents. Protestantism and the commercial spirit, that is, combined in a pervasive individualism that, whatever the vigor and rhetoric of its pietist strand, often leaves the material strand ascendant, projecting its values and emphasis into the very citadels of the spirit.[28]

For example, as New England emerged from the half-medieval authority of John Winthrop, both a pietistic puritanism and a growing commercial spirit exerted strong influence. Social historians have described seventeenth- and eighteenth-century New England as a "pre-modern" culture of "homogeneous, organic cohesive communities" where people "subordinated their individual self-interest to the good of the group," where "consensual authority was possible because the community, through its town government, dispensed benefits to all as needed," where goods were bartered and sold at "the customary just price," and where dealings were among people all "knew well in all their social roles."

This sense of community, however, gave way under the pressures of a commercial economy. As material concerns and zeal for profit became more central, farmers shifted from subsistence to commercial agriculture, market-established prices replaced "just" ones, "town meetings became occasions of strident competition for access to privileges and limited resources," and parishes and precincts were formed "to accommodate the needs and desires of particular groups." More and more, "individuals brooked no restraints on their pursuit of self-interest," the legal system began more to prohibit crimes than to enjoin duties, and people's relations with each other "became contractual and impersonal, shaped by competition, calculation, and self-assertion." The individual was left to stand alone, "isolated, sharply defined against others."[29]

Theologies then arose that satisfied both the still strong attachment of New Englanders to cohesive, moral values, and their attraction to the expansive, prospering world of commerce. One revealing convergence came in the New Divinity of Samuel Hopkins (1721–1803) and his followers. They insisted, in an extreme pietism, that *only* an inward, *willing* acceptance of the grace of Christ could save a sinner. Nothing else was possible or efficacious. The individual thus faced absolute, universal distinctions between good and evil. Movement away from traditional, communal concerns and restraints became possible without lapse into anarchy and moral dissolution, but the rescue was entirely personal. The law of a sovereign God would prevail in the world, person by person, restraining human depravity, even as the pursuit of commerce and wealth came to overshadow the political community. A radical, pietistic theology furnished an effective and convenient moral shield for individuals in an age of competitive, impersonal commerce.

The New Divinity, then, by "condemning those varieties of self-interest that threatened to...weaken the authority of [God's] law," enabled New Englanders "to venture into the marketplace with something approaching [moral] confidence." By making personal piety and benevolence the key to salvation, New Divinity theology put acts of grace accepted by individual wills in place as guards against immorality and social decay. As Hopkins himself put it, a "person who exercises disinterested goodwill to being in general must have a proper and proportionable regard to himself, as he belongs to being in general, and is included in it as a necessary part of it."[30] A certain self-attention, then, received theological as well as economic validation. But though self-interestedness aimed at material well-being was supposed to complement moral and spiritual individualism, it soon exhibited a strong tendency to overshadow and even pervert or manipulate its more pious companion. A moral universe had been turned upside down and portentous movements of private enterprise and political diminishment had been set loose. After studying the growth of a New England town from its founding in 1636, a social historian concluded that by the American Revolution "men were speaking and even thinking in terms of an old ideology, but they were living a new one. Whether they liked it or not pluralistic democracy was replacing the democracy of homogeneity, freeing the individual from the dictates of the social order, and laying the foundations of the ideology [liberal individualism] which was to become America's pride."[31]

SCIENCE AND EMPIRICISM

Another basic foundation of the modern world, the growth of science and technology that so accelerated from the seventeenth century onward, has also contributed crucially to the ideology of individualism. The powerful, critical ability of scientific investigation and discovery upset ancient orthodoxies. When hoary beliefs that had long restrained human adventure and progress, such as the geocentric hypothesis and the supposed flatness of the earth, fell before the irresistible evidence of the astronomers and explorers, vast scope for human enterprise and ingenuity opened up. Also, the understanding of the physical world that came with such breakthroughs as the anatomical discoveries of the dissectionists, Harvey's theory of the circulation of blood, and Newton's demonstration of the laws of motion, intensified the sense of man's ability to cope with and even control the world he lived in. As the technology that went hand-in-hand with the science led by the middle of the eighteenth century to the beginning of the Industrial Revolution, the dawn of a new era was apparent. The role and self-conception of the individual would be as transformed as the landscape of West Yorkshire.

The modes of thinking of the scientists, furthermore, proved as liberating to human initiative as their discoveries. Science, A. N. Whitehead has pointed out, "recoloured our mentality, . . . [and] altered the metaphysical presuppositions of the imaginative contents of our minds."[32] Though the scientists were much impressed with the collective, universal nature of their inquiries and took the lead in forming new societies to "promote useful knowledge," the connections they had with each other and the very organizations they spawned embodied new notions of individualism. Bacon's inductive method required individuals (any number of them; singly or in groups; the more the better) to gather data, assiduously and endlessly, in order to frame hypotheses that other individuals would then test by gathering more data, in order to posit new hypotheses, *ad infinitum*. The implicit assumption was that there were no final truths imposed on the human race from above, or anywhere else, but rather that the parts, ultimately individuals in their particular endeavors, were of the essence. In laborious, multitudinous, minute, critical inquiries, Bacon asserted, humankind would find the knowledge that was power over nature itself: "the true and lawful goal of the sciences is none other than this: that human life be endowed with new discoveries and powers."

Descartes made the same confident, forward-looking point when he scorned "the syllogisms...of the Schools" as capable only of "explaining to others those things that are [already] known," while the inductive method was effective in "learning what is new." The scientific, practical philosophy, he declared, was a "more powerful instrument of knowledge than any other that has been bequeathed to us by human agency." It would, if properly understood and applied, enable men to "render [themselves] the masters and possessors of nature."[33]

Baconian science, and particularly its inductive methodology, then, required the ceaseless collection of data received through the empirical senses of unnumbered individuals. Further, assuming that the rational, critical minds of human beings applied to those data would yield laws and truths useful to progress, it emphasized individual effort within an atomized world-view. Powerful intellectual tools had been fashioned that allowed critical analysis to devastate dogma and ancient systems. The New World, moreover, so open and unformed that it became, repeatedly, "a disproving ground for utopias," was especially congenial to this modernity.[34]

An Enlightenment, an Age of Reason, flourished, then, as Newton's mathematics and laws of motion seemed to make the inductive method and the accumulation of knowledge not fractionalizing and disordering, but rather encompassing and all-consuming. To Newton and his popularizers and followers, the world (terrestrial and celestial) was a vast perpetual motion machine subject to universal laws. In Pope's famous couplets, in the Newtonian synthesis,

> All are but parts of one stupendous whole,
> Whose body nature is, and God the soul.
>
> All nature is but art, unknown to thee;
> All·chance, direction which thou canst not see;
> All discord, harmony not understood;
> All partial evil, universal good.[35]

Though the poet exalts God's universal design, not entirely grasped (yet) by humans, Pope celebrates as well an efficacious *human* (individual) role in the design.

At the same time Locke worked out the epistemology and politics of the Baconian and Newtonian systems. Hobbes had already brought the perspective of science to the study of politics by declaring that "the rights of states, and duties of subjects" can, like a watch or an engine, only be known when "taken in sunder," that is, "considered as if they were dissolved." Then, continuing the analogy to natural science, Hobbes supposed that "civil philosophy," like geometry based on "lines and figures. . . drawn and described by ourselves," could be as perfectly explained, "because we make the commonwealth ourselves."[36] Consistent with this confidence in the capability of the human knower and with Bacon's method, Locke argued that the human mind was blank at birth, ready to receive all its substance from impressions made on it through the senses; ready, that is, to perform as required by the inductive process. This meant, of course, since the array of sensory impressions received by each human being would be different, that diversity would be at the center of human nature, rather than any indwelling, innate sameness. Working out the implications of the diversity and emphasis on method, Locke was tolerant of different views, stressed education (as a means of developing the varying talents and skills of maturing human beings), supposed, as he put it, that "all can choose differently, yet all choose right," and argued that government should in some fashion rest on the consent of the infinitely varied parts of the body politic. It led him further to assert as natural law the inherent freedom and equality of human beings: how, having posited the infinite variety of humankind, could one justify the oppression of one person by another or the denial of an equal esteem in the eyes of the law to beings not essentially or inherently categorizable?

When Jefferson took Bacon, Newton, and Locke as his "trinity of immortals," he accepted the buoyant, forward-looking, individualized, yet harmonious world-view that crystallized in the half century 1680–1730, when British science, literature, and philosophy were the envy of the western world. He believed, as a man of the Enlightenment, that the presumed calculation of long-range rational self-interest by individuals that made possible marvelous increases in productivity, "was actually complimentary to human nature." It "enhanced the worth of labor – what ordinary men and women did." Thus it seemed possible to Jefferson that, in politics as well as economics, life might be "undirected but patterned, uncoerced but orderly, free but predictable."[37] Such a vision informed the founding documents of the United States.

This pattern of thought, moreover, made forthright and explicit the often only implicit movement, since the Renaissance, toward an individual-centered moral and political life. Locke himself regarded America as a virtual "state of nature" blessedly unfettered with the hoary restraints and irrationalities of older societies. In a perhaps fateful way, then, a vigorous, unabashed individualism, beyond what was common even in western Europe to say nothing of the rest of the world, existed in the United States not so much as the upstart foe of ancient hegemonies, oppressions, and social bonds (the usual posture of liberalism), but rather as the foundation of the national edifice itself. What sort of meaning would it have, as the virtually unquestioned basis for a polity, rather than as a challenger of settled, traditional patterns?

ROMANTICISM AND DARWIN

As people extolled and experienced the Enlightenment ideals of reason, harmony, natural law, and human efficacy, however, there seemed to be something amiss. Were science and reason, facts and critical analysis, expressive of anything like the complete range of human potential and individual fulfillment? Just as Aristotle had asked whether one could be fully human without being political, and Jesus had asked whether man could live on bread alone, Goethe and other critics of the Enlightenment asked whether facts and reason and science were the full measure of humanness. Physics, chemistry, astronomy, and anatomy, enlightening as their study was, Goethe wrote, were not enough. "How hollow and empty did we feel in this melancholy, atheistical half-night, in which earth vanished with all its images, heaven with all its stars. . . . We took a hearty dislike to all philosophy, and especially metaphysics," Goethe wrote of himself and his young friends. Instead, they "threw [themselves] into living knowledge, experience, action, and poetizing, with the more liveliness and passion."[38]

Later, reacting against the same Enlightenment ideas, Emerson, Theodore Parker, and other young Americans, inspired themselves by Goethe, Wordsworth, Coleridge, and other European romantics, made the same points. Emerson wrote that the intellectual climate of his youth was "Timid, imitative, tame," and scholars were "decent, indolent, complaisant. . . [causing] the mind of the country. . . to aim at low objects." Parker complained that "the common books of Philosophy" of his student days, deriving from Locke's *Essay on Human Understanding*, "gave little help" as he and his friends sought to understand the "great primal [questions]. . . of human nature."[39] Romantic individualists believed with Emerson that science, since it accepted evidence only of the five senses, was "superficial," and that "nothing was further from fiction than poetry." Individuals were thought of as more unique than the findings of science discerned, or even conceived. Romanticism strove, then, to enlarge and diversify human experience, to probe all the wonders and mysteries and fascinations of what Kant termed the transcendental and noumenal realms and Hegel called a realm of "absolute spirit" – art, religion, and philosophy. The goal, as Rousseau had boldly set forth in the *Émile*, was the fullest development of the unique potentialities of every person.

As a general rule, of course, this would have been accepted by Aristotle, St Paul, Locke, and many others. What the romantic ideal added was both an enlarged range of human endeavor and an emphasis on the individual for his own sake. It paid little attention to social responsibilities or even the cultural context, except to condemn existing institutions and customs as oppressive and pathological. Rather than life having an essential social context fulfilled within some political or religious cosmology, the aim of society and of the state came to be merely the protection and enhancement of the freedom, self-expression, and creativity of each individual part of the polity. The goal became simply lives like Goethe's or Byron's or Thoreau's, lived often in separation from and in resistance to cultural norms and social institutions. This kind of individualism exalted artistic, literary, religious, spiritual, and moral capabilities – intrinsically private and idiosyncratic – more than political, commercial, or even scientific ones. As the hero-worship and "great men" ideas of Carlyle and Emerson show, however, remarkable, towering individuals in any field – for example Napoleon, Sir Humphry Davy, Cromwell, Mohammed, and Josiah Wedgwood – could "represent" the potential for individual accomplishment. The romantic outlook, then, condemned both the calculating, materialistic individuality of the Age of Reason and the whole idea of beneficent society and government, at least in anything like their traditional forms. "Every actual state," wrote Emerson, "is corrupt. Good men must not obey the laws too well. ... To educate the wise man the state exists; and with the appearance of the wise man, the state expires. The appearance of character makes the state unnecessary."[10] Left was an atomized, unrooted, emotional understanding of human nature that validated a radical individualism.

The final stone in the ideological foundation of American individualism was set in place by mid nineteenth century with the publication of Darwin's *Origin of Species*, which itself in part simply gathered together the emphases on relentless, competitive struggle of Thomas Malthus, David Ricardo, and other British thinkers. Jeremy Bentham, for example, had noted that "the boundless range of human desires, and the very limited number of objects... unavoidably leads a man to consider those with whom he is obliged to share such objects as inconvenient rivals who narrow his own extent of enjoyment.... This naturally engenders antipathy towards the beings who thus baffle and contravene his wishes."[41] Such thought, fraught with deterministic, impersonal, diminishing overtones and implications, also heightened the sense of the lonely, calculating individual. Darwin's theories of evolution, growth, and survival of the fittest seemed to synthesize these strands of thought and to spawn ideologies of man against the state and of society as an arena of steady, competitive progress. The model of Darwinian "struggle" gradually replaced Newtonian "harmony." The individual was pictured as in a lonely, ceaseless battle against both nature and society. In the eyes of some at least, "social Darwinism" complemented the self-interested competitiveness of Adam Smith's economic man and the self-reliance of Emerson's "one man is the counterpoise to a city,...[whose] solitude...[is] more beneficent than the concert of crowds." It thus gave a further boost to the ideology of liberal individualism that achieved its full, mature expression in the Anglo-America of Gladstone and Lincoln. Moreover, under the further stimulus of the opening of the frontier, of the waves of immigrants seeking new lives, and of the growth of industry, rugged individualism on the Darwinian model seemed peculiarly appropriate and right in nineteenth-century America. To those caught up in the spirit of vigorous growth and progress, moreover, Darwinian individualism often seemed consistent with Puritan diligence and with scientific rationality, as well as with romantic aspirations of self-fulfillment.

JOHN STUART MILL AND NINETEENTH-CENTURY LIBERALISM

This heightened individualism became the dynamic core, the *raison d'être*, for the wider ideology of liberalism that flowered in the nineteenth century. In 1859, in *On Liberty*, John Stuart Mill, following Wilhelm von Humboldt, declared boldly that "the end of man, or that which is prescribed by the eternal or immutable dictates of reason ...is the highest and most harmonious development of his powers to a complete and consistent whole." From that it followed that every human being should work for "the individuality of power and development" in himself and in every other person. (There are ways, of course, in which Aristotle and Augustine, thus far, would agree with this argument.) But then Mill (and Humboldt) argue further that "freedom and variety of situations" are conditions requisite for the "individual vigor and manifold diversity" which produce the creativity and originality indispensable to growth and progress.[42] In this extension of the argument Mill becomes wholly and characteristically modern rather than either Classical or medieval. Instead of supposing that the "harmonious development of...a complete and consistent whole," for example, required a primary concern for the polity as Aristotle assumed, or that enhancing the "individuality of power and development" meant seeking salvation in Christ's Church as Augustine and Aquinas and Calvin believed, Mill simply made the individual the starting place and center of both society and the cosmos. "Men in a state of society," he wrote, "are still men; their actions and passions are obedient to the laws of individual human nature. Men are not, when brought together, converted to a different kind of substance, as hydrogen and oxygen differ from water. . . . Human beings in society have no properties but those which are derived from, and may be resolved into, the laws of individual men."[43] Though Mill condemned "selfish individualism," and acknowledged the validity of social obligations, he saw social purpose and progress as no more than the sum of individual accomplishments.

Mill thus gathered together all the varieties of individualism that had moved and stimulated people since the dawn of modernity. The self-confidence of the Renaissance, the Reformation emphasis on will and conscience, the commercial validation of competitive energies, the critical spirit of scientific inquiry, the faith in reason of the Enlightenment, the romantic preoccupation with the eccentric, creative individual, and the evolutionary view of progress through struggle, are all echoed by Mill and are embodied in mature nineteenth-century liberalism. Indeed, looking backward, and with the benefit of Mill's own compelling argument, individuality as he understood it appears as the entirely plausible, even inevitable fruit of four centuries of western history.

One can see, again retrospectively, that while the progress was steadily toward a purer, more unalloyed individualism, older conceptions persisted. Renaissance individualism, for example, left man comfortably within a Christian cosmos, just as the Reformation sought not to weaken man's devotion to religious purpose within a universal Church, properly understood, but rather to strengthen it. Even the increasingly secular movements toward competitive capitalism and scientific inquiry often saw themselves as fulfilling rather than undermining the divine will. Then "the heavenly city of the eighteenth-century philosophers," in Carl Becker's illuminating characterization of the Enlightenment, seemed to be a synthesis as orderly and encompassing as that of Thomas Aquinas five centuries earlier. However humanistic and secular the philosophers proclaimed themselves to be, they nonetheless seemed more akin to the Church Fathers than to "liberal pluralists." But with the less harmonizing, less socially bonding outlook of the romantics and the evolutionists, the stage was set for the uncompromising individualism of J. S. Mill, where it, standing by itself, is "the end of man."

One can think, then, of European liberalism (including its American offshoot) as a "single coherent movement" whose broad assumptions were dominant, Isaiah Berlin argues, down through the speeches of Woodrow Wilson, David Lloyd-George, and Thomas Masaryk in 1918–19. This liberalism insisted, Berlin wrote, that

> man is, in principle at least, everywhere and in every condition, able, if he wills it, to discover and apply rational solutions to his problems. And these solutions, because they are rational, cannot clash with each other, and will ultimately form a harmonious system in which truth will prevail, and freedom, happiness, and unlimited opportunity for untrammelled self-development will be open to all.[44]

Put this way, the liberal outlook includes not only Jefferson and J. S. Mill, but also Edmund Burke, Herbert Spencer, and even Marx as well, as they accept the essential starting points of rational argument and of ultimate concern for individual well-being.

The peculiar force and vigor of Mill's idea of individualism in the United States are evident in the outlook and thought of Justice Oliver Wendell Holmes. Though his Civil War battlefield experience left him with a "soldier's faith" in idealistic commitment and the comradeship of battle, his post-war studies, especially of the law, were strongly Darwinian. He rejected Lockean formulations of natural law, and upheld the rights of freedom of expression, privacy, individual opportunity, and competition under the Constitution. In fact, as he pondered the purposes and powers of law and government, he became the foe of all orthodoxies, statist or *laissez-faire*, and the defender of all eccentricities and experiments, including those by all levels of government to deal with particular social problems according to the will of the majority. Notions of the general will or the body politic were to him delusive, mystical abstractions.

In a famous Supreme Court dissent Holmes stated an American version of Mill's argument in *On Liberty*: "The best test of truth is the power of thought to get itself accepted in the competition of the market." When men realize that "time has upset many fighting faiths," the Justice argued, they will realize as well that the "ultimate good," each generation discovering its own truths, "is better reached by free trade in ideas." Holmes thus regarded the Constitution, like all of life, as "an experiment." It was essential to "be eternally vigilant against attempts to check the expression of opinions we loathe and believe to be fraught with death" lest the new truth be suppressed without a chance to prove itself in the marketplace.[45] Only a "clear and present danger" to the survival of the government (to him, democratic process), Holmes wrote in another opinion, could justify interference with freedom of expression.

By so pragmatically defending individual expression and individualized politics, Holmes spoke in a characteristically modern voice, clearly distancing himself from both Classical and Judeo-Christian understandings of individual dignity. For Holmes there is no *polis*, no publicly-oriented good life to which individuals contribute in order to find their fulfillment as human beings. Instead there are only individual efforts that might or might not include some socially-accomplished tasks. Nor is there any cosmic purpose or eternity within which men and women find salvation from their otherwise alienated, anxious lives and toward which conscience and moral conviction offer compelling guidance. Rather, Holmes was scornful of notions like moral purpose and natural law. Time, he was fond of noting, had upset many fighting faiths. "Life is an end in itself, and the only question as to whether it is worth living," he concluded in a blunt statement of uncosmological individualism, "is whether you have enough of it."[46] John Stuart Mill might not have quite agreed, but the idea is not substantially different from his view that "the end of man [was]...individuality of power and development."

The mundane, uncosmological individualism of Mill, Darwin, and Holmes more and more denigrated the role of the state and made the political in its rich Classical sense very nearly disappear. The individual, and a complex, evolutionary entity usually referred to as "society," were seen as having existences and growth patterns that were more likely to be perverted than nourished by political action. A Scottish economist had declared flatly in 1825 that society had as its main goal "to obtain the greatest possible amount of wealth with the least possible difficulty," and that the gaining of this "wealth is independent of the nature of government."[47] At most, government within such an outlook was an auxiliary, simply another component of society, that could perform such functions as might be from time to time convenient or practical. With government thus subordinated to the more important wealth-producing and progress-engendering aspects of society, the basis of citizenship had shifted. Universal suffrage was validated because, in Herbert Spencer's dictum, "each is the only safe guardian of his own rights and interests." But citizenship no longer meant taking part in a politically sustained common good – because such was no longer thought to exist. In the same way, individual and group *interests*, idiosyncratic and subjective, gradually gained the sanction personal conscience had once had: they were to be protected, to be valued in political discourse, and to be viewed as essential manifestations of individual potential and creativity.

AMBIGUOUS LEGACY FOR TWENTIETH-CENTURY AMERICA

As the twentieth century opened, then, a thoroughgoing creed of individualism was in place, able, so it seemed, to stand as the basis of democracy as a form of government, of private enterprise as an economic system, and of liberalism as an attitude toward life. Humanistic psychology, progressive education, and conflict of interest politics are more recent expressions of that creed. In each case, when analysis pushed toward the "end," the purpose of this or that enterprise, the answer increasingly was simply that it allowed greatest scope for individual choice or influence or fulfillment. Democracy was valued because it gave individuals a voice in and some degree of control over collective measures seen as the vector sum of the needs of the parts of society. Since "only he who wears the shoe can tell where it pinches," the argument goes, it is necessary to involve all the (individual) wearers to achieve proper diagnosis and remedy for social (aggregated individual) "pinches." (The metaphor is telling: what phenomenon is more idiosyncratic and unsocial than a pinching shoe?) Any concern for the good or glory of the whole was viewed as a dangerous, illusory abstraction.

Tolerance, pluralism, open-endedness, free inquiry and expression, procedural safeguards, pursuit of knowledge, and other liberal hallmarks all received validation as sustainers of individual dignity, opportunity, and growth. And, more and more, such words as "dignity," "opportunity," and "fulfillment," when used as a noun after the adjective "individual" in a statement of a goal or a purpose, came to mean mainly unfetteredness – the absence of restraint by any tyranny, orthodoxy, set pattern, custom, "truth," or whatever. Drawing on a variety of rich if not wholly consistent accents on the individual, twentieth-century thought came, then, to regard such emphasis as self-evident and axiomatic, and thus capable of becoming the grounds for additional parts of the individualist creed. In 1960 Archibald MacLeish expressed unselfconsciously this modern version of individualism when he rephrased Jefferson's statement of the national purpose: Americans believed it to be the right of all men and women "to think for themselves, speak for themselves, govern themselves, pursue happiness for themselves *and so become themselves*" (emphasis added).[48] The end, then, for MacLeish was that people might be free to *become themselves*, that is, to achieve what they might possess individual potential to become – an idea to which Jefferson would not have objected. It would not have occurred to him, however, to add the string of "themselves" to the Declaration of Independence ideals because he still retained ideas of *polis* and higher law within which the emphasis on self would have been jarring.

Nonetheless MacLeish was able simply to rephrase the 200-year-old Declaration in explaining what Americans all knew to be their national purpose because the agreement on a "basic individualism" and its envelopment in liberal attitudes and institutions had always been so pervasive.[49] As Louis Hartz has explained, the "tradition" in the United States has always been "liberal." At least since the preponderant presence in the British colonies of the more Whiggish, dissenting, self-governing aspects of English public life throughout the eighteenth century (and in some respects even earlier), one could, that is, best describe values and institutions in the United States as non-feudal, non-aristocratic, and non-traditional. All the things that liberals in Europe struggled against in the eighteenth and nineteenth centuries were, comparatively at least, weak to the point of non-existence in the United States. One need only recall the battles of liberals in France, Germany, Italy, and even Great Britain in the 150 years between 1764 and 1914 to see the point: all they had to resist most powerfully – an entrenched nobility, an established Church, a powerful monarchy, and hereditary privilege – were largely absent in the United States. (The fact that slavery in the *ante bellum* South, a classic liberal target, seemed so anomalous, to friend and foe, in the United States, in a way reveals the liberal character of the nation generally.) Thus, though there were and are severe disputes and basic disagreements aplenty in the United States, in a wider perspective they have been within the consensus set forth in the founding ideology and documents – all of which in successive formulations have stated and restated the tenet of individualism.

The significance of the American consensus on a "liberal, atomistic, individualistic ideology," as many analysts have put it, is highlighted if one contrasts our public life with that of other nations. In the first place, respect for authority, the degree to which individuals feel they have a primary duty to the nation and to obey its laws, is sharply lower in the United States than in much of Europe. Though Americans in many ways are at least as *law-abiding* as citizens of other nations (as for example in paying taxes and adhering to traffic laws), they do so without any sense of awe or of the omnipotence of those in authority. Instead, they have in mind more practical considerations – a simple realization of the convenience of certain rules. Even less is there in the United States very much of the deference and even reverence accorded to the national culture and polity one finds in the Confucian-influenced societies of East Asia. (see chapter 3).

Second, though American politics has been characterized by a consensus on liberal goals, how to reach these goals has been contested bitterly. Reform movements, for example, have seldom disputed the validity of the ideals of the Declaration of Independence. Rather, calls have issued for their fuller achievement in society as a whole (as in the Jacksonian era), for their application to previously excluded groups (as in the civil rights movement), or for a revised understanding of their meaning in a changing society (as during the New Deal). In each case the emphasis was not on a new or a foreign ideology, but on the realization of the traditional liberal and individualistic goals. Ronald Reagan's economic and social programs, however much they might seem to require sweeping change, nonetheless fitted the same pattern: he sought the achievement of what he thought of as old, liberal values, not new departures. His defense of voluntary prayer in public schools, for example, rested on an argument that Supreme Court decisions in the 1960s changed the traditional American belief that "the state was tolerant of religious belief, expression, and practice." The Court, in a dramatic innovation, "removed religion from its honored place." Those who tried to outlaw prayer in the schools, he said, were "intolerant of religion," and thus violated a basic *liberal* principle.[50]

In Europe, on the other hand, political parties have often seen themselves as having communist, socialist, fascist, liberal, Catholic, monarchical, and other clearly-defined ideologies that challenged the existing polity. And when these ideological parties found support overwhelmingly in particular classes, long-standing social groups, or religious persuasions, the stage was set for sustained conflict over the basic national purposes and values. Such a pattern, of course, is in some respects more pluralistic and divisive than the American one; it contains less consensus. In another way, though, the great passion and expectation of basic change aroused in the United States, periodically at least, by fervent, indignant appeals that existing circumstances be made to live up to professed ideals, have been sources of disorder and instability. The opportunity for intense conflict is evident when one considers the force of the demand, characteristic of American politics, that hypocrites who fail to practice what they preach close the gap between what existed shamefully and what was proclaimed ideally.[51] The turmoil and fervor of the populist crusades against economic privilege and of the civil rights movement against racism each arose from the alleged violation of hallowed American (liberal) principles.

The result is once again paradoxical and revealing of the place of individualism in American public life. The Constitution of 1787, the oldest in continuous use in the world and the basis for a strong consensus in the United States on how the nation should be governed, rests itself on a liberal tradition that for two centuries has repelled as alien any competing ideology. Yet, the almost mystical reverence for culture and nation (even where none exists politically) seen among such diverse peoples as Japanese, Russians, Arabs, Poles, Frenchmen, and Mexicans, has no real parallel in the United States. Lacking such an anchor in the spirit of the whole, American public life has tended to sway and lurch as interests, passions, and impulses of all sorts have surfaced and spread among large numbers of people. Americans assume, for the most part, that their own needs and values warrant political influence even, and *especially*, when they have no strong sense of themselves as part of a national body politic. And the American "tradition," liberal, atomistic, and individualistic, validates this cacophony of interests, passions, and impulses as fair, democratic, and, in a way, even purposeful. Somehow the interplay of diverse forces and interests is raised to a level of principle which becomes a surrogate for the spirit of the nation. But can such an (anti?) principle really serve as the spirit, or public philosophy, of the nation? Is this not the trap liberalism builds for itself that Max Lerner, in ultimate irony, both celebrated and warned about in explaining the "cement" of "America as a civilization" (see pages 29–32)?

The critical spirit of modern liberalism, which has usually had to challenge the status quo, has in the United States been itself the established, entrenched pattern. Americans then become alternately complacent about the freedom and openness of their society and agitated about the threat some existing circumstance – slavery, or the power of the trusts, or the military-industrial complex – poses to those values. And the cycles of agitation, moreover, have been infused with the peculiar intensity of those who feel their opponents have betrayed shared values or destroyed a common destiny, rather than the more straightforward, less psychically disturbing energy of those intent on supplanting the old with the new.

This sort of impassioned, fractured politics, furthermore, may especially suit the individualist tradition in the United States. Encouraged to think of one's self as a separate entity, as possessed of individual motivation and will, as validated in pursuit of self-interest, as having a personal moral responsibility, as having an effective critical intelligence, and as being altogether a unique embodiment of human potential and creativity, what would be more fitting than a politics whose dynamic was the drives, interests, and aspirations of such individuals? In the relative absence of institutions and ideologies to restrain or counterbalance its liberal tradition, American society has been fluid and diverse, and American politics the jumble of the "multiplicity of factions" that Madison had predicted, welcomed warily, but also never ceased to fret over.

Another way to express this peculiarity of American public life is in the preponderance of what has been called "exit" over "voice" in the United States. That is, in the face of need, dissatisfaction, or deterioration, Americans have tended to move away, make another choice, or seek a change – *exit* – rather than to complain, confront, organize, or argue – *voice*. This has been especially true in economic affairs, but has also often characterized public life. The effect has been to heighten and sensitize habits of (individual) choice and mobility, and to underuse and atrophy skills of public argument, community organization, and attention to the long-range common good. Thus a parent might choose another school rather than organize to revive an inadequate existing one, or a subway rider might switch to a private auto instead of taking part in efforts to improve the public transportation system. Religious groups often splinter from mainline churches rather than work for institutional reform. Exit, of course, requires choice, and liberal, individualistic public culture values that greatly. Conversely, though, and especially in the United States, pre-occupation with exit as a solution can seriously erode both a sense of what the public good might be, and voice, that is attitudes and skills needed to sustain it.[52]

For nearly two centuries, then, individualistic values have been welcomed enthusiastically as the wave of the future. The advance of the frontier, the flood of immigrants, the exploitation of resources, and the building of a vast industrial system, all seemed both to flourish in and encourage these values. So much so that up through mid twentieth century, and including the aftermath of the great victory over the Axis powers so validating to American individualism, the basic assumptions were rarely questioned. Indeed, individualism seemed the fruit of a progress under way since human conceptions of it were fashioned in Greece and Judea millennia ago. As Bishop Berkeley had put it grandiloquently as early as 1725,

> Westward the course of empire takes its way;
> The four first acts already past,
> A fifth shall close the drama with the day;
> Time's noblest offspring is the last.[53]

Yet, all the paradoxes of the 1950s and 1960s (noted in chapter 1) so enlarged and intensified that in the 1970s there seemed to be, for the first time in American history, not a trauma or crusade over a betrayal or a falling-short, but a crisis over the goal itself. Was liberalism overrated; at the end of its tether; collapsed? Was a radical individualism not as all-sufficing as it had been cracked up to be? Were there serious, long-overlooked flaws in the very idea of the self-reliant individual? Was voice needed more than exit? The United States confronts, perhaps for the first time in its history, not a need to fine-tune, enlarge, reapply, or update its individualist ideology, but rather the limitations of the ideology itself. The need is not to somehow further extend the ideals of individual freedom or fulfillment, the opportunities for exit (though such might still be desirable for some people), but instead to supplement or enrich that ideal with emphasis on relatedness and the public good – use of voice. Even if individualism were to achieve the depth and fulfillment sought by many people, basic causes of *public* disarray would remain.

The problem is parallel to that noticed by J. K. Galbraith in 1958: "We must find a way to remedy the poverty which afflicts us in public services and which is in such increasingly bizarre contrast with our affluence in private goods."[54] The continued preoccupation with individualism may, in the 1980s, be a pathological distraction not because it is wrong in itself, but because it both enfeebles an already seriously infantile public concern and exacerbates a disproportion in individual lives that in fact hinders the creative fulfillment of human nature, of man as a political animal. On the other hand, should American society find ways to move toward values and habits less self-oriented and starkly individualistic, then some of the paradoxes might enough resolve themselves to improve public life.

3

East Asian Counterpoint: The Shadow of Confucius

THE DIVERGENCE OF WEST AND EAST

Western Europe and its offshoots around the world, as well as much of eastern Europe, the Middle East, the Mediterranean world, and Africa, strongly influenced by Greece, Rome, and the Christian and Islamic projections of the religion of Abraham, have thus been so permeated with western individualism that counterpoints to it are hard to find. Wherever one turns, from Patagonia to Siberia and from Alaska to Zanzibar and Iran, the moral and cultural energies of Athens, Rome, Jerusalem, and Mecca predominate. In this vast area, according to Huston Smith's large picture of the world's cultural spheres, the Word, religion as doctrine, and the sanctity of the individual, are pervasive. (Christians, Jews, and Muslims are each people of the Book and all see individual faith and righteousness as the means of salvation.) In South Asia, however, in what can be termed the Hindu-Buddhist sphere, the realm of the spirit and the unworldly, suffused with a pantheistic oneness, loom larger than doctrine. In East Asia, under the sway of the ancient Confucian culture of China, the social, the society of humans on earth, is pre-eminent. Liang Chi-chao made similar distinctions in a 1922 study of Chinese political thought: "China has none of the religious fervor of the Hebrews or Indians; she takes little interest in mystic or metaphysical thinking in which the Greeks and Germans excel. . . . The central thesis of [Chinese] literature is the ethical conduct of mankind in this life."[1]

There are, then, two large cultural alternatives to western emphasis on the Word and on the individual. The South Asian sphere, though, is more linked to the West. Its ancient language, Sanskrit, for example, is Indo-European, and Greek and Islamic intrusions have been influential for millennia. This cultural configuration, with its spiritual and other-worldly preoccupations, is also less relevant to a study seeking insight on *public* philosophy. (The large influence of Buddhist and Hindu practices on counter-cultural quests by contemporary westerners, though, reveals the importance of South Asia for those intent not on the public, but on the private, spiritual needs of western society.)

East Asia, on the other hand, offers a vast, ancient, and fascinatingly relevant counterpoint in public practices. Its traditional culture is both almost entirely distinct from that of the West, and of special interest as a socially- or publicly-oriented way of life. Individualism, in both its ennobling and more problematic manifestations, is so deeply imbedded in western habits and ethos that outside perspective or fundamental critique is difficult. Marxism, anarchism, and "New Age" humanism, for example (and even Khoumeinite Islamic fundamentalism for that matter), are all clearly within the western cultural ethos and sphere; viewed from East Asia, at least, they all appear foreign and irretrievably western. (Asian Marxism, in its Maoist form and others, furthermore, has never seemed much like its European counterpart.)

It might help, then, to truly "look from the outside" by making an extended comparison and contrast with a radical alternative, a culture the assumptions and values and ways of which are as distant as possible from those of the West. What might public life, citizenship, attitudes toward the state, be if the individualist assumptions and ethos so pervasive in the West were simply not present? Without suggesting at all that it is either possible or desirable for "the West" to become like "the East" (or vice versa), we may find that the Confucian cultures of the Far East afford us highly useful perspectives on the paradoxes of "advanced case" individualism in the United States. There are 3,000 years or more of recorded political experience to observe, in a region extending from northern Japan, Korea, and Manchuria through the mainland and islands of East Asia southward through some of Vietnam and westward as far as the Buddhist and Islamic regions of Central Asia, including as well islands of Chinese predominance such as Singapore.

One must be careful, of course, about over-generalizing in making wide-ranging cultural comparisons. The important differences among the cultures of China, Korea and Japan (as well as differences in their current regimes) make caution necessary in statements encompassing all of them. The place of Confucianism in each, evolving in time, by no means results in a common pattern. For example, for some centuries after AD 1400 or so, Korean Confucianism was more rigid and pedantic than was the case in either China or Japan, and during the Tokugawa era in Japan (1600–1868) the regime deliberately encouraged an exceptionally hierarchical (and from the then dominant Chinese understanding, unorthodox) variety of Confucianism.[2] In China itself, the neo-Confucian philosophers of the Sung dynasty (AD 960–1279) made far-reaching reorientations that eventually had great impact in Korea and Japan as well. Indeed, Confucianism has always been much more than the writings and teachings of Confucius. He himself was a synthesizer of earlier legends and intellectual traditions, and many important ideas and institutions of "Confucianism" evolved long after his death. Thus, it is not the "ideas of a single philosopher set down in a specific body of writing, but a long and dynamic intellectual tradition with a number of conflicting cross-currents."[3] This evolving character, both changing and changeless, has also been conditioned by style of scholarship and discourse that required every new direction to be traced back nonetheless to some earlier (more or less) Confucian scholar, to the master himself, or even to legendary sages or kings in the mists of China's prehistory who had themselves been extolled, embellished, or invented by Confucius or his disciples. Furthermore, Chinese thought has always contained an indigenous antithesis, Taoism, but its focus beyond the social, in the realm of spirit and spontaneity, often distances its influence from politics and public concern.[4]

Another complication arises because all of East Asia has been strongly influenced by Buddhism. At least as far as explicit religious rites and practices are concerned, this vast region might be regarded as within a Buddhist sphere, and as part of a larger cultural area also including most of South and South-East Asia. Indeed, it is possible to interpret "ways of Asian thinking," and understand national patterns in East Asia by fathoming how Chinese, Korean, Japanese, and Tibetan Buddhism differ among themselves depending upon the different national contexts – but nonetheless each being in its own way deeply Buddhist.[5] Thus one runs more or less risk, in speaking of Confucianism in East Asia, of failing to disentangle what at any given time and place (especially after about AD 500 when Buddhism moved into China, an important transition) might actually be a mixture of Buddhism and Confucianism, or, particularly in China, a Confucianism that had absorbed much of Buddhist values and ways. In China, and in Japan, millions of people find no difficulty, partly because they eschew labels and distinctions, in being devoted to both Confucian and Buddhist ideas and practices. Or, in Korea, the millions of people who regard themselves as Christians (25 percent of the population in South Korea) still seem, at least from the outside, as Confucian in their habits and relationships as other East Asians – and this despite the low standing of Confucianism as an explicit philosophy in modern Korea. In fact, to occidentals fascinated by the Orient in general, it has sometimes appeared that the whole of Asia, from Iran to the South Seas, had characteristics, values, and thought patterns that, at least compared to the West, amounted to a vast and distinct cultural homogeneity. Within this view, the obvious differences between China and India, for example, might be seen as less significant than their similarities and the even deeper chasm between the East and West as wholes.[6]

For a study looking for a publicly-oriented counterpoint to the western tradition of individualism, however, generalizations about the Confucian culture of China, Korea, and Japan still make sense. The point is to focus on the cultural area centered in and heavily influenced by China, which adopted the Chinese system of writing along with its learning, and which absorbed, deliberately and self-consciously, the Confucian values and social system of the Chinese "middle kingdom." This centrally important history, together with the racial and geographic affinities of East Asia, creates, all things considered, a remarkably homogeneous culture readily acknowledged by those within it and just as readily evident to outsiders. It also contrasts with South and South-East Asia which, except for the distinct and relatively recent establishment of Chinese enclaves, were little influenced by China and can be seen generally as within a Hindu-Buddhist cultural sphere. And in so far as East Asian culture possesses an integrity and wholeness, to see its foundation in the Confucian way illuminates its distinctiveness from the West, and also from South and South-East Asia.

Yet another complication arises from the widespread condemnation in the last century or two of Confucianism as a barrier to modernization. The notable campaigns by some Meiji era (1868–1912) intellectuals and officials in Japan to replace Confucian with western learning, and the denunciation during the Great Cultural Revolution in China (1966–76) of all Confucian influence, both rested on a conviction that it was a rigid, ossified, privilege-protecting system that stood in the way of a modern, pragmatic, scientific outlook (whether capitalist or Marxist). Liberal, dissenting groups in contemporary South Korea, too, often regard Confucian precepts as so tied to the authoritarian regime, or at least so manipulated by it, as to make praise of Confucian ways appear oppressive and illiberal. It has been partly pressure from the outside world, then, and the intrusion of foreign ideologies, that have brought modernizing changes to China, Japan, and Korea. This has left explicit Confucian learning and philosophy often more or less disgraced or moribund and has infused society with modern (western) values and habits that increasingly challenge and weaken the hold of ancient (Confucian) values. One can question, then, in philosophy and habit, how much any of the three nations in the 1980s is Confucian.

In deeper, less self-conscious, and indelible ways, however, the time-honored habits and mores remain and continue to pervade attitudes toward self, social customs, and the public, a circumstance which often leaves outsiders impressed with the common elements of East Asian culture. E. O. Reischauer has summarized the political significance:

The Chinese since antiquity have seen their civilization as centering around the political unit, and the Japanese and other peoples of East Asia accepted this concept of the primacy of a unified political system. This concept contrasted with the emphasis on religion as the unifying element in South and West Asia and the acceptance in the West, after the fading of Rome, of religious unity but political diversity. The East Asian emphasis on the political unit may help account for the fact that among the nations of the contemporary world those which first took shape as recognizably the same political units they are today are China in the third century BC and Korea and Japan in the seventh century AD.[7]

Though this emphasis on the nation has in some ways dangerous statist and dictatorial implications, it also implants in the polity a sense of the importance of society as a whole and of the transcendence of public good over private right. It is thus the polar opposite of the liberal, western conception of the state as resting on its "convenience" to the individuals making it up. Such a view would, in the East Asian tradition, be not so much opposed or denied as simply unconceived.

A MORALITY OF RELATIONSHIP

In one of the most famous and, to many westerners, most appalling comments in *The Analects* (ca. 500 BC) Confucius remarked that "no one properly raised need ever be left to improvise." That is, in the detailed, comprehensive, ethical and social system of Confucius, the well-educated person, the person fully conversant with and practiced in the manners, customs, and obligations of life, was one who would in every conceivable circumstance know a habit or a precept that would surely and steadily guide what to do. Or, what was the same thing, he would never be conscious of having a choice, of being in a quandary (if he acted rightly), because the Confucian cultural pattern and ethical system offered complete, precise guidance at every step. Put yet another way, the ideal was *not* to develop in human life a sense of maximum choice, flexibility, options, or indeterminate potential (what in the modern West is thought of generally, and positively, as individual opportunity and openness). Rather, the idea is to so organize, tutor, and guide human life as to make it clear, habitual, unmistakable, what was good, proper, and just. The cultivation of intellect and will so that an individual would be conscious not only of making choices, but of growing in proportion to his ability to decide and choose rightly among alternatives, even of finding pleasure and fulfillment in never-ending openness and moral wrestling, was simply antithetical to the intention and design of Confucius. Other "sayings" make the same point in other ways:[8]

A true gentleman, even in his thought, never departs from what is suitable to his rank. (*Analects*, XIV:28)

To learn and at due times to repeat what one has learnt, is that not after all a pleasure? (I:1)

A young man's duty is to behave well to his parents at home and to his elders abroad, to be cautious in giving promises and punctual in keeping them, to have kindly feelings, toward everyone, but seek the intimacy of the good. (I:6)

Govern the people by moral force, keep order among them by ritual, and they will keep their self-respect and come to you by their own accord. (II:3)

. . . When the way prevails under Heaven, commoners do not discuss public affairs. (XVI:2)

These sayings, of course, place little value on personally chosen creativity or even eccentricity, and are distant indeed from an Emerson who in "Self-Reliance" (*Essays*) proclaims "he who would be a man must be a non-conformist." Confucius found dignity, potential, and fulfillment in a different direction. To him the goal was *li* (理), a rich concept including connotations of principle, of rules of propriety, of ritual, of courtesy, of sacrifice, but above all of moral correctness.[9] This term by no means exalted or validated merely prescribed rules, or etiquette, or convention, or social customs, but, rather, had its essential meaning in an idealism, an adherence to principle, and an emphasis on the rightness of one's inner being. Central themes of western moral philosophy would, in a way, agree, but Confucian thought nonetheless is more mundane, more socially based, more practical, and more inclined toward faithfulness to specific customs and conventions than most Greco-Roman, Judaic, or Christian doctrine and teaching. The essence for Confucius was a moral-social amalgam of precept and practice designed to foster virtue, fidelity, social harmony, order, and political stability – and the individual would achieve meaning and fulfillment by finding his *place within* the principles (*li*) and the way set forth in the Confucian classics.

The profoundly different emphasis in Confucian thought from much of western moral and social philosophy is revealed through its basic teaching about five fundamental relationships and the distinguishing moral quality essential to each: father–son, characterized by affection;

sovereign–subject, characterized by righteousness (or duty); husband–wife, characterized by distinction; elder-brother/younger-brother, characterized by precedence; and friend–friend, characterized by faithfulness.[10] The whole of morality, right conduct, and personal worth depended on one's carefully prescribed fulfillment of the obligations and associated attitudes required throughout life in both sides of each of these relationships. For example, a good son would be always conscious not only of the multitude of specific obligations (and privileges) that were part of his role as his father's son, but also possess, earnestly and instinctively, the feeling of affection that went with the particular practices. Only the sentiment of affection could infuse the prescriptions with a richness that would make them more than mere rules. Becoming a father would move one on to different particular functions and obligations, but would sustain the quality of affection in all aspects of the relationship. In the same way, a younger brother would always be conscious, in deed and attitude, of his position below his elder brother, just as the elder one would think and act always aware of his precedence above the younger. But the sense of precedence would be accepted implicitly and willingly in ways that would benefit, fulfill, and please both elder and younger. Exploitation of either the dominance or the dependence would be a grievous default. Furthermore, many other relationships were subsets of the five major ones; for example, master–servant and teacher–pupil were modelled on sovereign–subject (and thus distinguished by duty), and senior–junior work colleagues followed the precedent-abiding elder-brother/younger-brother pattern and qualities. Sometimes, too, special emphasis is placed on certain relationships, as in pre-1945 Japan when the loyalty of children to parents and of subjects to sovereign was supremely important.

The Confucian system also emphasized five overall virtues in some degree overlapping the qualities associated with the five relationships: benevolence, righteousness, propriety, wisdom, and faithfulness. These virtues were embodied in the natural order of things ("Way of Heaven"), and, practiced earnestly throughout life, would result in moral greatness. Pre-eminent among these qualities is *jen* (仁), benevolence, love, or sympathy for fellow-beings, again making a posture or attitude or feeling the supremely valued center of human life. One brought up within the Confucian system, then, would not only be trained minutely in the etiquette and habits proper to particular roles, but also be imbued with the need to cultivate the requisite feelings that would transform the rituals into heartfelt, morally uplifting relationships. Arthur Waley, eminent translator of Confucius working at the time of the decline of the Liberal Party in Great Britain after World War I, noted this emphasis in a telling comparison. "The downfall of Liberalism," he thought, "has been due to its failure to associate the Middle Way with any strong trend of emotion," while Confucianism had succeeded almost from its inception because "it contrived to endow compromise with an emotional glamour."[11] Waley recognized that one could not *will* a feeling of benevolence in working for compromise and accord, but he saw that in the Confucian system constant inculcation and practice validating that sentiment could, over time, enlarge its sway.

Though the virtues and qualities extolled in Confucian thought are not unlike those often admired in the West (indeed throughout the world), and even the stress on proper relationships is familiar in some degree, there are two important differences in emphasis. First, the entire Confucian system is mundane. There are universal principles in a way, and the "Mandate of Heaven" conferred on the system is a kind of analog for higher, natural, or even divine law, but overwhelmingly the emphasis is on day-to-day relationships, the maintaining of harmonious social patterns, and the infusing of life here and now with correct moral feeling. If such matters are attended to properly, they embody their own reward and are the *summum bonum* of existence. Like the Greek outlook, then, Confucian cosmology and moral thought are thoroughly social in their context and assume the ultimate importance of life and relationships on this earth. Even here, though, there is a key difference: Confucianism disdains the sense of individual pride and hubris prominent in Greek thought from Homer onward. There is even less room in the Confucian way for the intensely personal, overtly self-preoccupying, autonomous emphasis in many other strands of western thought. The contrast is clear in the novel *Creation* where Gore Vidal has his Greco-Persian traveler to China of the fifth century BC find Confucius a rather shallow atheist who sought in vain for moral insight – "one of those masters of the commonplace who are always quoted at such length by the dull." To Vidal's hypothetical scion of Darius and Zoroaster, and confidant of Socrates and Pericles, the Chinese sage was almost ludicrously prosaic and uninspiring, lacking any idea of spiritual power or individual creativity – even though he had "the clearest idea of how public and private affairs should be conducted."[12]

Second, everything about the Confucian system is hierarchical, or vertical, emphasizing relationships "up and down" in pairs where there is clearly a higher and a lower position. One is thus conditioned to think always of whether another person is above or below, whether one's attitude and behavior in a particular relationship is appropriate to a superior, leading role or an inferior, following one. Once the respective positions are established (and there always is a specific obligatory relationship for any given situation), then the proper manners, language, and sentiments are carefully prescribed for the correctly educated person – and there is room for neither choice nor doubt about one's behavior. This ethic thus infuses society with a sense of order and of the satisfaction that arises from knowing and fulfilling one's stations or roles in life.

Yet, in a way sometimes difficult for the western mind to grasp, there are no connotations of oppression or inequity or exploitation in the relationships as understood ideally. Rather, stress throughout is on harmony, constructive interdependence, and mutual concern; *jen*, or love of fellow-beings. Even in the one relationship that is not entirely hierarchical, that of friend to friend (and this relationship can be thought of as "elder friend to junior friend", where the elder friend must be considerate and the younger one deferential),[13] the bonding quality is faithfulness, requiring that above everything friends be true and loyal to each other. Both the relatively unhierarchical nature of this relationship and its emphasis on loyalty, though, give it a peculiar, personal intensity within a Confucian culture. But the bond is seen as existing for its own sake, to fulfill in shared sentiment the lives of the two friends. Common service in an external cause, common belief in external creed or principles, or even encouragement of the personal growth of each individual, though perhaps present as part of the friendship, would not be central. Rather, the essence would be utter devotion each to the other, no matter what, thus again placing the individual in a web that was its own reward, entirely apart from anything else.

In the West there are more or less distancing aspects in even the closest ties; courts, for example, exempt only husbands and wives, and parents and children, from testifying against each other in order that justice be served. Matters of conscience or principle or love are regarded as legitimate, even obligatory grounds for limiting or breaking conventional bonds, and are the basis of many searching, heart-rending works in western literature – Antigone and Creon, Abraham and Isaac, Romeo and Juliet, and the brothers Karamazov, among countless others, come to mind. There is loyalty and steadfastness and heroism aplenty in the sagas and literature of East as well as West, but in the Judeo-Christian-Hellenic cultures the crux is more often faithfulness to conscience, while in Confucian cultures personal fidelity is usually central. More precisely, in Confucian thought conscience consists of faithfulness to the relationship *lived* in all its rich moral significance rather than adherence to abstract principle. Duty, loyalty, bonded commitment to a relationship, then, would in a Confucian outlook be stressed rather than individual conscience or autonomy or self-fulfillment.

The contrast with much of western thought and culture is especially stark in public life, which Confucius himself had so emphasized in his own career and teachings. Order, duty, wisdom, and morality – the marks of personal excellence and of social harmony – would have their largest application in the conduct of the centralized state. In the cultivation of relationships, ascending from those of family and close personal ties to those of livelihood and village and region and then to nation, the sustained emphasis on loyalty, hierarchy, and commitment to the welfare of the group leaves a broad, encompassing role for the nation-state. Lacking both the Greek preoccupation with the abstract ideal and the Judeo-Christian concept of divine law as separate from and superior to the state, Confucian political thinking has accepted a large sphere for the ancient nation or empire. In fact, as E. O. Reischauer has noted, throughout East Asia the state is regarded as "the highest embodiment of civilization," that is, the entity which orders the noblest and most sanctified aspects of human life.

Yet, the East Asian concept of the state (even that somewhat abstract and theoretical phrase is inappropriate because the state is not so much a concept as a pervasive given) is not totalitarian or mystical like either western fascism or communism. It is neither a manifestation of "God marching through history" nor an instrument on either side of a relentless class war. In Confucian thought, in the first Chinese dynasty the emperor ruled with a "Mandate from Heaven," but he also embodied the highest, ultimate bond and being of the people as a whole, and was thus sacrosanct in a mundane way as well. Yet, even the emperor was obliged to maintain his virtue and rule according to it. If he did not, he would, under "Heaven," be disqualified; not properly fulfilling his role, thus immoral, and thus unfit any longer to keep his place or office. In such a case a change or revolution is necessary (*kakumei* in Japanese, or "heaven changes its mind"), either to another branch within a dynasty, or to another dynasty. The idea bears a certain resemblance to western, especially Lockean, thought in that a ruler can lose authority by violating morality and can even be deposed legitimately under such circumstances. But the similarity is also limited severely by the vastly greater weight in the Confucian system given to the nation as a sanctified, encompassing entity. The ideas of the state as a mere convenience for its citizens, or as legitimated in any mechanical way by the consent of the governed, or as limited in its scope and function to certain designated powers, or as distinct from and even somehow antithetical to society/community, would be simply incomprehensible to Confucian-based public consciousness. From the time of the Hebrew prophets and the earliest Greek philosophers for whom we have surviving texts (both roughly contemporaneous with Confucius, about 500 BC), all the major movements of western thought traced in chapter 2 as contributing to our idea of individualism have not been part of the intellectual heritage of East Asia.

EASTERN AND WESTERN IDEAS OF SELF

In sharp contrast to Confucian emphasis on relationships, much of western thought begins with an idea of the individual essentially as "on his own", seeking communion with God, enlightenment, purity of conscience, profit, creative fulfillment, or some other personal aspiration. A model that finds fulfillment in life in faithfulness to carefully structured relationships with other human beings leads, on the other hand, in different directions. Incessantly, many times a day, in the latter pattern impulse and concern would flow toward others and find unnatural and incomprehensible any inclination to begin with "I" or exalt the separate, the unique, or the abstract. In the grammar of the Japanese language, for example, there is often no need to indicate a personal subject for a sentence. When the first person singular is used there are dozens of words for "I," depending on the context and the relationship between the speaker and the hearer. The structure of the language itself, then, denies a unique or willful "I" and instead defines "self" in terms of context or relationship. In an even more subtle neglect of individuality, the language makes no distinction between singular and plural objects; it does not matter whether there is one or many. The Chinese character for the primary Confucian virtue *jen* (benevolence), 仁 , is formed by combining the characters for "human" and "two."

Within the western ideal, oppositely, a sense of self grows steadily more vigorous and forthright, producing all the fruits in so many fields of endeavor that have been the glory of western civilization. This sense is esteemed so pervasively, and often so unquestioningly, that westerners, and especially Americans, take it axiomatically – for granted, as given. Yet, from another perspective, put rather extremely, the same assumption might seem like so much arrant nonsense, so much plain selfishness, so much moral turpitude, so much interference with public duty, social harmony, and even personal satisfaction or fulfillment.

In contrast one finds in East Asia what Robert Barnett calls an "utterly natural acceptance of the age-old Confucian tradition of subordinating individual liberty to collective obligation – for example, to the family."[14] Evidence of this subordinating characteristic appears everywhere, especially in folklore, daily life, and literature. It also permeates neighborhood, occupational, and national life as well as family life.

Two young Chinese university students, one preparing to return to his post at a Beijing Institute and the other in the process of emigration, arriving at an eastern American university in September 1981, were equally startled that a prominent, entirely unashamed concern of their American contemporaries was *choice* about so many things in their lives. Americans pondered, even agonized endlessly, about this or that vocation, political orientation, religion, marriage (or non-marriage) partner, region of residence, and so on. To the young Chinese both the emphasis on choice and the orientation toward *personal* concerns were at once novel and appalling. Could it be that in propriety and self-respect Americans in their early twenties could be facing, relishing, and insisting upon such elemental choices? Could it be either moral or patriotic, furthermore, to make such choices with individual rather than social requirements uppermost? To them, it seemed self-centered in the extreme to suppose such questions might be open for individual choice in the first place, and that they be made, in the second place, with little or no thought of "subordinating individual liberty to collective obligation." (Even in Japan, where choice exists, a persuasive social pressure often very nearly compels young people, far more powerfully than in the United States, to make "choices" not really their personal preference.)

And it was not (at least before being influenced by Western perspectives) that the Chinese students felt themselves to be oppressed, or denied purpose and fulfillment, or kept from making decisions rightfully theirs. Indeed *their* sense of purpose, fulfillment, and right was as much tied to "collective obligation" as the attitude of their American counterparts generally ignored or subordinated such obligation. And it is not that the young Americans were necessarily less idealistic; they simply saw their idealism in individual terms, and assumed that social improvement would follow from their personal growth and fulfillment. Furthermore, though each of the young Chinese had grown up in Mao's China (each, however, scorned the Great Cultural Revolution), there was very little in their attitudes that seemed particularly Marxist, but a great deal that reflected the ancient East Asian view of "the state as the highest embodiment of civilization," of the individual as having identity largely within relationships and groups.

To take another example, an article in a 1979 issue of a Korean magazine, appearing at a time of astonishing modernization and economic progress in Korea, nonetheless extolled the virtues of the "Korean family system," especially as they appeared in the customs of the New Year's season. People everywhere, more likely to be in traditional dress than at any other time of the year, returned to original homes to honor ancestors, parents, and seniors, while those with "seniority and authority" stayed home to receive the compliments and respect of "younger and subordinate people." (The same custom, more or less, is common in China and Japan.) The effect was to cement personal ties of many kinds by reinforcing the "emotional attachment" and moral bonds that all knew, ideally at least, were supposed to characterize both directions of the paired relationships. The author went on to point out that these family life customs extended to many other social situations. Basic "dependency relationships between a senior and a junior," building "order, trust, and propriety," were essential to the many small groups in neighborhoods, schools, and places of employment that enabled people to work together effectively.

Furthermore, far from being obstacles to modernization, these traits and habits were viewed by the author as linked to the diligence, willingness to sacrifice for the sake of family or group well-being, respect for authority, paternalistic management practices, political stability, and keenness for education that many observers saw as responsible for the remarkable social and human resources that in turn undergirded Korean economic progress. The author concluded by lamenting the "extreme individualism" growing in many large cities where people neither knew nor wanted to know their neighbors in big apartment buildings, where senior citizens were "estranged from their own sons and daughters," and where the small nuclear family was becoming the norm. These tendencies were regarded as pathologies, dangerous alike to "customs well worth preserving, to healthy social life," and even to the very success in modernization that some linked (wrongly in the author's opinion) to the alienating aspects of urban, industrial culture. Indeed, the author thought the diligence, group solidarity, and loyalty to one's station that characterized traditional mores, were responsible for Korea's swift adaptation to complex, modern organizations.[15] One can easily imagine almost exactly the same sort of article being written in a Japanese or Chinese context – including even the innuendos favorable to the interests of established authority and the state, whether dictatorial, democratic, or communist.

Contrasting reactions of Japanese and American students to movie heroines also reveal the deeply different attitudes toward individualism and social responsibility prevalent in East Asia. Japanese students seeing the motion picture version of Pasternak's *Dr Zhivago*, though impressed with the idealism and romantic intensity of Yuri and Lara, nonetheless could not really find them very admirable because they were so "selfish." That is, they were so preoccupied with their own desires for creative fulfillment and for joy with each other that they abandoned both their own family responsibilities and the imperatives of the tumultuous social and political revolution going on around them. Pasternak evoked poignantly the tension (endemic in western civilization) between social obligation and the personal quest for romantic love and creative achievement, and he finally justified that quest. The young Japanese, even though studying in the United States and thoroughly modern in many ways, simply didn't respond in the way that made Pasternak's novel so popular in the West.

On the other hand, a group of American students watched a motion picture version of a traditional Japanese tale (as re-told by Lafcadio Hearn) in disbelief and finally scorn and contempt. For Japanese audiences the same picture generally evoked sympathy and understanding, if not any longer, in the last half of the twentieth century, admiration and enthusiasm. The story told of a devoted, loving wife whose husband becomes increasingly "bad": he squanders family resources, becomes an insolent drunkard, consorts with prostitutes, neglects his children, beats his wife, and loses his job. The wife, in response, is patient, understanding, and enduring, as might be expected in a culture emphasizing dutifulness and subordination in wives. More than that, though, and simply appalling to the American students (especially the young women), the story pictured the wife as increasingly noble and heroic the more she endured and the more her response to the abuse was determination to fulfill her obligation as a wife. The Americans thought unanimously that the woman owed it to herself to abandon such a wretch and find satisfaction and realization for herself in another life apart from him. They could not imagine that even beyond the formal requirements of the "role as wife," so important in a Confucian society, there might exist a sense of self that would find fulfillment – even growth and creativity – in accepting and living through outwardly dreadful circumstances in order herself to exemplify essential virtues. To the Americans the tragedy in the story was the unfair and damaged life of the abused wife, while to the Japanese attention focused on the derangement in the relationship – and hence the sympathetic understanding for the sacrificial, virtue-sustaining efforts of the dutiful wife. (Modern, westernized Japanese women, of course, might not be as sympathetic.)

Even aspects of the story that seem to have western analogs, such as heroic self-sacrifice, do not really reflect similar outlooks. In a western story the self-sacrifice might be personal in that one individual, most commonly a parent for a child or an older sibling for a younger one, would give up or endure even to the point of death in order that a loved one, presumably with a long and hopeful (individual) life yet to live, might survive and grow. Or, the sacrifice might be for the sake of a principle or a cause, as in devoting one's life to the sick or the poor, in refusing to repudiate one's religious faith under threat of torture, or in willingness to die on the battlefield for God or country.

Though there are often overtones of the self-disciplining, morally ennobling benefits of the sacrifical posture in its own right, the more profound justification is found in the external goal achieved: the saving of a valued life, the triumph of a glorious cause, and so on.

In the Hearn story, though, there is, at least in western eyes, no noble cause or potentially creative life to "save." After all, the dissolute husband is a thoroughgoing cad hardly worth saving. Nor is there any particular implication that the wife's devotion might rescue the marriage, preserve the family, or in some other way lead to a happy or constructive ending. According to traditional Japanese values she is heroic and admirable in a way *precisely because* there are no such external rewards or purposes. Her moral elevation and human dignity arise because she is faithful to a relationship, because she retains and strengthens the virtuous attitudes (distinction, loyalty, benevolence) that the relationship requires, and because she has no thought of reward, ulterior motive, or ultimate vindication. As with such Japanese "failed heroes" as Minamoto-no-Yoshitsune and Saigo Takemori,[16] it makes no difference that the struggle of the wife is doomed to failure; that is, she does not rescue or reform her husband. Indeed, it is not her business or role or in a way even her purpose to do that. Her conduct is probably even counter-productive in that her indulgence may have encouraged her husband's bad habits or have imposed unnerving and unjust hardships on the rest of the family, but that is of little significance. What matters is the ennobling subordination of self to duty, "fittingness," and the necessarily associated virtues.

But even putting it that way – natural to a westerner – gets the Confucian idea of self wrong because it somehow implies that there *is* an independently existing self that can be consciously sacrificed or subordinated. This is a tension of which the East Asian is generally not cognizant, as the Chinese students revealed in 1981 by their surprise at the agonies over choice and individual fulfillment that so preoccupied their American counterparts. Their astonishment seemed to ask, "is there really a 'self' that is that unique or important apart from the ties and relationships that give life meaning?" Indeed, much of far eastern psychology rests on achieving what in Japanese is called *muga* (無我), "no-self" (the same characters with much the same meaning are used in Chinese and Korean), literally denying what in the West is often regarded as most essential. In Tu Wei-ming's summary of neo-Confucian thought, "the self . . . is not a static structure but a dynamic process. It is a center of relationships, not an enclosed world of private thoughts and feelings. It needs to reach out, to be in touch with other selves and to communicate through an ever-expanding network of human-relatedness."[17] Thus we can find in China, Japan, and Korea patterns of culture where the individualistic mores now so dominant in the United States not only have had little sway, but have not even been valued (except recently in response to western influence). If some of the flaws and pathologies we discern in our public life, then, are related to deficiencies in our long-valued traditions of individualism and liberalism, it might be enlightening to observe some of the guidelines of a public life that, whatever its characteristic weaknesses, nonetheless permits us to see things from another angle.

EASTERN AND WESTERN IDEAS OF THE STATE

The conceptions of self (or lack thereof) in East Asia lead to different assumptions and postulates about the place of the individual in the state. In keeping with the pervasiveness of the family model in the Confucian scheme of things, the state in East Asia has been understood traditionally as a great family. The ruler is at once legendary progenitor, paternalistic authority, affectionate protector, sage-like conselor, impartial arbitrator, stern punisher, revered ritualist, and efficient manager. That is, the good ruler possesses all the qualities and prerogatives, writ large, of the good father of the traditional extended family. Political conceptions and practices, deriving from elaborate "histories" laden with accounts of more or less mythical kings, warriors, sages, and other heroes, hark back, also like veneration of a family's past, to the beginning of time. There, the "national family" had its origins (descended from the gods), and then grew to become a universal, unified empire that as much gives life and meaning and succor to its people as a family does to its members. Moral, affective meaning, moreover, permeates the collective, whether family or state. Formal connections, specific duties, and reciprocal arrangements, far from being of the essence, are seen as being insincere and corrosive if not carried out with benevolence, loyalty, and selflessness.

Within such a framework one would as little think of the state in terms of contract or convenience or compulsion as one would suppose a family to rest on such notions. Nor can the individual be thought of as somehow pre-existing morally with certain rights apart from the polity (or government), or even thought of as a unique creature of conscience and possessed of a suprememly valued soul. Rather, the family model regards the individual as deriving from, utterly enfolded in, fully dependent on, morally completed within the large family of which he was entirely a part. Though there are significant differences in the legends of the origins of the Chinese, Korean, and Japanese peoples, each nation posits its derivation from a dynasty existing from the beginning of time, and each has endlessly elaborate overlays on its history by dozens of generations of Confucian-oriented philosophers and historians that sustain the idea of "individual subordination to collective obligation" – as is true within a family.

The East Asian sense of the state, then, rests upon moral values and a social system sharply at odds with those in process of evolution in the West also over a span of two or three millennia. The East Asian tradition embodies ideas of public virtue, political obligation, and membership that are not so much opposed to those dominant in the West as simply outside them. And it is not that the mythic origins of East Asian states do not have parallels in the West; divinely related or inspired chieftains as founders and progenitors of a people are common enough, as in Egypt, Rome, and Israel, for example. Rather the tie to the historic state, through the habit of Confucian scholarship to elaborate the mythic history and to repreatedly recur to and refurbish it, makes the sense of continuity and incorporateness very much stronger. The first great ruler of Korea, Dangun, for example, is by legend the grandson of God, the father of the nation, and "the guiding genius of Korean national inspiration through all subsequent ages."[18] The feeling of close and real relationship between the ancient, legendary Hsia and Shang dynasties in China, and the model rulers Yao and Shun (endlessly retold, elaborated, and idealized by later generations of "historians"), and the sense the Japanese have of being one, distinct people descending from an emperor-father, convey a far stronger political immediacy than is true for most national origin myths. This, plus millennia-long historical records of the ruling dynasties (in the case of Japan, even a single dynasty), make the state ancient, organic, nurturing, and encompassing in ways not readily comprehensible in nations that evolved along different lines.

In East Asia, then, the starting places for understanding the nature of political life are on the whole very different from those common in the West. The basic propositions are the subordination of individual preference and choice to collective obligation (whether family, village, or nation), and the position of the state as the ultimate, or highest, most encompassing embodiment of civilization. Even stating these basic concepts in terms commonly used in western political discourse, though, is in some degree misleading because there is no way the western mind can read (or write) them without freighting them with their western history, usage, and connotations.

For example, as has been noted in discussing the Classical origins of western political ideas, the Greeks, without denigrating the individual, exalted public life and assumed a necessary, proper subordination of the citizen to his political (collective) obligations. Aristotle (to say nothing of Plato), as much as Confucius, insisted that "a state exists for the sake of the good life, and not for the sake of life only."[19] Yet differences in assumption and connotation are also quickly evident. There is very little Confucian parallel, for example, for the Greek emphasis on the direct, meaningful, ennobling *participation* of "freemen" in the political process. (The parallel, though, to the Platonic notions of fulfillment of proper function and of philosopher-kings is closer.) Instead, Confucian practice puts government and administration in the hands of "heaven-mandated" scholar-bureaucrats, leaving the populace (including even substantial, middle class or land-owning elements) with little to do but accept and obey – and that willingly, loyally, and sincerely. The Greek-derived word "citizenship" is largely untranslatable into East Asian languages (it exists in Japanese, for example, but is seldom used), and there is virtually no place for it in the Confucian cultural scheme. Thus, though Greeks and Confucians each exalt the state, the similarity is limited by the Greek emphasis on individual fulfillment *through* political participation for relatively large segments of the populace, a proposition simply absent from Confucian-derived political thought. (Though there is emphasis on the obligation of officials to "see with the eyes and hear with the ears of all," and then to rule wisely and disinterestedly on behalf of all the people. In another version of the same idea, the Mencian tradition insists that Heaven sees as the people see and Heaven hears as the people hear.) Thus Liang Chi-chao observes that though Chinese thought gives high honor to government "of the people and for the people," government "by the people is a thought left untouched. . . . Neither the method nor the theory . . . [of self-government] has been studied."[20]

To take another example, to see a parallel between the Confucian view of the state as "the highest embodiment of civilization" and the western concept of totalitarianism, though in some ways plausible, is also inappropriate and misleading. The Hegelian idea that "the State is the Divine Idea as it exists on Earth,"[21] the highest and most encompassing of earthly syntheses, is altogether too mystical, abstract, and imposing to suit the Confucian outlook, which is much more mundane, taken for granted, and focused on the relationships among the parts. It is hard to imagine any writings on the state more different in tone and approach, at least, than those of Hegel and Confucius, despite, so to speak, independently arrived at conclusions about "highest embodiment."

Similar limits are apparent when the Confucian-style state is compared with the reality of modern totalitarian governments, whether fascist or communist. The definition of a totalitarian state as one where "everything that isn't forbidden is compulsory" has a certain applicability to East Asian practices. The elements of choice and idiosyncrasy are largely and deliberately absent – Tokugawa Japan (1600–1868), particularly, comes to mind. Yet, the western and eastern systems do not work the same way. Western totalitarianism is generally explicit, "up front" and "laid on," under a highly visible, charismatic leader who deals with and, indeed, often assembles "the people" *en masse*. Even the bureaucratic state that has repudiated the "cult of personality" creates an aura of direct, explicit contact with and control over the populace. Within the Confucian context, however, the omnipresence of public authority and the insistence on unquestioning submissiveness by the people may be no less rigorous, but it is at the same time somehow implicit, built-in, assumed, unexhorted. Thus Japan moved from the Tokugawa shogunate to Meiji oligarchy to military dictatorship and, in a way, even to modern "Japan Incorporated," Korea went from her ancient Yi dynasty to Japanese occupation to the authoritarian regimes of the post-1948 republic, and China moved from Manchu absolutism to Kuomintang dictatorship to Maoism and even to Deng Hsiao-ping's "four modernizations" campaign, each without ever becoming really comparable to western fascism or communism. The state loomed large at each stage, but throughout it was implicit and largely non-ideological, at least as far as the people were concerned. Even the most dictatorial regimes – Japanese wartime militarism, Japanese-occupied Korea, and Mao's Great Cultural Revolution – reflect their western "models" more in general results than in how they actually worked and impacted on the populace.

Rather, all stages in each country can be best understood as under-girded by an assumption of individual subordination to collective obligation built into every level of society.

Confucian emphasis on the *personal* aspect of hierarchical relation-ships, though requiring loyalty and obedience no less exacting than that required by *der Führer* or the party in western statism, nonetheless results in important differences. In the East Asian model, the place of the state is built in at the top of a complex of personal relation-ships woven through society and resting finally on the structure of the family itself. In general, relationships go only one step at a time, as from son to father, or pupil to teacher, or villager to "head man," leaving the connection to those "above" the responsibility of those more immediately "below" the higher authority. There is a strong sense of being part of the whole, especially so far as the nation is concerned, but of more intimate and day-to-day importance are the bonds to family, village, school, and work place. The distinction is between what Nakane Chie calls in Japan the "vertical" society, dependent on interlocking chains of higher–lower relationships, and the essentially "horizontal" (class, party, or large interest group) character of western society (or of India's caste society), including totalitarian systems where leaders relate to vast layers of officials (or party members) and then to the people at large. Thus the "totalness" of the system in the East is on the whole passed down from one binding relationship to the next, rather than, as in the western model, being a matter of personal or party edict, mass meeting, and charismatic influence.

The demise of Japanese and German totalitarianism at the end of World War II (as well as the rise and character of the two regimes) illustrates the difference. Displays of charismatic leadership were absent in Japan 1931–45; in fact, at times it seemed unimportant who the "up front" leader was, and the public had little consciousness of per-sonally dynamic guidance (though of course the symbolism of the largely powerless emperor was immensely significant). When, in the fall of 1944, it became clear to General Tojo that he had failed in the responsibilities of both his superior (the emperor) and his inferior (the officers and soldiers of the army) relationships, he withdrew meekly, willing to face the consequences (required by the nature of the relationships themselves) – almost sure at some stage to be *seppuku* or ritual suicide (bungled in Tojo's case; he was subsequently executed as a war criminal). Hitler, on the other hand, though he too ended in suicide, clung to his totalitarian system to the bitter end, conceiving of it as his personal instrument still dedicated to Nazi ideals, and he had no sense of responsibility for any of the relationships closest to him.

The most profound and revealing difference, though, between East Asian and western conceptions of the state arises from the intense infusion, insisted upon by the Confucian way, of moral precept into the very idea of polity and nationhood. The Confucian classic, *The Great Learning (Ta hsueh)*, in a passage cited and elaborated on endlessly by later generations, holds that

> If there be righteousness in the heart, there will be
> beauty in the character.
> If there be beauty in the character, there will be harmony
> in the home.
> If there be harmony in the home, there will be order in
> the nation [state].
> If there be order in the nation, there will be peace in
> the world.

Within such precepts there could be no separation between morality and politics, between family and government, or between any of the ennobling qualities – righteousness, beauty, harmony, order, and peace – and their associated family and political relationships. This working upward from personal moral qualities to the well-being of the nation and the world does emphasize the individual in that his own good character is essential to the public welfare. But the progression, instead of leading toward more and more lonely grandeur (e.g. Francis of Assisi and H. D. Thoreau), becomes increasingly social: individual righteousness and beauty lead to (social) harmony, order, and peace.

The distance between this Confucian ideal and ideas of government common in the West in the last century or two is evident in the thought of the Japanese anti-Confucianist of the Meiji era (1868–1912), Nishi Amane. He wrote in 1874 that the "root of the evil" in Confucian thought linking politics and morality was its supposition that "cultivating the self and ruling others are the same thing, based on the doctrine in the *Ta hsueh* of cultivating one's self, ordering one's family, governing the country, and pacifying the world."[22] Following closely ideas he had absorbed from J. S. Mill and other admired English utilitarians, Nishi thought these connections hopelessly confusing because "politics and morality are two distinct phenomena." To mingle them impeded the objectivity, scientific analysis, and calculation of individual and group self-interests that were properly the concern and method of politics. But in a Confucian context the separation of morality from politics in order to gain objectivity and clarification of interest in molding public policy vitiated the moral integrity of society. To separate essential, built-in relationships was itself profoundly immoral. Many ideas valued in the liberal West, furthermore – experimental science, self-determination, and individualism, for examples – Nishi saw were not valued in the Confucian order he had grown up in and learned at school. Hence, it seemed an obvious proposition to him that if Japan was to be a modern, liberal nation it would have to reject its Confucian-oriented past and adopt not only the industry and technology of the West but also important elements of its values and political ideas.

The entirely different East Asian concept of the state is everywhere apparent in Liang Chi-chao's 1922 comments on western nationalism, capitalism, and Marxism. Liang, an active reformer as well as scholar in the China of Sun Yat-sen, saw the development of European nationalism as resting on the principle of "consolidation of forces within to withstand those without, so that hatred for foreigners is the means of arousing patriotic feelings. Under the nourishment of emotional racial-hatred groups, the bud of nationalism grows into full foliage. The more it develops, the more pronounced the disorders of modern society,... culminating in the disaster of the Great War." After explaining the Confucian idea of *jen* (仁) (benevolence), Liang observed that in contrast the "narrow [western] conception of patriotism ...brings hatred...and beguiles people into thinking of war as glorious." Furthermore, under capitalism "the capitalist class ignores all considerations of reciprocity, giving to labourers what they themselves dislike. On the other hand, the protagonists of labour, notably the followers of Marx, are also daily advocating retaliation, again giving what they themselves dislike." Thus violating the basic ethical rule of "not doing to others what you do not like yourself," Liang declared it "unthinkable that a social revolution, inspired by such motives [either capitalist or Marxist], will uplift mankind." It was grotesque, Liang thought, to validate ethical or social systems that celebrated alienation among people or depreciated "fellow-feeling among men."

Thus, the polity should not condone parochialism, self-interest, alienation, class conflict, or even convenience and individual opportunity, but rather should emphasize "the doctrine of *jen*, or fellow-feeling." Though never attained in Chinese history, the ideal was an ever-present aspiration, as set down in the ancient *Book of Rites* (quoted by Liang):

When the Great Doctrine prevails, all under heaven will work for the common good. The virtuous will be elected to office, and the able given responsibility. Faithfulness will be in constant practice and harmony will rule. Consequently mankind will not only love their own parents and give care to their own children. All the aged will be provided for, and all the young employed in work. Infants will be fathered; widows and widowers, the fatherless and the unmarried, the disabled and the sick will be cared for. The men will have their rights, and the women their home. No goods will go to waste, nor need they be stored for private possession. No energy should be retained in one's own body, nor used for personal gain. Self-interest ceases, and thieving and disorders are not known. Therefore the gates of the houses are never closed. This state is called the Great Commonwealth.

Liang also pointed out that the western doctrines of utilitarianism, pragmatism, and scientific efficiency, as bases for government, were all deficient. Paraphrasing the Confucian disciple Mencius, Liang stated that "we should reckon life not in terms of material value but by spiritual standards. . . . The sum total of the efficiency of mankind is not measured either by the addition or the multiplication of the efficiencies of all the individuals." Even worse was "the standard of rights upon which is based all the political thinking of Europe and America. . . . Even the relationship between father and son, husband and wife, is not free from its influence." From the Confucian standpoint, the western concept of rights seemed "founded on the feeling of antagonism; its very nature is acquisitive and insatiable." Parents and children or husbands and wives would not be able to live in the essential affection and benevolence if they were preoccupied with the protection of the separate rights of one individual as over against another. On the other hand, a people imbued with *jen* as underlying all human relationships would be "incapable of understanding the importance of individual rights, municipal rights, institutional rights, class rights, and even state rights." "It is evident," Liang concluded, "that the expression of rights can only be conflict and murder. That a society built on such foundations will ever be safe is inconceivable. No wonder that men of vision in Europe should predict the collapse of civilization."[23]

Though Liang spoke in hyperbole, largely ignored the violent, oppressive, and ethnocentric aspects of Chinese history (perhaps nourished by some elements of Confucian thought), and overlooked the valuable aspects of western ideas of human and individual rights, there is a profound point to his critique. From a perspective that sees the good and moral life as resting on relationships and inclusion in family and nation, the ideologies of individualism, utilitarianism, and even natural rights have deeply troublesome, even frightening implications. Would it be instructive, then, to reassess the western ideologies to see if they do indeed, as Liang argued, contribute to "the disorder of modern society?"

THE JAPANESE ENCOUNTER WITH THE WEST

We can see further how this Confucian counterview might help us understand our own practices, values, and dilemmas if we look more closely at the meeting of East and West in Japan since mid nineteenth century. In that nation this encounter has resulted in a democratic polity and a sophisticated modernity that in revealing ways is both like and unlike anything we know in the West. In Japan, as in China and Korea, the dominant reaction of those first excited by a knowledge of western ideas and culture, and eager to bring their nations into the modern world by learning from the West, was to see Confucian philosophy and habits as barriers to be overcome. This was true not only because Confucianism was the basis for the anciently established society and government. More particularly, especially as a few men began to fully understand western thought and values, they saw that these ideas, intriguing, even appealing in themselves, also undergirded the technological and military superiority that at once awed and frightened the far eastern nations. If these nations were to survive the threat from the West, then, and also perhaps absorb some new and valuable ideas and ways, then Confucianism in all its manifestations seemed an obstacle that had to be set aside. It buttressed the state, dominated education, controlled access to officialdom, furnished a rigid philosophical orthodoxy, sustained the family, defined the social system, and dictated ethics, all in ways antithetical to modernity – and to national survival as well.

Confronting this circumstance, Fukuzawa Yukichi (1835–1901), the leading interpreter and exponent of western learning in Japan during the Meiji era, came early to believe that "Chinese [Confucian] philosophy as the root of education was responsible for [Japan's] obvious shortcoming." It was altogether a "retrogressive doctrine" whose influence had to be eliminated as much as possible and replaced with western learning. It would be necessary, he thought, if Japan was to learn the vital lessons from "the true spirit of western culture," for scholars and teachers to "rise up and denounce the all-important Chinese [Confucian] influence."[24] It had for too many centuries dominated life in Japan and the rest of East Asia. In pursuit of this goal Fukuzawa learned Dutch, and then English, traveled to America and Europe, translated English documents, wrote books introducing western ideas to Japan, advised the reformist elements in the Meiji government, and founded a university (Keio) emphasizing western studies.

Fukuzawa's encounters and battles as he waged this campaign reveal again and again how deep seated Confucian precepts were and, increasingly, the complexity and ambiguity of his effort. While studying western medicine, he and his colleagues became aware that they were gaining possession of a vocabulary, and a scientific understanding and technology, that allowed them to treat many disorders that baffled even the most learned practitioners of what he called "Chinese medicine." Since in Confucian thought there were no disconnections between medicine, social customs, ancient learning, ethics, or anything else – the schools of "Chinese medicine" were philosophically encompassing, devoted as all Confucian schools were to passing on the learning of the presiding "master" – Fukuzawa "came to dislike everything that had any connection with Chinese culture."[25] At the most straightforward levels of scientific investigation and of understanding the physical world, that is, Fukuzawa found Confucian learning so inferior that he, like many others, saw it as discredited also in every other way. The path to survival, progress, and modernity required its wholesale extirpation. (How ironic these objections seem in the light of the recent holistic health movement in America and Europe, seeking now to redress the chemical and technological emphasis in western medicine.) The pall that fell over Confucianism was akin to the general stigma Roman Catholic Christianity sustained when for a time it clung to Ptolemaic astronomy, opposed dissection of the human body, and otherwise found itself on the wrong side of increasingly impressive scientific, material achievements.

Fukuzawa thus sought to help his countrymen to learn and think and act in the western ways. In one revealing incident he talked about an elementary western economics textbook to a government official who asked for a translation so he could show it to his superiors. Seeking to comply, Fukuzawa came to the key word "competition" for which, he discovered, "there was no equivalent in Japanese," at least with appropriate connotations. He had to invent his own word, *kyoso*, composed of two Chinese characters meaning "race-fight" (競争). When the official came to the word in the translation he commented "here is the word 'fight.' What does it mean? It is such an unpeaceful word." (The Chinese character for "fight" had connotations of war and battle as well as struggle more generally, while "race" referred to contests in comparative ability such as running, climbing, and the like.) Fukuzawa explained that the concept he had in mind was nothing new or alarming, even in traditional Japanese ways. It meant the effort, as was common among Japanese merchants, to sell things more cheaply, or improve them, or display them more attractively, in order to increase sales. In this way all merchants "race and fight" (compete), fixing terms of trade and the value of merchandise. That was all *kyoso* meant in the science of economics. When the official objected that there seemed to be "too much effort [striving in frantic, divisive ways] in western affairs," Fukuzawa responded that there was not since it was "fundamental to the world of commerce," where to "compete," to seek self-advantage, was valid and laudable. Still, the official insisted that "the word 'fight' is not conducive to peace." He could not, therefore, show a paper with that character on it to his superior; could another one be used, he asked. Piqued, Fukuzawa said he supposed the high official would rather see phrases about "men being kind to each other" or being loyal to their lords, or merchants being generous "in times of national stress," as Confucian rhetoric of statecraft required. But that would be unfaithful to the idea in the western textbook, so he would have to leave it out. Fukuzawa thought this incident showed how hopelessly backward and unenlightened the old ways of thinking were.[26]

Actually, of course, a profound cross-cultural exchange had taken place. Embedded in the relationship between superior and inferior, in attitudes toward commerce and national polity, and in the language itself were deeply variant attitudes toward what in the West is thought of as "competitive individualism." The western economics textbook, in the tradition of Adam Smith and classical economic theory, extolled the idea, finding it both morally defensible and the foundation of "the wealth of nations." Accepting these arguments, Fukuzawa sought to transfer and translate them into Japanese culture, but there simply was no framework for understanding, or even vocabulary for explanation. As the official revealed, everything about the idea seemed repugnant: it was self-assertive and aggressive; it upset social harmony; it injected separateness into vital human relationships; it lowered moral tone and sensibility. And, as Fukuzawa's explanation also revealed, it was *not* that Japanese merchants (and customers) were unfamiliar with, or unpracticed in, the realities of competitive exchange, but rather somehow the cultural and moral placement was vastly different. Well into the twentieth century the Japanese words for freedom, *jiyuu* (自由), and for individualism, *kojinsyugi* (個人主義), were scorned because they implied selfishness. With such deep difference in perspective and evaluation, it is not surprising that in myriad ways the Japanese encounter with the West produced vivid contrasts and intricate misunderstandings.

Even such an avowed foe of Confucianism as Fukuzawa, though, remained in many personal ways more traditional than perhaps even he realized. At Keio University he abolished the old custom of students making elaborately wrapped ceremonial presents to revered teachers according to family wealth and status, and instead set a fixed tuition fee. Fukuzawa nonetheless reported that the teachers, all former students at the school, followed his example and took from the fees collected only what they needed for subsistence. At the end of each month Fukuzawa watched the sessions where each teacher sought to *diminish* his share, and would finally intervene. He urged his staff not to argue (even in reverse) over the trifling matter of money but instead to simply take a little for their own needs and then trust all would come out well for the good of the school.[27] Thus he preserved the ancient guidelines of deference to the master, absence of contract, unconcern for material rewards, attention to the quality of human relationships, and faithfulness to the collective body, because they embodied social and moral values too ingrained for Fukuzawa to disavow. It was simply impossible even for so westernized a person as Fukuzawa to conduct a school in East Asia according to the precepts of Bentham and Ricardo.

Again the point is neither that selfishness and insincerity did not exist among the Keio faculty (doubtless they did), nor that generosity and sacrifice for the good of the group are not valued in the West (of course they are). Rather, the basic relationships and emphases are somehow very different. In the Confucian context an exchange of money disconnected from the feelings and obligations incumbent on both giver and receiver was vulgar and immoral. Even the idea of a fixed contract providing payment for services rendered, regardless of the particular individual – a simple arrangement, fair, efficient, and businesslike in a commercial culture – was instead thought deeply offensive because personal feelings were ignored. Oppositely, the preoccupation with the wrapping paper and the unwrapping ceremony, the elaborate distinctions made among individuals and families, the deference to authority, the emphasis on sentiment and attitude, the gift-giving posture, and all the other rich subtleties of the traditional relationship between teacher and pupil, did not carry the negative connotations of favoritism, arbitrariness, obsequity, or even near-bribery as they would generally in the West.

Fukuzawa's eye-opening encounter with western ideas in Meiji Japan, then, reveals a stark and stunning juxtaposition of sophisticated cultures, especially in their ideas of self and society. The historical accident that it took place at a moment when Anglo-American philosophies of liberal individualism were at a flood tide of influence and self-confidence, and Japan had been imprinted with two and one-half centuries of a firmly imposed, Confucian-oriented cultural stasis, heightened the contrast. It was almost as though John Stuart Mill and Justice Holmes confronted Confucius himself (or at least Tokugawa Ieyasu's teachers of official Confucian philosophy) in the new schools of "western learning" that flourished in Tokyo after 1868. And as the serious and learned Japanese in these schools (like Fukuzawa generally with thoroughly traditional Confucian training) absorbed western ideas, an intense light is shed on the contrast. The Japanese learned as they were so eager to do, and became leaders in the modernization of their country (necessary for survival in the face of western imperialism), but again and again their searching critiques and explicit repudiations as well as their implicit reservations and subtle transformations showed how different the values and perspectives were.

The Meiji official, for example, in disdaining Fukuzawa's translation of "competition," in a way simply asked him to consider "the other face" of the ideas of assertive individualism and social contentiousness. In the confident models Fukuzawa was learning from England and America, the ideas seemed entirely constructive. The effort and energy of individuals were stimulated, people found opportunity for creativity and change, society became more fluid and open, trade and industry flourished, and citizens learned the self-reliance and responsibility required to make government by consent work. The ideology of liberalism seemed to Fukuzawa vigorously unassailable. Yet the whole notion seemed wrong-headed to the official. It was inimical to precepts of peace and harmony that to him were the essential foundations of a good society.

The western, liberal ideology was, to the Confucian outlook, simply appalling. It asserted that economic competition provided a benign outlet for instinctual human selfishness – but was that *really* so basic to our natures? It supposed that forces contending in the marketplace resulted in "public benefit" as an "invisible hand" guided economies toward "the wealth of nations" – but could good thus come from greed? It proclaimed that strenuous, divisive striving was good for the mind and spirit as well as the body – but was "so much effort" really conducive to human well-being? And it insisted that the general good could rest on the assertiveness of the parts – but was not the wisdom and guidance of a learned, exalted officialdom the necessary basis of a morally correct public life? Even the very idea that a public official might bring his superior a paper so freighted with virtually immoral brush-strokes (however "true") was inadmissible because it would upset, even violate, a relationship dependent on a deep sensitivity to its inherent values. Kindness, loyalty, order, and generosity (Confucian benevolence) were to be encouraged – not effort, self-assertion, contention, and change as the western model upheld. And however much each outlook also in reality contained rationalization, self-deception, and hypocrisy (and each did, of course), the contrast and tension between each at its best is considerable and holds the other up to a standard that questions its value even in ideal form.

Another element in Japanese contact with the West, the writing in the Meiji era of so-called "I-novels" (that is, novels using the first person singular, or injecting the author into the story), shows how long-standing, widely admired literary conventions of the West might appear both strange and problematical from another perspective. The novel in some form was centuries old in Japan, and notable heroes (and heroines) such as Prince Genji and the faithful samurai Benkei were fixed firmly in its literary-legendary imagination. Yet, there was no real counterpart, traditionally, to the western focus, growing in eighteenth- and nineteenth-century thought and literature, on the individual as possessing an inner uniqueness, an energy and morality and creativity interesting and valuable in its own right, entirely apart from loyalty to others, political leadership, martial courage, or any other connectedness with society. As Fukuzawa and other advocates of western "enlightenment" introduced Samuel Smiles, John Stuart Mill, Herbert Spencer, Orison Swett Marden, and other proponents of western-style individualism to Japan, as part of campaigns to liberalize Japanese public life, Japanese writers began as well to absorb the import of such introspective western authors as Goethe, Hawthorne, and Dostoyevsky.[28]

Futabatei Shimei (1864–1909), for example, wrote in a novel *Ukigumo* (1889) of the inner life of Bunzo, a young man who was dismissed from his government job. He then agonized over the effect this had on the plans of his aunt-guardian to have him marry her daughter, just coming of age. The plot is conventional and predictable, involving a rival suitor, changing relationships, and so on. It was also startlingly new in Japan for its long scenes which have Bunzo sitting alone and desperate in his room as he ponders his situation – as if this lonely, inner life was of great importance and as if it was possible to live meaningfully in the isolated world of one's feelings, moral struggles, and personal development. Despite Bunzo's continued reflection of the traditional samurai values of family loyalty, social harmony, and so on, Futabatei nonetheless departs boldly from the conventions of Confucian-based stories. In that genre characters essentially fulfill roles associated with certain virtues, and the action ordinarily reveals (good) characters living up to such patterns, and others (bad) not – all clearly intended to affirm social values and to provide moral (that is, socially acceptable) instruction to the reader.

Ukigumo was path-breaking, then, not in plot or overt message but in its shift of focus from the social and the connected to the inner and the isolated, a viewpoint deeply alien to the long-dominant Confucian culture.[29]

Eighteen years later, after further extensive influence on Japanese writers by a whole range of western "egoists" from Rousseau and Emerson to Zola and Tolstoy, Katai Tayama wrote in *Futon* (*The Quilt*) another apparently conventional story of an elderly teacher. He yearns to make love to a young pupil, resists the impulse, and then is asked by the pupil and her modern, city lover to defend their illicit romance. In a mixture of jealousy and righteousness, he reveals the affair to the girl's father, a stern traditionalist, who at once brings her home in disgrace. The novel ends with the tormented teacher, while knowing all is lost, yet unable to forbear a self-pitying clutch at the girl's bedding. Conventional morality triumphs, but not until Katai has explored in all three characters (but especially in the teacher) a deep psychic turmoil that had little or no precedent in Japanese literature.[30]

In another novel written at about the same time, Toson Shimazaki's *Haikai*, the author dwells on the inner life of an outcast *eta*, Ushimatsu. He had, by concealing his origin, become a teacher and won the love of a girl from a simple but respectable family. In a sub-plot, another *eta*, Inoko, courageously acknowledges his status in order to fight openly against their degraded condition amid the corrupt beginning of parliamentary politics in Japan. This inspires Ushimatsu to reveal his own standing, which results in dismissal from his teaching post and emigration from Japan. Though the novel is in part a social one, protesting Japanese prejudice against the *eta* and corruption in politics, its dominant theme is Ushimatsu's "rebirth." Through honesty and self-revelation he achieves a true identity that enables him to hold his head high rather than have to hide and evade in the face of social convention. Ushimatsu's triumph, that is, is an inner one. The novel often depicts Ushimatsu, amid suitable scenes of nature, achieving insight into himself and making self-strengthening decisions. In the end the point is not so much his struggle in society against *eta*-hood, as it is his discovery of the inner strength to be his own real, honest person – a state Japanese critics of his work have often referred to in their westernized compatriots as "the awakening to modern selfhood."[31]

To the western mind the struggles of these Japanese "I-novelists" (the force of the appellation itself arises from the minimal presence in Japanese language and culture of the first person singular; hence the notableness of writing emphasizing the "I") is at first glance odd because one thinks of Zen Buddhists, for example, as highly introspective. Also, ancient Japanese literature is filled with subtle evocations of inner feelings and sharp delineations of personality. The characters' lives, though, are always strongly contextual and filled with fidelity to relationships. Like the monk, they aspire not to egoistic fulfillment (however idealistic) but rather to mastery over or escape from individuality, or separated identity. And the I-novelists of the Meiji era, strongly influenced by western models, seemed revolutionary precisely because they gave expression to an ideal of individuality, an emphasis on "true", real, inner identity conceived of as over against what tradition or society or status or relationship required, simply unheard of in the centuries-old Confucian culture. Thus one sees excruciating travail, by both the authors themselves and the characters they create (often clearly autobiographical in the accepted western mode but shocking in Japan where self-revelation was still seen as vulgar and immoral), as the utterly alien ego exaltation of the "confessions" of a Rousseau or a Tolstoy or a "Raskolnikov" breaks into East Asian consciousness.

SOCIETY AND PSYCHE IN MODERN JAPAN

Modern analyses of Japanese character and society, though often increasingly preoccupied with how Japan is losing its customary ways, nonetheless describe a culture very different from that of the United States, especially on deeply held attitudes toward society, relationships, and the individual. As Japan's economic miracle of the 1960s and 1970s changed the face of the nation, overt or explicit Confucianism seemed virtually to disappear even as a topic of discussion. It was the unlamented symbol of Japan's backwardness and stagnation. The hope of Fukuzawa that Japan would discard "Chinese learning" and replace it with modern, western science, technology, and thought thus seemed fulfilled.

Yet despite their obvious transformation into the Orient's most advanced people, the Japanese still seem different and inscrutable to westerners, especially in everyday habits and attitudes. How deep, then, has the transformation really been? Are there profound ways in which Japan still bears the mark of its 1,500 years as part of Confucian-derived East Asian culture? Modern Japanese high schools, for example, still require two years of classic Chinese language and history, where Confucian discourse is implicit throughout and Confucian teachings are included in the textbooks. Japanese universities, though, pay as little attention to Confucius and Chinese as Harvard and Ohio State do to Cicero and Latin, and western seekers often know more about eastern philosophy than their Japanese counterparts. Can Japanese character and society, then, still be understood in some degree by seeing not how modern or western they have become but rather how "Confucian" they still are?

Nakane Chie, for example, in analyzing how Japanese groups work, explains that even in modern industrial organizations the interplay of people and the relationships among groups are starkly different from those usual in the West. In Japan the basic unit or group is always tightly bonded emotionally as well as in purpose, composed of generalists rather than specialists, and "vertical" rather than "horizontal." That is, higher–lower personal relationships are fundamental rather than broad affinities of specialization or function or class. Thus, a work team usually consists of a leader (*oyabun*, or *joshi*), perhaps some subleaders, and then a group of subordinated (*kobun*, or *buka*), whose main allegiance or connection is upward toward the immediate superior. The functioning of the group, then, rests on the loyalty, obedience, and willingness to serve of the *kobun* and on the authority, guidance, responsibility, and concern for all of the *oyabun*. The model is the family household where the father is the head and all others are linked hierarchically to him. There are thus clear higher–lower relationships, but there is also a pervasive sense of the classless membership of all in one organization where everyone puts its welfare uppermost. The authority of the leader is not unconditional, and emotional feelings on all sides are very important. Indeed, the leader risks the effectiveness of the group if he rejects the consensus of his followers. In large corporations, this closeness and, in a way, equality, is symbolized when company presidents wear the same uniforms as low-level workers; one can scarcely imagine this at a General Motors or British Steel plant.

The key to being part of the group, then, is not skill at a specialized role or representation of a particular constituency. This would make it a committee, where the attributes – quality control engineer, economist, union member, Chase-Manhattan representative on the board, etc. – of the people involved are of the essence. Instead, the crux is a pervasive, emotional commitment to the group as a group. Everything depends on the closeness and assurance of the bonds within the group, and the willingness of everyone in it to share its tasks and accept the moral and emotional responsibilities that go with prolonged, intimate association. The group develops a keen sense of camaraderie and commonly spends long hours together, day after day, at work and in relaxation. Individuals are valued and trusted, all speak up and make important contributions, each member knows the abilities and weaknesses of the others, personal idiosyncrasies are acknowledged, and the needs of all are attended to thoughtfully – yet the essential verticalness is never relinquished. All are deeply aware of, utterly imbued with the clear hierarchies of every relationship within the group. They control language used, order of speaking and acting, mode of participation in decision-making, and relations and attitudes for every circumstance that can arise. (Recall Confucius's aphorism, "no one properly raised need ever be left to improvise.") And all of this takes place, traditionally at least, without overt feelings or display of resentment, or inferiority, or injustice that would often characterize such relentless hierarchy in the West, and perhaps especially in the United States with its strong ideologies of equality and individualism. It is not that people are less valued or important in one culture or the other, but simply that how and why they are valued are different.[32]

Yet, despite the pervasiveness of hierarchy and thus the multitude of leader–subordinate relationships, there is no word in Japanese that conveys the assertive connotation of the English word "leadership." The common Japanese word *shido* (指導) is literally "finger-guide," and thus connotes more guidance than overt leadership. In fact, western qualities of leadership – charisma, extraordinary genius, easy dominance of others, public eloquence – are not characteristic of Japanese leaders because such qualities would not nourish the all-important *emotional* relationships within the group. Thus heterogeneous groups of specialists gathered to "solve a problem," even if given strong (in western terms) leadership, "almost invariably blunder," Nakane asserts, because the vital qualitative ties are missing.

Furthermore, the existence of a legal contract to define task and responsibility is usually a severe obstacle to effective group work. "One might say that fundamentally the concept of contract does not exist at all" in the customary outlook of either those undertaking a task or those commissioning it. Again, this is because everything depends on the intimate, personally sensitive, trusting (yet always hierarchical) relationships between leader and subordinates. To emphasize legalities, impersonal expertise, and contractual clarity in such a context appears cold, inefficient, tenuous, rigid, and authoritarian. Expertise, of course, is not unappreciated, but instead of being a quantitative contribution that could come from anybody, it is typically a qualitative attribute, loyally acquired, by someone within the group.[33]

Within customary groups (those of about ten or twelve people work best), decisions are thought to be fair and democratic when consideration is given to the views and needs of "the weaker or lower." Discussion begins informally, not necessarily logically or directly on the issue at hand, but with "much indulgence toward individual feelings at stake." Gradually, as all listen to each other, consensus grows and all have a feeling of having been heard and having made a contribution. Subtly, leaders absorb as their own the views of subordinates until it seems that the initiatives come from the leaders. Roughly, when agreement passes the two-thirds point, the group will sense a decision is near and the need for cohesion and solidarity will take over. In the interests of loyalty, all will readily agree to cooperate, satisfied that at any rate all have been consulted and heard. Two features of western decision-making are notably absent: the idea of deciding by majority vote, which seems inconsiderate and domineering, and the notion of continued, principled opposition as a vital part in an ongoing search for truth, which is regarded as a breach of the all-important emotional well-being of the group and its need to draw together loyally.[34]

Though the dazzling success of Japanese industrial management and the remarkable stability of the Japanese political system since 1951 demonstrate an ability to function effectively in a thoroughly modern way, it is also evident, then, that ancient values and habits infuse the inner dynamic of how groups function. The key, in a Confucian pattern centuries old, is the instinctive dependence on relationships at once firmly hierarchical, intensely moral, and deeply emotional. The whole sense of fitness, dignity, value, and purpose in life is bound tightly to the quality and fidelity of these relationships. Neither abstract principle nor practical efficiency, to take two common western pre-occupations, are sufficient reason for violating this quality and fidelity. To put it oppositely, there are simply no grounds for asserting individuality as over against the imperatives of proper relationships and group cohesiveness. Thus, though Japan may *seem* modern, or westernized, ancient values and habits, strongly Confucian, make her people and the way her society works deeply different – and thus afford Americans a useful counterpoint and critical perspective for pondering their own ways.

Seeking another way to understand cultural differences, the Japanese psychiatrist Doi Takeo has explained how the concept of *amae*, meaning dependence on or seeking or expecting the indulgence of others, gives to the Japanese sense of self (or individuality), of the group, and of relationships with others connotations very different from those common in the West. Dr Doi points out, as an example, the difference in Japanese and American customs in entertaining guests at a meal. He had been made nervous, and had unpleasant reactions, he recalls, during his first visits to American homes when the host commonly offered a range of drink choices before the meal. Dr Doi had first to choose between hard or soft drink; then, having selected liquor, between Scotch and bourbon; having chosen Scotch, between mixture with soda, water, or ice; and having selected soda, between strong or weak dilution of the drink. Dr Doi sensed at first not the intention of politeness and respect for individual preference, but rather the burden of being obliged to make trivial choices about which he could not have cared less – or choices, at least, which were far less important than the need he felt to simply depend on the host to take care of everything. It seemed further that the whole performance revealed not a sensitive anticipation in advance by the host of the guest's needs and hence an ability to conduct him caringly and without perplexity through the opening ceremonies, so to speak, as Japanese etiquette would require, but rather it seemed designed to display the abundance, prodigality, and freedom of the host. The same discomfort arose at the end of the meal when more choices were required: tea or coffee, regular or decaffeinated, sugar or cream or both or neither, and so on. (Customarily at Japanese meals, the diner assumes the food is properly seasoned, and enjoys and values what has been prepared – without making personal choices or changes.)

Then, at the meal itself, especially if it were a buffet of some kind,

Dr Doi was told "please help yourself." Instead of the phrase having the generous connotation of "please take what you like without hesitation," again the words rang unpleasantly in his ears. They somehow sounded like "nobody else will help you," or "you're on your own," or "place your desires above all other considerations," and thus, to him, hardly seemed expressions of kindness or goodwill or concern for others. He felt, rather than the inclusion in a welcoming, informal openness and freedom the host intended, only abandonment, inconsiderateness at being left unguided in an unfamiliar place, and, finally, an almost desperate loneliness.[35]

Clearly, Dr Doi is describing situations, perhaps trivial in themselves and permeated by the good intentions of all concerned, where deep differences in expectations, values, and psychic satisfactions are present, and where opportunities for both misunderstanding and insight abound. Most profound, perhaps, is the gap between the assumption of the American hosts that choice, freedom, and individuality would of course be gratifying to and appreciated by the guests, and Dr Doi's *opposite* desire. He expected and would have appreciated guiding kindness (in a degree that would have seemed childish and even insulting to most westerners), empathy and dependence (rather than choice and independence), and a selfless anticipation by the host arising from a keen sensitivity for the *quality* of the morally-oriented host–guest relationship. Rather than the coldness and lack of concern he felt in the words "help yourself," and the discomfort of making endless choices, Dr Doi's cultural foundations left him longing for "help from others," a thoughtful attentiveness that would have relieved him of making decisions, and a kind of encompassing inclusion that would have eliminated choices and distinctiveness. This sense of discomfort at making endless choices, moreover, arises especially for a Japanese male because traditionally his wife would have attended, unasked, to all his preferences, and he would never complain about such trivial matters as meal selections. For a woman, the discomfort at expressing preferences would arise from her traditional role of *never* injecting her personal desires or views into any situation, especially where men ("superiors") are involved. Young Japanese women are often told by their grandmothers that "it is vulgar for women to have opinions." Deep down Dr Doi did not *want* to "be himself," or to maintain his "private space," or exercise his right of making choices – all qualities his American hosts, within their cultural context, assumed he would value as much as they did. At least, as he recognized, there was not the slightest *intent* to discomfort, exclude, distance, or disrespect him. In fact, by western standards, there was exactly the opposite intention on each score.

Dr Doi emphasizes, then, the importance for the Japanese of *amae*, the pleasure, comfort, and assurance experienced when others (either above or below in hierarchical linkages, but especially notable in "above" relationships) allow and invite an indulgent, even child-like dependence. Also important is *ninjo*, an intensity of human feeling and emotional attachment that dissolves any sense of unworthiness or presumption in the claiming of dependence and can even infuse the *giri*, or duty, that characterizes more formal or contractual relationships, with feelings of willing fulfillment, gratitude and warmth. Closer dependence and tenderness and obligation is expresssed by the *on* one feels toward parents or other superiors (especially teachers) who give special benefits with care and affection. One does receive "credit," of course, in allowing (accepting or even welcoming might be better words) the dependence, in that the matter is "not ended." But the obligation is infused with feelings of greater closeness, heightened empathy, and assurance of support and loyalty in general rather than being like holding an IOU that can be claimed at some later time.

One who has experienced a favor or act of kindness from another, then, incurs *on* or an obligation that entails a dutiful response (*giri*) of some sort and that establishes an interdependence. But ideally this interdependence evokes *ninjo* in both directions; that is, warmth, human feeling, and goodwill flow back and forth in a way that conditions and encompasses any more straightforward, formal, or tangible aspects of the relationship. Without this *ninjo*, furthermore, going through the formalities, though still "required" and perhaps undertaken or received perfunctorily, becomes troublesome, nerve-racking, and even contempt-breeding. The formalities are false and enervating because the positive emotion and moral attitude are not present. In fact, they generate *enryo*, restraint or holding back, that has the effect of distancing people and is a sort of "negative yardstick in measuring the intimacy of human relationships."

The ideal is relationships that are as much as possible devoid of *enryo* ("arm's length" or "with reservations" would be other connotations in English), but instead are infused with warm *ninjo*. Then one can feel an acceptance, indulgence, or dependence of *amae*, most fully embodied in the parent–child (especially mother–child) bond but more or less aspired to in family, work, school, neighbor, and friend relationships. Thus various *giri* relationships, perhaps initially expressing a rather "distant" sense of duty, can, as Dr Doi says, "have *ninjo* brought to them", and indeed will only be satisfying, become untroublesome, if that human feeling comes to infuse them. Rather than thinking of them as opposed, then, one should understand *giri* (duty) as a vessel into which can come *ninjo* (warm feeling). This in turn nourishes the welcome and enjoyable feeling of *amae* (dependence).[36]

In some degree, of course, the bonds and sentiments here described are evident and valued in western culture, just as the Japanese words can be translated, more or less, into English. But the imprecisions, the different weight and tone given to the words in the different languages, and varying emphasis, centrality, and context also mark important cultural distinctions. These can help us understand key psychic and emotional aspects of a society that defines human existence in terms of relationships. The five basic Confucian relationships, including their refinements, subdivisions, and modernizations, for example, in Japan must be infused with the vital feelings, emotional currents, and moral sensitivity if they are to achieve the requisite dimensions, quality, and psychic satisfaction. (Chinese and Korean embodiments of the relationships are not identical, but once the Japanese versions are in some degree understood, other Confucian-based ones seem similar, especially as compared to either South Asian or western conceptions.) The relationships must encompass much more than formality, duty, ritual, and habit (though those are all present). Only then can they achieve the moral and emotional content that can make them so deep and ennobling that they can become the ethical, religious, and spiritual basis of a civilization – a surrogate for "god," for an abstract higher law, for the "Thou" beyond "I" and "You," or any other western concepts of *summum bonum*.

THE PUBLIC, THE PRIVATE, AND DEMOCRACY
IN EAST AND WEST

An understanding of the morally enriched idea of relationships in Confucian-based societies can help the western observer get beyond a tendency to view hierarchical, group-oriented values and customs as somehow inimical to freedom and individual dignity and fulfillment. The idea is *not* that one denies or suppresses one's freedom or fulfillment by being subjected to an array of inferior–superior relationships, or by putting "Group ahead of individual." Instead, dignity and meaning *come from* the very structure and dynamic of the relationships and group emphasis. Rather than being impediments or obstacles, hierarchical linkages are enhancements and vehicles. One might even say that individual fulfillment comes from the heartfelt observance of the duties and responsibilities that go with such linkages. And this understanding of relationships is further permeated with rich affective and moral overtones in a culture where the *"amae* mentality" dominates social life.[37]

This point is relevant to the extensive commentaries in western social psychology, from Erich Fromm's *Escape from Freedom* (1941) onward, about the psychological hazards and unfulfillments of individual freedom. The *amae* mentality in Japan, for example, recognizes implicitly the deep longing in the human psyche for attachment, dependence, and inclusion, even to the point of fearing and rejecting endless freedom, choice, and autonomy. In Doi Takeo's words (written in 1971),

> Despite the preference [western man] gives in theory to the individual over the group, there must exist inside him a psychological desire to "belong." This is, in other words, *amae*. And this desire, one suspects, is gradually coming to the surface of consciousness now that western faith in freedom of the individual is breaking down. He views this fact, however, with mixed feelings.[38]

On the other hand, there is a certain pathology that goes along with the *amae* mentality, in its tendency to deny or resist one's sense of self. The psychological posture of *amae* is a classic embodiment of "escaping from freedom" in that the person amaeruing has absolved himself from self-reliance or independent responsibility by claiming, presuming on, the indulgence of another and then by accepting the dependence and attachment that goes with it. A culture that encourages and rewards such a posture is not likely to have a highly developed sense of self, and will perhaps be deficient in the qualities of self-reliance and individual creativity so much valued in the West, and especially in the United States. But this tension is precisely the paradox that Americans face as they ponder the legacy of their individualist (anti-*amae*) tradition at a time when its blessings seem not to be as unmixed as they once were.

The point can be made in another way by noticing the difference between the Japanese sense of what is most precious or personal, that is, the inner circle of family or intimate friends of which one is a part, and the western sense of one's *privacy* as most precious and personal; that is, one's aloneness, one's individual consciousness, one's conscience or soul as most sacred and inviolable. Thus, while in the West there is great value placed on this lonely sense of "private space," it is a concept uncherished or scarcely even recognized as existent by Japanese. This is plausible, perhaps even inescapable, though, within the Japanese emphasis on the group, preoccupation with relationships, and yearning for dependence. These qualities loom too large, occupy too much psychic and emotional space, to leave much room for the ideas of individual privacy or independent choice – notions which, as Dr Doi experienced at western dinner parties, simply feel like uncaring abandonment to one used to an *amae* culture.[39]

At the same time, though, the emphasis on intimate, intense, encompassing relationships inside the group tends as much to preclude any very meaningful awareness of public spirit in a principled or abstract sense, as it does a private realm of conscience and ego-centrism. The western idea of public, harking back to its Greek origins, has always, at least in its ideal form, even more required transcendence of groups than of the individual. The group, carrying connotations or partialness (party), of parochialism, and of special interest, has generally been viewed as the antithesis of the public good. The individual, though, if endowed with conscience or a sense of principle (moral code or philosophy), has seemed suited for and fulfilled by engaging in public life. In fact, such participation is often seen explicitly as a way to allow an individual to *transcend* his group or his narrow interests by bringing his principles to a larger, less parochial (public) scene.

It is precisely this ability to conceive and take seriously a public realm as a larger place where one can give effect to one's (morally based) political nature, or conscience, however, that is hindered by

the omnipresent Japanese sense of the group and of the sufficing quality
of his web of relationships. Two Japanese words sometimes used for
"public," or "the public sector," *oyake* or *honke*, have different meanings,
neither of which has connotations suitable for the English words. *Honke*,
for example, referred originally to the imperial court, or the original,
main branch of a family, and thus could mean simply the most
encompassing group, or even the "most time-hallowed clique" in charge
of "publicness," relations outside the family. *Oyake* is also linked to
the main branch of the family, but is now a rather vague, neutral
"public," not belonging to anything, having the connotations of the
usage "don't do such a thing in public;" that is, "in the open," the
opposite of private. Thus the idea of public has connotations simply
of dominance, or "being in charge," when it means more than not
part of anything, especially family. It is not surprising, then, that
democratic politics in Japan has often been largely a matter of the
interaction of factions, or groups, and that public policy has often
meant the will of the primary faction. Within such a conception of
the public, there is little room for notions of individual conscience
or choice any more than such postures are valued in more primary
groups. There is even less room for the idea that some large principles,
or abstract, encompassing public good, is the justification for the
nation-state any more than such ideas are essential to the definition
or function of primary groups. Emphasis on group loyalty and on
the quality of relationships on "the inside" push out to diminish both
"the private" and "the public" as those terms have been understood
(and honored) in western political dialogue. Japanese, and generally
East Asian, sensibility, then, exalts a middle dimension of relationships and group consciousness that differentiates it sharply both
from western reverence for abstract principle and from western
individualism.

Indeed, looking at western and far eastern ideas of "the state" and
"the public good," one can see two contrasting pairs of conceptions.
In a large, macrocosmic sense, one finds in the Far East an ancient
notion of the state or nation as the immemorial, encompassing family
of the people as a whole, and hence "the highest embodiment of
civilization." Within this idea there is simply no being or existence
for individuals apart from inclusion within this large entity – family
or nation. Relation to it is indelible (notions of choice or contract
would be utterly foreign) and essentially defining, but also is without

explicit ideology or commitment to abstract principle. Yet, the people or culture as a whole (nation or empire in western terms, but the comparison is imprecise) is thought of as distinctive and superior, as in the traditional Chinese idea of themselves as the "middle kingdom" to which others are tributary, or the Japanese sense of *gaijins*, "outside persons" or foreigners, somehow lesser beings.

The macrocosmic conception in the West, on the other hand, tends to be more abstract or ideological. For example, in the Enlightenment ideal, embodied in the American and French Revolutions, universal principles become the basis of the nation. Marxist ideology (by now, at least) is similarly viewed as a grounds of nationhood. In either case the essence is an abstraction definable in words or doctrine, that has inclusive applicability, and thus inherently transcends nationhood. Somewhat analogous conceptions of doctrinal universality inhere in both Christian and Islamic ideals of worldwide conversion and empire. Though assumptions of superiority exist in both eastern and western conceptions it is noteworthy that the far eastern version is understood as an entity or large, immemorial *group*, while the western version is, doctrinally, at least, an abstraction, a universal or absolute *idea*. The former is at bottom a matrix of relationships (a society), while the latter can be seen as intellectual or conscientious acceptance of a faith or ideology. The former emphasizes inherent "belongingness," while the latter emphasizes, even within secular and religious ideas of inevitability and providence, choice and personal commitment. The former also, then, sees the public in unarticulated, implicit terms, while the latter tends to suppose that certain ideas or principles to which one assents define the public good.

Microcosmically, there is another contrasting pair of conceptions. In Confucian cultures the group – family-clan, village, work team, school, etc. – is the essential, defining entity. One's being consists literally of the emotional and social relationships nourished and fulfilled within such groups. These ties, moreover, are prior both to more remote national policy (though an implicit sense of obedience to the nation can be rendered very real through pyramids, or hierarchies, of groups), and to individual conscience or will. The obligations to and within the group, that is, require individuals to transcend selfishness and to find personal fulfillment in the common (group) good. The strength and primacy of sentiment and relationship within the group thus encroach to squeeze out both universal principle and individual conscience that have loomed so large in the West.

In the western microcosm, however, this sense of individual conscience, of inner conviction, choice, and commitment, has helped define the public good. The capacity of individuals, through reason or a sense within themselves, to have some understanding of shared values and needs is regarded as a vital element in ennobling public life; indeed, making it possible at all in any large, civic way. Convictions of conscience, though personal, are part, so to speak, of the universal principles that define the public good in its broader conceptions. In Lord Coke's words, the higher law embodying "the first principles of civil society...[is] written with the finger of God in the heart of man."[40] This phenomenon provides a link between the smaller entity (the individual) and the larger conception (the principled state or empire), and suggests in a way how the idea of the public good can work and gain legitimacy and force even in an individualistic society.

The four ways of discerning public good, then, in two pairs of greater and lesser conceptions, arise from fundamentally different views of human nature and society. The persistence and in some degree manifest validity of the far eastern ideas, moreover, compel us to consider which views, or which combinations of them, are more profound and fulfilling and appropriate for human beings. Western ideas and ways of politics, for example, though in part nicely tuned to ennobling conceptions of public life (especially in Classical thought), in other emphases may not do full justice to human nature. The West, and especially contemporary ideology and practice in the United States, perhaps neglects latent qualities in human beings – capacity to rise above self-preoccupation, talent for affective, morally-based relationships among people, and ability to ask public questions of themselves, for examples. And the under-encouragement of these very qualities may be at the root of troublesome pathologies in our public life. At least the different way human relationships and group life work in the Far East reveals both that western assumptions about autonomous individualism are not really indelible in human nature and that it is possible for social concerns and public opportunities to be dealt with less on the basis of individual will and special interests and more with group vitality and the common good in mind.

The profoundly unwestern sense of the individual and the group in Confucian cultures, furthermore, raises an interesting question about democracy: what form might it take if it were separated from foundations often thought of in the United States as essential to it? Explanations of American democracy often emphasize the formative influence of the philosophy of John Locke (or other *British* thinkers), or the Puritan ethic, or the impact of waves of immigration, or the open land of the New World that made the frontier experience possible. As noted in chapter 2, for example, British empirical philosophy, from Bacon and Locke to Adam Smith and J. S. Mill, is generally regarded as *the* foundation for the ideas of government by consent, liberalism, and individuality that have been strong in America. The inductive mode of thought, the preoccupation with facts and observation of the material world, the exaltation of the methods of science, the celebration of technology, the welcoming of diversity, and an appreciation of competition and conflict of opinion, all find validation in the British philosophic tradition and are seen as essential for democracy to flourish and for individuals to find fulfillment. Or, it has seemed to other observers that the Puritan ethic, with its emphasis on personal piety, diligence in one's calling, thrift, honesty, and serious purpose in life, offers the moral qualities vital to a progressing, prospering, democratic society. Or, still others have suggested, perhaps the essential dynamic of American democracy arises from the diversity, the ambitions, the openness, the energy, the restless tensions, and the creativity of millions of immigrants to the United States from four continents.

Finally, Frederick Jackson Turner and others have held that the consuming experience of settling the open lands of the west promoted in the United States an intense and unique "individualism, economic equality, freedom to rise, [and] democracy." The "striking characteristics" of the American mind, Turner wrote in 1893, "that coarseness and strength combined with acuteness and inquisitiveness; that practical, inventive turn of mind, quick to find expedients; that masterful grasp of material things, lacking in the artistic but powerful to effect great ends; that restless, nervous energy; that dominant individualism, working for good and for evil; and withal that buoyancy and exuberance which comes with freedom," were shaped by the influence of the frontier. Thus, Turner asserted, American society had become "a mobile mass of freely circulating atoms, each seeking its own place and finding play for its own powers and for its own original initiative,...[a place where] there was freedom of the individual, in which there was the vitality and mobility productive of originality and variety."[41]

Almost as often as some observers have speculated on how these ideas and experiences advanced individualism and democracy, others have wondered whether their absence might not seriously impede such growth. Is it so that the absence of something like the British empirical, liberal ideology makes democracy and individualism virtually impossible? Fukuzawa thought so – and so did J. S. Mill. In seeking to explain why "the progressive principle,...the love of liberty or of improvement" flourished in some parts of the world but not in others, Mill blamed its absence of "the sway of custom." "The whole East," he asserted, had been unprogressive for centuries because "custom is there, in all things, the final appeal, justice and right mean conformity to custom." China, he noted, was an ancient nation "of much talent and, in some respects, even wisdom,...with a particularly good set of customs." In its history were many eminent "sages and philosophers" who had often occupied "the posts of honor and power." For centuries, though, "the Chinese ideal" had been to make "all people alike." The effect had been stagnation, oppression, and degradation. Oppositely, western Europe, since the Middle Ages, had moved toward another ideal: to expand liberty so there would be "as many possible independent centers of improvement as there are individuals." The empirical mood, tolerance of diversity, the spread of science, freedom of movement and expression, and a faith in progress, Mill thought, had enabled western nations to prosper, grow, and improve all aspects of civilization. As for the Chinese, "they have become stationary – have remained so for thousands of years; and if they are ever to be further improved, it must be by foreigners."[42] Something like the Anglo-American ideology of liberal individualism, then, was for Mill a necessary foundation for freedom, progress, and democracy; its absence, at least, seemed fatal to such aspirations.

Other analysts, especially of American experience, have thought that the absence of infusions of immigrant diversity, energy, and creativity make the emergence of an open, individualistic society problematical. Still others have wondered whether a nation without a frontier experience (at least in relatively recent times) would be likely to possess the "striking characteristics" Turner asserted arose in the United States from that experience. (Many continental European observers of America have thought not.) In any case, there has been a strong tendency to see individualism and democracy (especially in the extreme American form) as tied to patterns of ideas, cultural foundations, and historical experiences present in the West (and, again, especially in the United States) but largely absent in much of the rest of the world. (The generalizations are in many cases very rough, of course: British empiricism and the Puritan ethic are of European origin and have spread to or have equivalents in parts of the world besides North America, and many areas have had waves of immigrants or frontier experiences, but the peculiar combination and concentration in the United States may still be significant.)

Particularly intriguing and instructive, however, especially in view of what Turner acknowledged nearly a century ago was the ambivalent "for good and for evil" aspects of frontier-engendered individualism, is the fact that for three or four decades now a stable, democratic government has flourished in a Confucian-based society (Japan) with little or no experience of a Lockean tradition, a Puritan ethic, waves of immigrants, or settlement of a frontier. And, though certainly not a culture one can call individualistic, it is nonetheless a society of vigorous enterprise, mobility, and growth. One can enter caveats, of course, about the influence of empirical philosophy in Japan (considerable under the zealous promotion of Fukuzawa and many others), or the equivalence in certain ways of the Confucian and Puritan ethics, or Japan's own "frontier" in Hokkaido, and so on. One can point as well to shortcomings or incompletenesses about Japan's democraticness or openness as a society, and to the benefits of American vigilance for individual rights. Yet, the Japanese experience since World War II remains a vast laboratory for observing a democratic polity struggling with modern problems of public policy in a culture still markedly different from that of the United States. Furthermore, one can discern, by looking at contemporary Japan, how elements of democratic government such as the nature of representation, or the idea of citizenship, or the role of leadership, or the modes of making decisions, simply work differently, and thus offer Americans alternate conceptions of those important components of their political system (see chapter 4). And in a very broad sense the baffling paradoxes of American public life, increasingly troublesome since 1945 (see chapter 1), might be illuminated by the ways similar problems of modern, democratic societies are handled when the cultural foundation is so different.

PUBLIC RESPONSIBILITY, ORDER, AND LAW IN EAST ASIA

To notice how the Confucian-based culture of Japan makes almost every aspect of public life work differently, suggests many intriguing, alternate possibilities. For example, soon after a Japan Air Lines plane crashed into Tokyo Bay in 1982, killing 24 people and apparently caused by a mistake made by a pilot known to be suffering from "psychosomatic disorders," the president of the company set out on a trip around Japan visiting the families of most of the crash victims. He "apologized profusely and paid homage on his knees before the Buddhist funeral altars in the homes of the bereaved." The official was politely received by the families and accorded respect for his acceptance of responsibility for the crash both on behalf of the company and personally as its chief executive. Though a law in effect at the time limited liability to $140,000 per victim, Japan Air Lines indicated settlements would not necessarily be limited to that amount. Furthermore, it promised that separate settlements would be offered, without law suits, to each family depending on the victim's age, salary, and family responsibilities.[43]

The incident highlights the oft-noted group-oriented, non-litigatious nature of Japanese society, but it also reveals something of the personal and emotional overtones that make things work differently in its culture. Even though the president was in no way directly responsible for the crash, he accepted his inseparability from the company and the need for it to show visibly and at once sincere concern for the families of the victims by a taxing personal pilgrimage. The families, for their part, then responded with respect and gratefulness both for the acceptance of responsibility and for the personal attention from so high an official. Direct, emotional bonds had been forged that were regarded as proper, necessary, and morally fulfilling by all concerned. And once these had been experienced, a basis for negotiation had been established that would exert a strong pressure on both parties to reach an amicable settlement.

Now, if one asks what made this kind of outcome possible, it is clear that highest priority for proper relationships is essential: all parties understanding their roles and obligations, and, even more important, expressing emotional conviction and goodwill (benevolence) in fulfilling the roles. This made the visits to the bereaved families something more than mere going through the motions (doubtless there was some of that in actuality, but it would not have been displayed, admitted, or condoned by anyone). Then, once these personal, morally uplifting ties were present, if matters did not move ahead free of confrontation, litigation, or rancor, it would cause distress, failure, and even disgrace for all involved. Feelings of trust, obligation, and sympathy, regarded by everyone as of the utmost importance, would have to be sustained to preserve faithfulness to the relationships and to all the group associations present – that is, to give effect to the deepest sense of one's identity and personal fulfillment as those concepts are understood within Japanese culture.

From the viewpoint of western culture and values, there are limitations and grave dangers, of course. The situation is virtually closed to any independent or out-of-protocol appeal by the victim's heirs once the proper steps have been taken and potent social pressures supporting them have built up. Furthermore, the capacity of leading personages to manipulate and cow lesser people is ever present and at least potentially liable to abuse. In many ways the leeway for individuals is slight, either to protest unfair settlements or to disavow what the system (i.e. proper relationship and group responsibility) sets in motion. Built in, too, is an attitude of deference, even obsequiousness, toward higher authorities, especially those representing the government (importantly present because the Japanese government, as all were well aware, owns 40 percent of Japan Air Lines). Furthermore, far from there being an adversarial system assumed and in place, where it is accepted that an individual has a right to object and defend himself against all authority including the government, the stigma and sense of "rightness" is generally in the opposite direction. Though in practice officials are often viewed as inefficient or stupid, the authorities, the higher-ups, are ideally thought of as possessing the wisdom, the judiciousness, the power, and the larger perspective that can properly settle matters for all concerned, especially common people whose role, ordinarily, is to accept and to obey, loyally and willingly. And any assertive or contentious departure from that role, however much justified on grounds of abstract principle or individual rights, would be viewed widely as unseemly, rude, ungrateful, socially unsettling, and even, in a way, immoral. Ideas of justice, of proper procedure, of protection of rights, and of the authority of government, in any case, are clearly far different from those common in the West. But are they necessarily less humane? or less fair? or even less democratic?

In many respects an analogous attitude toward litigation exists in China. In imperial China, where, under the Confucian code, harmony was the central value, the emphasis in settling disputes was often less on deciding who was right or wrong, and in assessing penalties accordingly, than on restoration of proper, amicable relationships. Moral honor, moreover, arose not from insistence on righteousness and exaction of a just penalty, but from a willingness to sacrifice something of even a just or legally valid position in order to restore harmony and goodwill. Thus, traditionally, much use was made of "go-betweens" and mediators, formal and informal, who brought prestige to themselves for discerning resolutions and for encouraging the end of hostility and bad feelings. Parties to disputes, go-betweens, and village elders would often celebrate the return of harmony with a feast. Even more formal proceedings conducted by elaborate, all-powerful layers of the imperial bureaucracy were suffused with opportunities and pressures to settle disputes locally and by mutual agreement. Overburdened district magistrates pressured subordinates and local officials to conduct business without recourse to the coercive measures they alone were authorized to apply. These magistrates were then valued by their superiors not for the number of cases handled or penalties exacted, but for the relative absence of litigations; a sign that harmony existed in their district. The omnipresent awareness of the power of the authorities to settle disputes and to inflict punishment (often draconian), doubtless explains partly the willingness to seek informal mediation. The widespread cultural emphasis, however, on harmony, and on proper social relationships and emotional attitudes, also had a decisive impact. In a way, the effectiveness and even the severity of imperial power, and the pervasive, unquestioning acceptance of authority, encouraged families and villages to settle their own disputes. Not only would that avoid a possibly painful brush with officialdom, but it conformed to the deep sense of being part of a polity that guided social well-being in ways far transcending merely legal or official constraints. This also diminished the need for "legal experts" (i.e. lawyers) and re-enforced the premium on those skilled not at litigation but at cultivation of harmony.[44]

Despite vast changes wrought by the communist regime and the upheavals of the Cultural Revolution, the values and practices of this ancient system are still evident in modern China. As in Japan, lawyers are much less common than in the United States (fewer than one lawyer per 10,000 people in China or Japan, compared to one for every 500 people in the US), and their function, according to regulations given to Chinese lawyers in 1982, is "first to protect the rights of the state, the collective, and the individual, and to safeguard the implementation of the laws." (Notice that in the instruction the rights of the state and of the individual are *not* set in opposition, as would be near canonical now in the United States.) More bluntly, the *People's Daily* asserted that lawyers arc "an important force for upholding the legal system of the state." Within such understandings, defendants are not presumed innocent (virtually all confess to their crimes and are found guilty by the courts), and defense lawyers seek not to prove innocence but to point out mitigating circumstances or seek lighter sentences based on the client's contrition, that is, his willingness to reform his attitude so he can resume an orderly position in society. "Trials," furthermore, are not open affairs emphasizing impartiality (defense lawyers do not have a right to see all relevant documents or evidence, or even to converse freely with their clients), but rather are occasions for warning the public against lawless behavior that has affronted social order and for publicizing the restoration of peace and harmony.[45]

As in Japan (there are, of course, many important differences between the modern Japanese and Chinese legal systems), the presumptions strongly favor the authority of the state, and procedures emphasize postures of loyalty and obedience, and settlement by negotiation. Individual assertiveness, adversarial stances, and holding out against the weight of the group or the state, on the other hand, are stigmatized. The limitations and dangers, from a western standpoint of cherishing individual rights and suspicions of those in authority, are again apparent. Nonetheless, one can see both the suitableness of the East Asian legal system to their relationship-oriented cultures, and even certain advantages that derive from an emphasis on negotiation and agreement; or, more graphically perhaps, the *disadvantages* of incessant, encouraged litigation, contention, and heightening of distinctions (even hostilities) between individuals and groups.

The role and conduct of the police in Japan, and the attitude of the public toward them, are similarly instructive. In the first place, the police in Japan (on the whole a national force) are seen traditionally as part of the officialdom that, because of its selection by examination, permanence in office, and link to the nation possess an aura of importance and authority that is vital to their effectiveness. As befits this status, recruits are carefully trained (for one year, compared to an average of eight weeks in the United States) and are subjected to strict discipline both on and off duty. The national police agency, furthermore, has the same system of "elite career tracks" for the top echelons that often seems to make Japanese business and government organizations operate with an almost awesome efficiency and professionalism. (This feature itself, of course, reflects a centuries-long tradition in East Asia.) Because of this training, discipline, and status, the police are given considerable discretion in investigation and even in settling disputes. Traffic accidents, for example, are often dealt with on the spot following immediate police assessment of fault and circumstances. Police corruption or misconduct is relatively rare, and the word of the police is seldom challenged or even received skeptically when cases, much less often than in the United States, are taken to court.

This professionalism is important to the generally cooperative relationship that exists between the police and the public. From mini-stations, unpretentiously dotting crowded towns and cities, Japanese police are very much present to ordinary citizens, make frequent rounds of their neighborhoods, and visit homes semi-annually to note changes in households. Both because they are commonly asked for directions (Japanese towns and cities are extremely difficult for strangers to find their way around in without local assistance), and because they keep careful track of coming and going, Japanese police also are intimately aware of the movement of people, especially newcomers, strangers, or even visitors, in their precincts. In general they are polite and businesslike in dealing with both local people and outsiders. Hence they do not ordinarily provoke attitudes of defensiveness or hostility, making it likely that they will receive ready cooperation in any investigations or efforts to curb crime.

Since there are about the same number of police per capita in Japan as in the United States, with far fewer crimes, major and minor, to investigate, Japanese police can be more present in a helpful way to neighborhoods (their unthreatening appearance resembles that of American mailmen), and more prompt, thorough, and effective in apprehending criminals. Crime solution and conviction is at a far higher rate in Japan than in the United States – in 1984, 65 percent as compared to 19 percent. It is even higher for serious crimes; 97 percent of the murders in Japan were cleared through the courts in 1984. Punishments, though, especially for less serious crimes, are in Japan at once more certain, swifter, and less harsh than in the United States, especially for criminals who are cooperative and contrite. Hence crime is severely stigmatized and firmly punished in Japan, but it is not surrounded with the attitudes of fear, of arbitrariness, of violence and brutality, and of suspicion and alienation that often entangle relationships among police, public, and criminals in the United States.[46]

That there are grave dangers lurking in some aspects of Japanese police attitudes and practices is apparent when one recalls the Japanese police state of the 1930s and 1940s. The combination of disciplined, national control of the police, omnipresent surveillance of the citizenry, thoroughness, wide discretionary powers, and habits of unchallenging obedience by the people (all more extreme 50 years ago than today), made it relatively easy for Japan's military rulers, once they had the will and power to do so, to turn the nation into a tyrannical state of daunting proportions. The exercise of police powers in both North and South Korea offers similar warning about the oppression that can accompany such practices. More broadly, abundant evidence from Chinese, Korean, and Japanese history makes clear the oppressive, totalitarian potential of a cultural base that gives so much deference to higher-ups, so heavy a duty of obedience to inferiors, so much scope to faithfulness to relationships, so much subordination of the individual to the group, and so much authority to the nation-state.

Yet, as the significant changes made by democratic governments in Japan since 1945 demonstrate, it is possible to reduce the oppressive aspects of such a police and justice system and still retain some of its more useful qualities. The strong bias built in for a cooperative relationship between the law-enforcing and the law-abiding elements in society, for example, shorn largely of arrogant, demeaning, and brutal features, has much in its favor. The emphasis on the need for the criminal to recognize his wrongdoing and his antisocial behavior, to be willing to seek rehabilitation, and to accept pressure to resume, as it were, proper relationships with others, can be seen as an almost ideal way to get at the roots of crime. Even the assumption that the nation-state has a broad obligation to nourish, perhaps require, attitudes and behavior conducive to public order and social harmony is not necessarily a purpose appropriate only for authoritarian governments. Might not democracies, especially individualistic ones, benefit from habits and institutions that effectively encourage such order and harmony?

Accounts of modern Singapore, an island nation of 2.5 million people, three-quarters Chinese and with the highest living standard in Asia after Japan, reveal further the intriguing public philosophy of Confucian-based societies. When asked to explain Singapore's rapid economic growth since its independence 25 years ago, one business leader replied, "it's our crazy Confucian work ethic. You don't need to make the Chinese work. They'll work anyway." This ethic has found expression in a vigorously entrepreneurial society that welcomes foreign investment and emphasizes profit, but it also infuses a strongly paternalistic government that guides every aspect of the nation's development. A highly successful "plastic bag magnate" notes that "one of the unique features of [Singapore] is that help from the government comes not strictly in monetary terms, but in moral support and infrastructure." Carefully planned, efficiently administered public services (all of which make money) are part of Singapore's Asian reputation as a "corruption-free, law-abiding, efficient, fanatically clean, often conformist and unquestioning society." Its leader, Lee Kuan Yew, in power for 25 years, prides himself on having created not a "culture of political bargaining and political struggle, [but a] petitionary culture, [where] political authority is seen as paternalistic, to be approached respectfully and which will react to demands benevolently, in wisdom and justice, where the national interest is not compromised." The result is "neither a democratic nor an authoritarian state, but rather an administrative state run by trusted managers." There was, at the same time, no "competitive and open electoral process, [and] an obvious lack of. . .political communication and links with the grassroots."[47]

To an uncanny degree, the generalizations are what one would expect of a society grounded on Confucian ethics and political philosophy. (In curious and in perhaps constructive ways, these same qualities can be seen in part as legacies of British colonialism, but Singapore, like Hong Kong, is culturally far more Chinese than British.) The moral tone, the devotion to success and hard work, the paternalistic bureaucracy, the deference to public authority, the respect for wise, vigorous leadership, the strong sense of national unity – and the general lack of democratic process and grass-roots participation – are all characteristic of far eastern polities. The valuing of harmonious group relationships above individual or group self-interest, the guiding of competitive energies by public authority, and the conducting of government wisely and efficiently are ancient Confucian precepts, perhaps linked to conceptions of human nature more social and less autonomous than those celebrated in the West in the last few centuries. And as numerous critics have observed, there may be some connection between these cultural foundations and the astonishing accomplishments of "the East Asia edge" in recent years.[48]

From the viewpoint of western open and democratic society, of course, warnings and ambiguities also stand out. An emphasis on individual rights can counter an often intrusive, overbearing public authority, a certain skepticism about demands for obedience may be useful and even healthy in any society, and the presumption of innocence until guilt is proven restrains over-zealous police and public prosecutors. There may even be some benefit in complicated, decentralized police and legal systems that keep justice (or oppression) from being administered too swiftly, too energetically, too efficiently, and too single-mindedly. A too "petitionary culture" and too much deference to the administrative state can result in dangerous arrogance and neglect of grass-roots needs. The tendency of all the Confucian-based societies to accept authoritarian regimes, to over-emphasize conformity, and to denigrate active citizenship are palpable warnings to those who cherish freedom and self-government. Modern liberal nations are peculiarly aware of such threats – but they may not be so alert to the need they have for a sense of the "whole as more than the sum of the parts" in their public life. The liabilities of a too clamorous insistence on individual prerogatives seem apparent – and make it eye-opening to consider ideas of public order and leadership that rest on different cultural assumptions about individual rights and social obligations.

A DIFFERENT DEMOCRACY IN JAPAN

A comparison of Japanese and American assumptions about democratic decision-making affords further insights. As noted earlier (pages 19–20), the whole western way of making decisions democratically – open, assertive advocacy to air and identify individual views, an assumed wide variety of self-interests, carefully tallied, secret balloting to let the majority rule, and the continuing of dissent on both principled and self-interested grounds to sustain the search for truth – has unwelcome, morally debilitating, socially corrosive overtones in the context of Japanese culture. To make such a process *essential* might make democracy itself an abhorrent idea. The Japanese simply could not think of democracy as essentially structural or procedural, where new, differentiated roles, groupings of previously unaffiliated people, and formal majority decisions defined a "process of democracy." To do so would have compelled them to think and act in ways deeply hostile to age-old traditions. One doubts that democracy, exclusively so defined, could ever have operated meaningfully in Japan. Rather, the essence there became "a change in the direction of the motion of energy" within the familiar primary groups (still hierarchical) and the pyramids of groups that have always been basic in Japanese society.

Consideration, voice, that is, must be given to the "weaker and lower" and the sentiment and energy thus generated must be conscientiously and sincerely attended to as discussion and decision-making continues according to the traditional (hierarchical) way. Within such an understanding, democracy is *not* present when a "dominant clique" ignores the energy from below, when decisions are made by narrow majorities and more or less imposed on everyone else, and when dissent goes on and on in a way that interferes with the harmony and emotional closeness that are the all-important, *morally essential* qualities of any associational life.[49] Thus, neither the demise of the hierarchical, vertical pattern (inconceivable in any case on both customary and moral grounds) nor the establishment of democratic procedures on western models is of much use in measuring the reality or vitality of democracy in such a Confucian-based culture.

Since 1948 Japan has possessed a formal structure of government and of political practice borrowed from Great Britain, the United States, and elsewhere. Yet traditionally in Japan, as E. O. Reischauer observes, "absolute obedience and loyalty" were expected of "inferiors," "superiors" exercised "unlimited authority," and "there were no inalienable rights, no concepts that might have underlain a Magna Carta, and no experience of any sort with representative bodies."[50]

Thus one finds an incongruous mix of western democratic institutions and Confucian-oriented attitudes apparently unsuited to them. This makes the formal structure work differently because the dynamics within it are so different. As Mishima Yukio's novel about a Japanese election campaign, *After the Banquet* (1960, and based so closely on an actual incident that it provoked a libel suit), displays graphically, everything is at once much the same and very different. There are nomination caucuses, noisy, elaborately planned campaigns, enormous expenditures of money, strenuous exertions by dedicated workers, "deals" of all sorts to gain support, struggles within parties, and other similarities to American political contests. The nuances, relationships, and dynamics, though, are repeatedly surprising to American readers.

At one point Mishima observes, after a candidate for office had made a particularly poor campaign speech, that it likely did little harm, especially among older voters, because of the instinctive Japanese "trust in inept talkers."[51] Why this trust? Because eloquent oratory and even lucid, forceful analysis each convey something direct, objective, and perhaps overpowering. There is little attention to personal feelings, special nuances in relationship, and the sort of indirection that allows others to "move closer," avoid confrontation, and resist clarifying verbal distinctions. Fukuzawa had noted in opening the first "oratorical society" in Japan (1874) that many people opposed giving "western-style speeches [because]. . . it is awkward for a person to give a speech in the Japanese language, and. . . his speech cannot, therefore, take a respectable form."[52] The "inept talker," that is, observing traditional deferences, invited all the ambiguities and space for display of feelings and personal respect that strengthen emotional relationships within groups. (That Prime Minister Nakasone both is more western in his speeches and political style, and is regarded as very much a new and atypical leader, illustrates the traditional bias of Japanese public life.) Equally offensive to Japanese ears is the incessant hostility of political campaigns. The aims "to score verbal points, to overcome one's interlocutors," and to make speech "a form of aggression, . . . a war of all against all carried on by other means,"[53] seem to Japanese poisonous both to personal morality and to the public good. The high value placed on vigorous oratory, debate, and lucid argument in most western models of democracy, then, in Japan works largely in reverse; there the democratic model requires attention to the very feelings, indirection, nuances, and "energy from below" that public oratory and debate largely bypass.

To take another example, though party politics in Japan are in some ways exceedingly divisive (the party in power since 1955, as well as its socialist opposition, has long been characterized as simply a collection of factions), almost all important decisions are made by behind-the-scenes, consensus agreements among party, bureaucracy, and business leaders. Debate in the Diet and even interaction among its members amounts to very little. Two-thirds of the legislation is passed unanimously. Furthermore, the most unacceptable and scorned behavior in the Diet is for either the majority to take advantage of its technical power to ram through votes by a narrow margin, or for a minority to keep obstructing or even dissenting after it has lost on a vote.[54] All these actions reveal a propensity for proceeding by agreement and consensus, and for acknowledging the need both for consultation before and for conciliation after decisions. Rejected are the mechanism of repeated efforts to achieve narrow majorities and the just as incessant continued disagreement and attempt to reverse decisions. The Japanese way, furthermore, vertical throughout, is in a sense highly oligarchic because decisions are made by elite "higher-ups," and there is by Anglo-American standards very little of the open, direct, significant debate among representatives and ministers exemplified by "question time" in the House of Commons. Yet, in less formal ways there is wide discussion of public issues in Japan (especially in the mass media) and a constant monitoring of responsiveness to sentiments among myriad groups and organizations. There is similar incessant effort to mollify and reconcile those once in opposition, successful in part because the culture so strongly requires those formerly in opposition to give up a stubborn or hostile "standing outside" in the interests of harmony.

Something of the ancient cultural roots of these rather puzzling political practices is evident in a memorandum written in 1877 for the Meiji emperor by his official reader-tutor, Motoda Eifu, a learned Confucian scholar and no friend of the new vogue of western learning in Japan. Precept number six in the document, on "creating public discussion," began, typically, with a quotation from a Confucian classic (*The Book of History*): "throw open all the doors [of communication between the court and the people of the empire]....See with the eyes and hear with ears of all." Then Motoda went on to interpret for the emperor as "sages" had done for East Asian rulers for millennia: "when avenues of expression are closed, the feelings of those below are blocked off. . . . The government should weigh the good and bad proposals, select the best discussions and most reasonable opinions, subject them to discussion in the cabinet, and have the decision made by the emperor himself." (Under ancient Japanese usage, this would mean, in fact, according to the advice of the officials governing in his name.) Two years later, elaborating on the question of "public opinion" that Japanese scholars struggled to understand as they read John Stuart Mill, Motoda reminded the emperor of an occasion in Chinese history where 800 advisors to a ruler had been wrong, and only one or two proved wise. Thus, Motoda observed, mass, majority opinion was not necessarily correct public opinion (*koron*) (公論), so even in a parliamentary system of some kind "the only way to decide what constitutes correct public opinion is for the emperor to choose among" the views expressed in the representative body. Motoda also emphasized the emperor's obligation to encourage proper teachings among the people, meaning especially proper "morals and human feelings."[55]

Motoda thus went as far as he could to accommodate ancient East Asian political precepts to what he was aware were swelling tides of pro-western sentiment in Japan, especially among the oligarchs who governed in the emperor's name and who were seeking, cautiously, to bring some of the forms and practices of constitutional government to Japan. But Motoda also strove to retain what were to him critically important traditional precepts: the need for rulers to be guided not by "mass opinion" (*shuron*) (衆論) but by wise, "correct opinion;" the essential agency of "sages" in discerning that correct opinion; the primacy of "morals and feelings" even in public affairs; the need for those in power to "see with the eyes and hear with the ears of all" so they might be aware of and responsive to those feelings; and the centrality of the emperor as the guiding, uniting spirit of the nation as a whole. The authoritarian, anti-democratic, highly conservative tenor of Motoda's advice, and his standing as an avowed, official Confucianist, dramatizes the strong association, throughout East Asia, of Confucianism with ancient, hierarchical practices. Japanese, for example, tend to link the fanatic insistence on obedience to parents and to the emperor of the 1930s and 1940s with officially promulgated Confucianism. Because of this, modern, democratically-oriented Japanese seldom regard themselves as "Confucianist." The same aversion is evident among Chinese and Koreans who also associate Confucianism as a school of thought with rigid, stultifying traditionalism; it is thus generally moribund or repudiated as a formal philosophy throughout East Asia. One can scarcely even imagine, for example, a century later, any such memoranda or substantial advice as Motoda's, but the peculiar features of Japanese democratic government in notable ways still bear the marks of traditional, Confucian-derived practices. And they may even suggest precepts and practices applicable to *good* democratic government anywhere.[56]

What Americans have in East Asia, then, as they contemplate public life in the United States and the problematic paradoxes imposed on it by their own individualist traditions, is a vast reservoir of alternate values and practices, some perhaps instructive and others not, that afford perspective on almost every question they face. Most particularly relevant to the United States is the strong emphasis in the Confucian way on the *quality* of public decisions, exemplified in Motoda's stress that the implemented policy be wise or correct. He insisted that the views of the people be "seen and heard," but the decision itself had to be made by the proper authority with the advice of sage counselors. Otherwise, how could it possibly be *right*, that is, in accord with "the Mandate of Heaven," the will of the nation (or the gods), or any other version of a higher, qualitative law or order?

To put it that way, however, makes the East Asian idea too much resemble Platonic and other western models of "philosopher-kings" ruling ideal states (though the Confucian pattern is much closer to Greek understandings of the active state pursuing the public good than it is to virtually all post-Hobbesian western conceptions resting on the will and interest of individuals.) The dynamic imbedded in Japanese practices, for example, before and after 1945, is less ideological and less attuned to logic and systematizing than either Platonic or Aristotelian political thinking. The emphasis on relationships, on moral energy within groups, on harmony and consensus, and on nuance and indirection rather than on precision and rhetoric, all make East Asian politics work differently from those that are western-based. Hence, modern western political practice (especially American) can learn not only another version of the Aristotelian dictum that "the state exists for the sake of the good life, and not for the sake of life only," but also the benefit that can arise from a more *social* dynamic of human relationships. Public life might be substantially different, and perhaps substantially improved, that is, if conceptions of a fulfilled human nature, and of how people understand and relate to each other, were to change (no small order, of course). The point is not that ancient cultural patterns can or should be transferred. Rather, it might be helpful if there was at least a conception or a model present possessing attributes that could suggest alternatives in some degree corrective of manifest shortcomings.

The largest ommision in traditional East Asian political ideas, by western standards, is any idea of citizen participation in public affairs akin to the obligations of either the classical freeman, or the modern democratic voter. In a way, though, this omission may help define the challenge of contemporary politics. We may need nothing less than the implanting within one political system of three basic axioms: the centrality of relationships rather than of individual autonomy, the need to attend directly and disinterestedly to shared public problems, and the capacity of *all* people to participate usefully in public affairs. Most polities, it would seem, have suffered from too much attention to one axiom to the impoverishment of the others. But might it not be possible to have something of the best of all worlds? The difficulties are great, of course, and the "cultural translations" required are enormously complex, but the opportunity, perhaps even the dire need as the twentieth century draws to a close, is also awesome. That, at least, is the beckoning, yet elusive lesson of a look at the political culture of this part of the world most unlike, and thus perhaps best able to enlighten, the paradoxical nationhood that has come into being in the United States, especially since 1945.

4

Individualism and the Public Interest in the 1980s

With these surveys of western individualism and of Confucian cultures in mind, then, what can we make of the paradoxes evident in American public life since 1945? Is it possible that the very depth and appeal of the individualist tradition, yielding as it has and still does rich rewards in openness, freedom, prosperity, creativity, and privacy, in a way also hinders us from coping effectively with the *public* realm? More profoundly, might that tradition itself, partly because it has had such a full and vigorous development through 2,000 or 3,000 years of western history, be in its late-twentieth-century formulation disproportionate and flawed? And does its very pervasiveness and attractiveness also serve to blind us both to its weaknesses and to alternate perspectives?

Perhaps two wisdoms, one ancient and the other modern, capture the central dilemma revealed thus far: the Biblical injunction, "he that loseth his life for my sake shall find it," and Erich Fromm's apparently incongruous title, *Escape from Freedom*. Each suggests a reversal of "first glance" truth. We do not find meaning or fulfillment in our lives by seeking such deliberately, for its own sake, or more to the point, self-centeredly, but rather by getting outside ourselves and relating ourselves, committing ourselves, to larger, transcending designs or purposes (see pages 25–9). Oppositely, mere freedom from bonds, being on our own, at liberty to do as we please (by ourselves), far from being welcome and satisfying as individualist ideology generally assumes, is often alienating and frightening and thus provokes us to want to "escape" from the very freedom we thought was our heart's desire.

But the quest, direct and unashamed, for (personal) happiness and fulfillment, and the yearning to be free of the bonds and restraints of custom or tyranny or provincialism or ignorance or whatever it is that hinders us (personally), are the commonplace foundations of the individualism venerated in western thought and in American culture. Is there not then a pervading tension, even a profound contradiction, between an emphasis on freedom from restraints and individualized fulfillment on the one hand, and the Biblical and the psychic insights on the other? If it is indeed true that we find meaning in life by reaching outside ourselves to other people and to larger purposes, and that the removal of restraints leading to an autonomous individualism results in an often intolerable loneliness and alienation, then is it surprising that the triumph of the individualistic values, and their embodiment in a vigorous post-war "America as a civilization" (see pages 29–32), has had paradoxical results spawned more fundamentally by success than by failure? The paradox, moreover, extends far beyond the peculiar crisis so much noted recently in American culture and public life. Its basis lies in the whole direction and deliberate intention of western society that, in the past three or four centuries especially, has defined modernity. This modernity, moreover, is increasingly a "global culture," linked to the material accomplishments of western technology and to liberal aspirations for individual fulfillment and national self-determination, that infuses the world-view of more or less westernized elites (Marxist and non-Marxist) everywhere. The paradox of unfulfillment amid "success," then, is in some degree worldwide and seems especially glaring in the United States only because it is the most "advanced" nation. The point is underscored if we note that social commentators in other nations, in virtual direct proportion to their "advancedness," remark on the same crises and malaise as those often noted in the United States. Comparison with non-western cultures further suggests that the paradox might rest on the inherent, often unacknowledged social and moral limitations which make the philosophy of individualism so meager and superficial, all things considered. The long-standing sociological critique of this insufficient philosophy by Durkheim, Marx, and others seems even more forceful in an increasingly interdependent world.

Yet, in the presence of immemorial impositions on human beings in the name of groups, tribes, dynasties, and nationhoods allegedly prior to individuals in some way, one can understand the use and attractiveness of starting, as Hobbes and Locke did, with the individual – willful, significant, and rational in his own right. Enthusiasm for this liberating idea of the autonomous, singularly-valued person found its most plausible context and most extreme expression, moreover, in the open and unformed societies of the New World; just to mention Daniel Boone, Henry David Thoreau, the Lone Ranger, Huckleberry Finn, and Horatio Alger (and, more recently, Lee Iaccoca and Rambo), gives one a quick sense of the idea's vigor. Yet, these same names evoke something of the limitation and shallowness of the pre-occupation with the lone individual – its "irretrievable absurdity" in Mark Roelofs characterization – and the diminishing utility of the concept in modern, interdependent society. Even one of Hobbes's early critics had complained that "he discourses of Men as if they were terrigene, born out of the earth, come up like seeds, without any relation one to the other."[1] Feminist writers who emphasize that women have been much less acculturated to be autonomous individuals than the assertive, striving men ascendant in western culture, and thus exhibit more social, nurturing values, simply underscore the disproportionate, perhaps pathological nature of the dominant, masculine ethos.

Even more problematical is the *moral* obtuseness of the individualist ideology. When, nearly three centuries ago (1714), Bernard Mandeville offered the paradoxical maxim "private vice: public virtue", the touchstone for an elegant analysis of the then-burgeoning commercial capitalism of western Europe, he provoked praise or scorn in his readers not because he had *discovered* or *revealed* the pervasive selfishness and competitiveness of human nature (these were ancient, often-elaborated facts of life), but because he saw that they might be *welcomed* and *celebrated*. He drew together and expressed forthrightly the steadily more insistent argument of the seventeenth-century economic theorists that the release and encouragement of human competitive and self-seeking energies resulted in both a rising material prosperity for individuals and an irresistible growth in national wealth and power. Mandeville thus asked mankind to confront a fateful moral revolution.

Could the ethical failure and political disease of selfishness (or at least so moral and political philosophers – and all major religious traditions – had always taught) really be converted into "public virtue," and eventually even into personal virtue? Could self-seeking and self-centeredness really be accepted as praiseworthy rather than being regarded as flaws in human nature to be curbed and guarded against? If this was indeed to be the case, then the western world had in prospect a moral revolution of Copernican dimensions: could man, individual man, rather than God, the Absolute, "the Mandate of Heaven," or the Eternal, be regarded as the center and measure of all things? Alexander Pope's scathing verses captured the audacity of Mandeville's system:[2]

> See nature in some partial narrow shape,
> And let the author of the whole escape.

> Or, at one bound o'erleaping all His laws,
> Make God man's image, man the final cause,
> Find virtue local, all relation scorn,
> See all in *self*, and but for self be born.

As this reaction shows, there was immediate, intense revulsion at the new ethic and its implicit world-view and assumptions about human nature. And reaction and debate are still not concluded. Yet, successive arguments that private vice yielded public virtue, that enlightened self-interest was a sufficient morality, that an invisible hand gave benign guidance to competing human selfishness, and that the moral universe consisted of an infinite calculus of individuals pursuing pleasure and avoiding pain, embodied the new egocentric hypothesis, and taken together increasingly defined modern individualism. Further arguments that politics had as its goal "the greatest good of the greatest number" (of individuals), that progress resulted from the ceaseless struggle (and creativity) of individuals, and that the public good was simply the resultant of the conflict of interests in a free, pluralistic society, eventually transformed the new ethic into a public philosophy. The autonomous individual, in this view, was the basic building block for the understanding of society as a whole that is no more than the sum of the parts – a sociological fact, one might say. Such an individual, self-seeking and self-celebrating, was as well the center of the moral universe – an ethical fact, one might say.

This continuing widespread acceptance, of course, rests on the *real* attractiveness and utility of the individualist ethic. It *has* undermined the assumptions of fixed hierarchy and status that have limited opportunity for countless people throughout most of human history. It *has* resisted political tyrannies of all kinds. It *has* stimulated stunning achievements in science, technology, and the arts. It *has* spurred growth in government by consent. It *has* nourished the values of tolerance, pluralism, and freedom of expression. It *has* celebrated human diversity. And it *has* often responded to the needs of outcast or disadvantaged minorities. Indeed, the more gross or blatant an oppression has been in the world, the more clearly the individualist ideology has seemed valid and attractive. In the West it has been the common ground for all kinds of liberal groups and parties in successive and recurrent reforms. In the non-western world, movements for national liberation and democracy have generally been led by those who had absorbed modern, western ideologies. And the American liberal tradition, thought of in broad terms as being the only ideology the nation has ever had, is simply this ideology in an especially vigorous, pervasive, and self-confident form (recall Willkie's *One World*) – at least, that has generally been the case until the hesitations and self-doubt of the 1970s and 1980s.

Alexis Tocqueville explained the problematic and paradoxical aspects of "individualism" in *Democracy in America* (1835–40), where the word was first used to define a distinct outlook. He noted that the word was "a novel expression, to which a novel idea has given birth." By this he meant that the "novel" idea of celebrating individual wants and intentions, discussed by moralists and social critics for a century or two, had reached the point where it needed a name of its own and could be regarded as the touchstone of a culture or national character – for better or for worse. Tocqueville's comment and vocabulary on the point reveal the ambiguities:

> Our fathers were only acquainted with egotism. Egotism is a passionate and exaggerated love of self, which leads a man to connect everything with his own person, and to prefer himself to everything in the world. Individualism is a mature and calm feeling, which disposes each member of the community to sever himself from the mass of his fellow creatures; and to draw apart with his family and his friends; so that, after he has thus formed

a little circle of his own, he willingly leaves society at large to itself. Egotism originates in blind instinct: individualism proceeds from erroneous judgment more than from depraved feelings; it originates as much in the deficiencies of the mind as in the perversity of the heart. Egotism blights the germ of all virtue; individualism, at first, only saps the virtues of public life; but, in the long run, it attacks and destroys all others, and is at length absorbed in downright egotism. Egotism is a vice as old as the world, which does not belong to one form of society more than to another: individualism is of democratic origin, and it threatens to spread in the same ratio as the equality of conditions.[3]

Tocqueville's point, then, is not that the modern, liberal spirit, the spread of freedom and democracy, the growth of the philosophy of individualism, have invented selfishness (what Tocqueville calls "egotism"). Of course not; it is "a vice as old as the world" and as characteristic of one place and one time as another. What *is* novel, and of great portent, is the "calm, mature," deliberate severing of each individual from the rest of the community on the grounds that such separations are best for the whole as well as for the parts; society at large is *willingly* left to itself. This novel proceeding, moreover, is not like egotism a "blind instinct" that indelibly taints human nature (Reinhold Niebuhr calls it "original sin"), but is rather an "erroneous judgment," a choosing of the wrong thing. Egotism, though, because of its clear moral inadmissibility, is readily recognized as "blighting the germ of all virtue," while individualism argues that it is morally acceptable to seek one's own ends when they are viewed in a sufficiently long-range and utilitarian way. Individuals, that is, could enjoy moral respectability under the ethic of "enlightened self-interest," in sharp contrast to a more traditional view that would see at once an inconsistency in the phrase itself: how indeed could "self-interest" be "enlightened" – virtuous or conducive to it – when the profoundest flaw in human nature is held to be selfishness? The same point is made in the accusation that the maxim "honesty is the best policy" is a "specious dogma" which lacks "that nice sense which revolts at wrong for its own sake, and that generosity of spirit which shrinks from" a self-seeking deviousness.[4]

Even heavier stigma is attached to the "novel idea" when Tocqueville considers how it "saps the virtues of public life." What did he mean by that? He first notes the bonding quality of traditional, aristocratic society, how it made inherent to its members, high and low, the vital interdependence with other, *different* parts of the living generation, and the complex connections with past and future generations. The problem was vexing for Tocqueville because, as much as he admired these qualities of aristocratic societies, he had little use for the inequality, the obedience to authority, and the oppression that usually went with them. Democratic societies, though, exalting individuals, "sever every link" of the communal and generational "chains." As some families "spring up," others "fall away" and all change their condition; "the woof of time is every instant broken and the track of generations effaced." Tocqueville thus sees a democratic, individualized society that "not only makes every man forget his ancestors, but . . . hides his descendants, and separates his contemporaries from him; it throws him back forever upon himself alone, and threatens in the end to confine him entirely within the solitude of his own heart." Observing the "ruins of an aristocracy" amid the growth of democratic societies in his own day, Tocqueville thought the "separation of men from one another, and the egotism resulting from it," struck the imagination most forcefully. Large numbers of "independent citizens in democratic communities," he thought, "intoxicated with their new power," entertained "a presumptuous confidence in their own strength, and as they do not suppose that they can henceforth ever have occasion to claim the assistance of their fellow creatures, they do not scruple to show that they care for nobody but themselves." Hence the unabashed setting of individual above communal claims, so personally liberating and also defended as producing "public benefit," in "the long run" shriveled private as well as public virtue.[5] Tocqueville saw great good in the multitude of "voluntary associations" that flourished in the United States, and he admired the friendly openness of many private groups, but he nonetheless sensed a social and moral pathology at work in American society.

Though Tocqueville is at pains both to put as good a light as possible on what he considered the inevitable spread of democracy, and to point out the many ways free, democratic government in the United States resulted in astonishing progress and benefit to humankind, he saw the ideology of individualism as a "deficiency of the mind," flawed both as a personal morality *and* as a public philosophy. A century and one-half of further experience of societies where the ideology has been ascendant (especially the United States) affords scant evidence that Tocqueville's reservations were misguided.

An intriguingly similar analysis has emerged 150 years later from the observations of another sojourner in the United States whose homeland provided a sharp counterpoint to American liberal individualism. Alexander Solzhenitsyn, a Russian exile who had been "pitched headfirst into hell" by the totalitarianism of his country,[6] is nonetheless profoundly ambivalent about the culture of the West to which he came after half a century of life in a communist state. He appreciated the guarantee in the United States of the individual against the many types of "state pressure" he had experienced all too much of in the Soviet Union, he told Harvard seniors in June 1978. He was impressed, too, with the "well-being" of the majority of the people beyond what their "fathers and grandfathers could even dream about," and with the "physical splendor, happiness, possession of material goods, money and leisure, almost unlimited freedom of enjoyment" that, comparatively at least, characterized American young people. Yet, in a turn that surprised and annoyed some of his listeners, Solzhenitsyn declared that he would by no means recommend the West as a model for his country. The tendency to find nothing wrong that was not illegal, the irresponsibility in leaving every moral and esthetic question to "free choice" ("invasion of publicity, TV stupor, and intolerable music"), and the shallowness and abuse of freedom by the media, were to him signs of cowardice, degeneracy, and spiritual disarray. He even thought the sacrifices and common effort required of the people in the socialist bloc nations gave them "a spiritual training" and a "stronger, deeper, more interesting character" than that "generated by standardized western well-being" and the "mechanical, legalistic smoothness" of life in the United States.

Solzhenitsyn also discerned what he termed a "psychological detail:" the "worry and even depression" that clouded many American faces in their "constant desire to have still more things and a still better life." The unreality of "prescribed smiles and raised glasses" despite the "decisive offensive [of] the forces of Evil" already well under way in the world was equally disconcerting. All the material progress and individual "fulfillment" achieved in the United States, Solzhenitsyn thought, rested on a "social system quite unstable and unhealthy." This revealed, as Tocqueville had also seen, an inherent flaw arising not from the failure of Americans to gain freedom and democracy, but from an insufficiency in these goals and intentions. Seen at first glance in the perplexed countenances and contrived joyfulness of so many people, the deeper trouble had to do with the inability of the ideology of individualism to understand and cope with the depth and complexity of the problems facing the planet – "a fight [for survival,] ...physical and spiritual,...of cosmic proportions."[7]

Tocqueville and Solzhenitsyn, then, half-astonished, half-appalled visitors to a nation distant in so many ways from their homelands, discerned distinguishing values and characteristics of individualist America. They also noted some of the same psychic and cultural dilemmas that emerge from a comparison of the West with East Asian society. Egotism, they admitted, was everywhere – East and West, ancient and modern, in democracies and in autocracies – but its conversion into a quality to be nourished and celebrated, to be made the foundation of the moral law, the economic system, and the political process, was "novel," audacious, exciting – and perhaps ill-advised. If one proceeds oppositely, as though proper relationships – with parents, brothers and sisters, spouse, children, friends, teachers, fellow citizens, and rulers – are the key to the moral, fulfilled life, then one has a different self-conception and a different ethic. If one sees the family as a whole, one's neighborhood and community as *indispensable centers* of meaning, rather than being adjuncts or conveniences auxiliary to one's personal growth or fulfillment, then one has different values and different notions of the place of society in one's life than one has when individual orientation is dominant. Finally, if one regards the state as a high "embodiment of civilization" acting under "the Mandate of Heaven," rather than as a mere compact of convenience among individuals to enhance private rights, social order, and national prosperity, then one's sense of public obligation will alter sharply. Within the Confucian understanding, that is, one sees the individual and the world he lives in from a perspective at 180 degrees from the novel viewpoint Tocqueville found both so liberating and so problematic in the 1830s.

The depth and subtlety of the different connotations of the idea of individualism are evident in the effort to translate the word "individualism" into Japanese. The word in English means literally "undivided," and hence carries a connotation of "getting it together" within a single person, an individual. This implies a certain pre-occupation with self, of course, and validates the idea of enlightened self-interest. But the more profound, moral intention is to so deepen and strengthen the single person that he achieves a kind of integration (undividedness) that is not a diminishment or partialness, but rather a fulfillment of human nature. To be an individual, furthermore, often means to assert one's own inner being and choices in life as over against ties or connections with a group – as, for example, when a young person becomes an individual (more complete and whole) by *loosening* bonds with family or school or business organization. In this conception, being part of a group is not enlarging or completing, but somehow is fragmenting because part of one's essential self is, in the group, taken over or coopted in a fundamentally dividing way. Thus, in English, to "be an individual" has positive, uniting, fulfilling connotations.

By contrast, the words used in Japanese for "individualism" – *kojin*, "one person," or *kojinsyugi*, "one-person-ism" (個人 or 個人主義) – has negative connotations, suggesting a person cut off from a group. It denotes the breaking down of a larger unity into atomic units, and is thus a residual idea of a lesser quantity after the whole has been fragmented. In Japanese, then, to "be an individual" suggests diminishment, breaking away, and lonesomeness – not at all the rich, positive connotations of the word in English. Even more pejorative are the connotations of another Japanese word sometimes used to translate "individualism" – *rikoshugi* (利己主義), literally "benefit-oneself-ism."[8] The English connotations arise readily from the long western tradition of taking the singular, core, choosing person as the starting point for both moral and social discourse, while the Japanese connotations are suited to the Confucian tradition of beginning with the human person in relationship and context.

The point is neither to condemn western individualism nor to ignore the manifest limitations and dangers of the Confucian outlook, but rather to get a more precise sense of the flaws in western ideology and the possible correctives that might emerge from a juxtaposition with East Asian culture. What might be "erroneous" about the "mature and calm feeling" that causes the individualist to "draw apart," to "willingly leave society at large to itself?" How might the subordination of the whole, so much a part of the individualist philosophy, first "sap the virtue of public life" and then spread so that a "downright egotism" more and more characterizes society in general? What might we learn about the health of our public (and perhaps private) life by looking carefully at both the insufficiencies of our individualist ideology and the alternatives available to us? If one re-examines, with these questions in mind, three basic elements of democratic public life – the idea of citizenship, the role of leadership, and the decision-making process – it is possible to discern the outlines, at least, of a public philosophy that challenges the conventional wisdom at many points and also suggests reorientations that might overcome some of the insufficiencies born of the disproportionate individualism characteristic of contemporary America.

EDUCATION FOR CITIZENSHIP?

Any searching look at ideas of citizenship current in the United States in the 1980s, and at training and socialization in the practice of it, must be bewildering and disconcerting. Amid earnest, often strident concern for participation, access, and "leverage," all in a way laudable and important in a democratic society, one finds as well widespread perception among citizens that nothing they do can have meaning or influence. Further, it seems that there is little or no correlation between more citizen impact on government and an improved quality of government. At the same time vigilance for one's special interests, skillful advocacy, manipulation of the media, and a sophisticated knowledge of how the political process works are offered as the pathways to effective participation in public life. Yet, such conceptions of politics may be responsible for the alienation and lack of interest in the first place. Citizens (and citizens-to-be) are taught that the "who gets how much of what when" definition of politics pretty much characterizes American government, that its institutions, processes, and results can best be understood by using that definition, and that such a conflict of interest model is both realistic and morally acceptable. They are then further taught that their effectiveness, and even discharge of their obligation, depend on active, single-minded participation in that system: to organize, maneuver, cajole, and bargain become the means of effectiveness – and even of fulfillment of duty. It should not be surprising, though, to find that such teaching and such urging lead to widespread disenchantment as its underlying cynicism becomes more apparent, and to widespread disillusion as fragmented, inexperienced, ill-financed groups and associations find themselves repeatedly outgunned and outmaneuvered by better-armed entrants in the battle for "how much of what when." Is it not apparent, then, that at least part of the malaise of contemporary American public life has to do with a theory and practice of citizenship which is the legitimate offspring of the "novel idea," the ideology of individualism that Tocqueville warned "saps the virtue of public life?"

What, then, would be better grounds of citizenship, a more proper idea of the *office* of the citizen? If one accepts, as any theory of democracy or government according to the consent of the governed must ultimately, that the sovereign authority, the final seat of decision-making power, is in the people, then the performance of the citizen is critically important. The citizen, the member of the self-governing body politic, *is* the ruler. As such as he must, ideally, have a measure of the careful education, the high sense of duty and obligation, the disinterestedness, and the deliberate training and apprenticeship always assumed essential for the good ruler, at least if the society is to experience wise and virtuous government. For the western world, the inquiry undertaken in Plato's *Republic* has properly set the question: how can virtue – wisdom, courage, temperance, and justice – essential to the good life, be made the foundation of a state? Plato's answer is that the state must be ruled, directed by those whose character embodies this virtue, that is, by philosopher-kings. Decisions that guide and mold the shared life of the community must be made according to the standards of virtue. Only thus could the essential qualities be made to infuse the society so that existence in it would go beyond mere survival, or material wealth, or imperial power, to the *good life* itself. Plato thus lavishes attention on the education and training of those who are to rule in order to insure that they will indeed be wise, courageous, temperate, and just. Decades of a thoroughgoing liberal education, firm distancing of rulers from the prejudicing temptations of family and ownership of property, and long practice in the efficient, disinterested administration of public affairs are insisted upon to insure the *quality* of rule required by the good of the society as a whole.

Plato, of course, in practice supposed that only a very few people possessed the talents and wisdom required in the ruling philosopher-kings (though his theory did not necessarily limit ruling to a few). To identify, select, and educate these people would be a vital task of the state; success in it would determine how "civilized" it was. He established the fundamental connection between the character, the virtue, the talents of the decision-makers in a state and the quality of life in the society at large.

Aristotle also examined at length the idea of citizenship, emphasizing its exacting nature, the leisure required for its proper fulfillment, the class and vocations most conducive to it, the appropriate rules of participation and office-holding in government, and the extent of territory suitable for effective exercise of citizenship. "All must have the virtue of the good citizen – thus, and thus only," he wrote, "can the state be perfect."[9] With the same connection in mind, Aquinas, Erasmus, and other Christian philosophers wrote of the "education of the Christian prince" as the key to a political society consistent with their world-views. The ancient Confucian system in China of elaborate examinations to qualify for government posts rested on the assumption that rulers should possess the wisdom and virtue expounded in the classic texts. The point in each system was to insure that those who ruled understood and embodied the virtues essential to the good life.

Thomas Jefferson's earnest concern for the education, vocation, land ownership, and political experience of those who would vote and otherwise take part in public life arose from a parallel conviction that democracy, government by the people, would be a tragic farce unless those holding the final power were wise, courageous, temperate, and just; that is, virtuous. He differed from Plato, Aristotle, and Erasmus only in his suppositions about who and how many would hold political power. He expressed the critical extension in writing that "I know of no safe depository of the ultimate power of society but the people themselves, and if we think them not enlightened enough to exercise their control with a wholesome discretion, the remedy is not to take it from them, but to inform their discretion."[10] In a more modern version of the same concern, John Dewey founded a movement for the "progressive" transformation of the public schools in order to better educate for democratic citizenship. He also worked endlessly to reform American political and economic life so that "the collective intelligence of the group," grass-roots groups of common people, might impinge knowledgeably and constructively on public affairs. In each case, the equation is the same: if human society is to be well, wisely, virtuously governed, then the governors must be wise and virtuous, whether they are one, a few, or many.

This perspective and emphasis differs in important ways from much modern discussion of political participation. First, and most fundamentally, recent commentary often assumes that there is no more or less objective standard of virtue – what Jefferson called "ideal right" and Swift "public good" – to which government might or ought to aspire. Indeed, much of the argument asserts that *because* there is no such objective standard, no body of principles, or "habits of civility," or "Mandate of Heaven," that can define the goals or purposes of a society, all votes, opinions, intentions, and interests must be accorded more or less equal validity and be given more or less equal weight in making decisions. "Input" is thus emphasized; the need is to register all views and take into account all interests, under an assumption that society is a heterogeneous aggregation of diverse parts.

This denial of any kind of objective standard in society has the effect of putting the emphasis on *quantity*, not *quality*, of participation. Plato, Aristotle, Erasmus, Confucius, Jefferson, and Dewey, whatever their disagreements, unite in declaring that government will be ill-conducted, and society will in consequence suffer, if those who govern are foolish, stupid, greedy, ill-educated, or short-sighted. Contrarily, modern governments are often evaluated merely in terms first of whether they *have* democratic institutions (elections of some kind, etc.) and, second, of the percentage of people who vote or take part in some way in political life. The assumption is that if the democratic forms exist, and if the people use them, then the essential standards of just (admirable, good?) government have been met. "Progress" toward democracy in Britain or the United States, for example, has often been recounted in terms of the expansion of the suffrage and the reform of institutions so that access to the process for all individuals and groups is made easy, and the principle of "one person, one vote" is more fully realized. Even when these reforms have been largely achieved, as is the case generally in Britain, the United States and other modern democracies, preoccupation continues with even further fulfillment: removal of literacy and residence requirements for voting, ease of registration, and participation by all groups in any way disbarred (ex-felons, illegal immigrants, mentally retarded, young people, etc.). The point is not that expanded participation is not desirable (powerful arguments on its behalf exist, of course), but rather that it may not be of the essence: one can readily imagine poor government in a society where "access" is easy and participation universal. Participation may heighten motivation to understand public affairs, and in that way might be of central importance, but access is at least as essential for corrupt, partial intentions. Mere taking part can be for good or for ill.

These propositions carry important implications for ideas of citizenship. If there is no concept of ideal right or public good or proper relationships even entertained within a nation's political consciousness, then the role of the citizen will quite naturally become that of the exerter of (private) will. What else is left, after all, other than "personal preference" if larger, transcending perspectives have been set aside? The point of view from which the citizen (the "ruler", ultimately, in democratic polities) considers her obligation or role, then, is individual, or at best group-oriented in the narrow sense of membership in a special interest of some kind. Within such a conception, preparation for citizenship would require little more than that members of the body politic know and seek effectively whatever they take to be their best interest individually, or the best interest of particular groups of which they feel a part. The essential training for citizenship would be intricate knowledge of how the system really works and shrewd understanding of how and where to exert pressure to achieve particular objectives.

The effect of such an idea of citizenship would be apparent from the earliest efforts to acculturate young people into a political system. In school the emphasis would not be on the polity as a whole, on understanding an "ideal right" or a "public good" that students might see as a basis for their society. Rather, it would be on ever-sharper perceptions of individual interests and objectives, on the identity and needs of the groups of which they were a part, on the skills of organization and campaigning that would gain power for individuals and groups, on studying political behavior, and on how power worked in the political process. Much is appealing and useful, of course, in this rather practical approach to political education, and one would find little to object to in any of the parts. Surely it is desirable, for example, for young citizens to learn how the political system works, formally and informally, to be skilled organizers and campaigners, and to see the political implications of their individual and group interests. There would also be use in helping citizens see how their own efforts and skills could be brought to bear on the political process and thus encourage them to be active citizens. Young people thus educated, we might assume, would be good defenders and advocates of their individual group interests, and thus effective opponents of efforts by others to exert undue influence and of moves to concentrate power in unfair or dangerous ways. As theorists of interest group politics from Hume and Madison onward have pointed out, the multiplicity of "factions" spawned by a free society and given voice in public life by democratic institutions are effective preventers of tyranny. There is, moreover, a simple plausibility in this scheme that can be grasped easily and felt readily in the give-and-take of politics in a free society (see pages 187–95).

Madison's model of contending factions each limiting the other in the public arena, and the emphasis on politics as give-and-take, suggest, too, a kind of working together and common interest essential even in a polity thought of as an aggregation of parts. In such a model citizens need, and would likely develop, valuable negotiating skills – seeking out areas of agreement, sensing where and how to concede non-essentials in order to protect more basic needs, displaying good humor to one's opponents, and all the other exceedingly useful means of working and living with people of fundamentally different views and interests. One can even speak of an "ethics of compromise," of a "spiritual amplitude," in accepting in good grace less than one earnestly sought, as noble and ennobling attributes of citizenship. But the skills thus emphasized, important and indispensable to life in a free society, are nonetheless mechanistic and akin to contract negotiating. They do not open up and enlarge the idea of citizenship as a shared, public enterprise, asking members of a body politic to explore and discuss, *together*, what might enrich the life of the community, and to seek, *together*, the ideals and aspirations that would enhance and fulfill both individual and social life.

The interest-oriented, accommodating model of citizenship also encourages a preoccupation with political behavior, with a description of what is happening politically, and with a quantitative analysis of political events and processes. If there are not thought to be any transcending, common purposes, consideration of which might be ultimately important in guiding a body politic, then what remains is largely "who gets how much of what when" – the dynamic of which requires grasp of the facts and realities of political behavior. Within this understanding the citizen must become as much as possible a social scientist, that is a sociologist with a knowledge of the groups, classes, and institutions of society, an economist conversant with the production and distribution of resources, a political scientist versed in the realities of the political system, and a social psychologist who understands and can work effectively with human behaviors.

Such knowledge is certainly valuable in its own right and highly useful to the citizen; democracy benefits when those giving consent are well-informed, realistic, and skilled in social dynamics. And it is doubtless fitting and important that those who are to be citizens (*all* people, whatever their occupation, extent of formal education, etc.) be schooled in this knowledge and understanding from an early age, and that ways and means exist to sustain the schooling (formal and informal) throughout life. Such an approach would convey both that knowledge about political behavior and how the system works was the essential foundation of effective citizenship, and that a praiseworthy participation in public affairs consisted in active support of interests and programs of some special, particular concern to an individual, or to groups of which he was in some way a part. Informed advocacy, tempered by a realistic willingness to compromise, would be the hallmarks of the good citizen.

An attractive model as far as it goes, to be sure; but is it enough? Like the idea of individualism, that conception of citizenship is not so much wrong as it is problematical, perhaps insufficient in a wider view of the world in the last quarter of the twentieth century and in a more profound understanding of human nature itself. To see the force of the first insufficiency, one need only recall Jimmy Carter's poignant assertion in his farewell address that the most serious obstacle he faced in trying to lead and govern the nation was the increasing tendency of "single-issue groups and special interest organizations to insure that whatever else happens personal views and private interests are protected." This was especially disturbing, Carter noted, since "it tends to distort our [national] purposes. . . . The national interest is not always the sum of all our single or special interests. . . . The common good is our common interest and our individual responsibility."

Carter's point (and other recent presidents have said more or less the same thing) is that he felt victimized and frustrated in his efforts to provide national leadership because the particular rather than the general loomed so large politically. This circumstance might not have been so harmful at some stages of our history, but given the urgent need for energy policy, improved industrial productivity, and expanded international trade he saw in 1976–80, it was simply calamitous, Carter felt, that he could find so little constituency for the general welfare. He emphasized three urgent, contemporary global problems – "the threat of nuclear destruction, our stewardship of the physical resources of our planet, and the pre-eminence of the basic rights of human beings" – that required a sense of the public good for responsible resolution.[11] The time, Carter insisted, when public policy could safely be left to the interplay of local or special interests had passed – and with it the comforting view of citizenship as requiring no more than the pursuit in politics of individual or relatively narrow group concerns. The interdependent world of the 1980s may make the special interest advocacy model of citizenship as pathological publicly as an atomized sense of individualism often is psychologically. To reverse Mandeville, private vice (self-seeking) is not only not public benefit; it is, all things considered, not even individual benefit.

PUBLIC-SPIRITED AND *LAISSEZ-FAIRE* UTOPIANISM

Even more problematic than the growing danger of this parochial view of citizenship in the sort of place the world has become in the 1980s is the impoverished, perhaps even "irretrievably absurd" conception of human nature embodied in it. In some sense this idea of human nature is the culmination, the logical fulfillment, of the understanding of the individual and of his relation to the state that has been gaining currency in the western world for many centuries. If the independence, the desires, the creativity of the parts (the individuals composing society) is emphasized, then it is consistent to emphasize a citizenship that projects individual concerns into public life. This justification applies, moreover, whether the individual concerns projected are thought of as moral (Thoreau's conscience-propelled part in abolitionism or evangelical support of prohibition, for examples), or are put forth candidly as special interests (grocery store managers opposing bottle-return laws or doctors opposing set fees for medical services). In both cases the political involvement is seen as an extension of private, personal values or needs into public life. If, as John Stuart Mill put it, "individual vigor and manifold diversity," the hallmarks of human progress, required "freedom and variety of situations" to flourish (see pages 60–2), then man's role as citizen would need to be defined consistently. That is, for this unique "self-actualizing" individual, the appropriate political obligation would be simply to project his personal needs or interests into public life. In fact, if society itself is thought of as an aggregation of parts, existing to enhance the freedom and fulfillment of those parts ("life, liberty, and the pursuit of happiness"), then the "projection of private concerns into the public arena" model of citizenship becomes inevitable – and laudable.

But this idea of citizenship fails to take into account what Aristotle insisted was the *political* nature of the human creature (or what Confucius saw as the indelibly social, relationship-based nature of human life). Within this understanding, participation in public life is not a distraction from individual fulfillment, or even a useful auxiliary to more important private interests and idealisms. Rather, it is the means, perhaps even the indispensable means, of personal self-development. Self-development – the achievement of a rich and satisfying personal identity – in this conception requires a sense of one's place in a cosmology or at least an orientation to a larger world than one's individual psyche. But this cannot be attained except through shared endeavors, involvement with others, acknowledgment of mutual interdependency, linkage to generations past and generations to come, and common concern and responsibility for the multitude of enterprises that are of collective interest to the public.[12] With this in mind, the civic humanist tradition, "part Aristotle, part Cicero, part Machiavelli, . . . conceives of man as a political being whose realization of self occurs only through participation in public life, through active citizenship in a republic."[13]

To speculate in this direction, though, runs counter to other ancient assumptions and emphases in western thought. The person of religious vocation, the spiritual seeker, for example, often feels politics and even any life in ordinary society must be given up in order to permit undistracted or untainted pursuit of transcending concerns and values. Rousseau observed that "Christianity as a religion is entirely spiritual, occupied solely with heavenly things; the country of the Christian is not of this world."[14] Artists, writers, scientists, mystics, and creative people of all kinds have often felt a similar need to be politically and socially unencumbered to allow an individed flow of energy into "their own thing." The romantic model of even the ordinary human being finding fulfillment in love or lonely wandering or communion with nature or pursuit of private hobbies or even with family or groups of friends is also largely devoid of public consciousness. In the United States the open land of the frontier and the awe-inspiring scenery of the west has afforded a vivid, compelling landscape for the fulfillment of these romantic impulses.

On a more material plane, the *laissez-faire* model of economic man, pursuing his own self-interest and requiring, so the theory goes, only to be let alone by government in order for both private and national benefit to be maximized, also depreciates politics. "We may fulfill all the rules of justice by sitting still and doing nothing," Adam Smith wrote, while a French liberal a century later noted simply that "individual existence has little embodiment in political existence."[15] Thus government and public obligation appear at best as necessary evils, to be pushed aside and diminished in order that private, intensely individual pursuits can have as much free scope as possible. As Emerson put it, when implored by a friend to take a more active part in politics,[16]

> I cannot leave
> My honied thought
> For the priest's cant,
> Or statesman's rant.
> If I refuse
> My study for their politique,
> Which at best is trick,
> The angry Muse
> Puts confusion in my brain.
>
> Let man. . .
> Live for friendship, live for love,
> For truth's and harmony's behoof;
> The state may follow how it can,
> As Olympus follows Jove.

There is, of course, a kind of politics that is often conceded to be a necessary adjunct to these individualized ideas of human nature. With only a fleeting sense of contradiction, it might even be called "the politics of privacy:" that is, a conception of government that accords with emphasis on personal fulfillment. It starts with a concession that certain things, regretfully, as a practical matter, are best handled by an overarching sovereignty of some kind – perhaps police to maintain domestic order, armed forces for national defense, courts to punish law-breakers and settle disputes, and a few services such as post offices and highways that seem ill-suited for private enterprise. The assumption even in these relatively few functions, moreover, is that each should be minimal and unintrusive in order that as little time, energy, and resources as possible be drained away from private pursuits.

Within this carefully restrained conception, there is a certain useful sphere of activity for both the citizen and the office-holder. The citizen must participate enough to assure that the (limited) public business is conducted honestly and efficiently, while officials are expected to furnish the necessary public services at minimal cost and interference in people's private lives. The citizen is thus principally a watchman, while the office-holder is principally the servant-administrator. Each is honored in part for the sacrifice each makes in order that most people (the higher proportion the better) can, unobstructedly, devote their energies to the private pursuits which embody what is enhancing, valuable, and fulfilling about human life. The office-holder, though, is held to a sort of double standard. He is expected to have some sense of and will toward the public good that is not assumed in the citizen – though why this is a valid expectation is seldom explained. Does it make sense to expect public servants, trained formally in schools of public administration attached to "multiversities" and informally in interest group politics, will transcend the outlook and values of those enterprises?

Generally, though, it is not supposed that there is anything *inherently* attractive or ennobling about being either a citizen or an office-holder. They simply approve and attend to the "necessary evils," those public services that there seems to be no way to get along without. This "public philosophy" is the common, unarticulated attitude about government accepted by many Americans – and by many office-holders who regularly campaign and rail "against government." Even bureaucrats, whose guiding tenet is often the preservation and growth of the tasks of their bureau (thus in a way enlarging public business), actually have made a private domain (a place of personal fulfillment *whatever* the common good) of their public station. Administrators thus positioned achieve a kind of quasi-private status where they do their jobs (and protect them with strikes, electioneering, etc.) for a going wage just as if they worked for a private corporation. And this model holds especially in the late twentieth century when the New Deal, the Cold

War, and the Great Society have vastly enlarged the necessary functions of government. Even though "minimal" has thus become very large, the rationale, and the postures of citizen and office-holder, remain as diminished and demeaned as they were in the *laissez-faire* state.

There is, nonetheless, a sort of grand, utopian idealism in the "politics of privacy," what we might term *laissez-faire* utopianism. If the public business can indeed be thought of in an auxiliary way, and if citizenship can be reduced to require only minimal distraction from private endeavors, then freedom, the absence of restraint, is maximized, and individual energies are given the widest possible scope. The utopian faith is that this aggregating of self-seeking and self-fulfilling parts will be both benign in its social effects and the sure path to the enlargement and creativity that is the great end of human life. Again, the analogy with Adam Smith's theory of the wealth of nations, with J. S. Mill's theory of truth emerging from the unrestrained competition of ideas, and with the conflict of interest theory of democratic politics is obvious: the good, or desired, result arises from a competitive interaction of parts whose motives are unashamedly self-centered. A plausible theory of citizenship, then, can be fashioned to accord with the liberal world-view that, especially since the late eighteenth century, has accepted the enchanting idea that truth, progress, fairness, creativity and other good things come, automatically and inevitably, from the unrestrained egotism of self-actualizing individuals. Deliberate public consciousness is unnecessary, usually misguided, and best unsought, or even unconceived. This is the wager of liberal individualism, what Robert Bellah calls "the most wildly utopian idea in the history of political thought, namely that a good society can result from the actions of citizens motivated by self-interest alone when these actions are organized through the proper mechanisms."[17]

But does this really accord with "the nature of man," the fulfillment of human potential, in *all* its rich and ennobling dimensions? Does this model of life, and its largely implicit public philosophy, do justice to human nature, to the development of the wide range of satisfactions that make life good rather than a mere matter of survival or even of lonely achievement? Does it make room for Reinhold Niebuhr's observation that "the veneration in which . . . the saints of all ages have been held, proves that, in the inner sanctuary of their souls, selfish men know that they ought not to be selfish, and venerate what they feel they ought to be and cannot be?" Is it possible that a fundamentally incomplete, or stunted entity, the private individual (however beautifully and creatively fulfilled *qua* individual), could, through a shared and practiced attention to common interests, be transformed not into a diminished or sacrificing watchdog but into a *citizen*, an enlarged and fulfilled human being whose private creativity is complemented by his exercise of public responsibility?[18] Persons become richly human, and individuals in a fully actualized sense, perhaps, only when they are also citizens, that is, participants, trusted and practiced, in sustaining and improving the shared life of the society.

This view embodies a faith and an assumption perhaps as utopian as the individualist doctrine that self-oriented competitions and aspirations of all kinds are socially benign and the sure path to "progress." What we might term "civic utopianism" is the assumption that people do indeed have a basically social nature and that their inclinations and capacities are such that, under proper circumstances, they will be willing and able to discharge their public roles effectively, disinterestedly, wisely and even pleasurably. Both utopianisms contain an optimistic faith that a cynic or realist can move quickly to debunk and undermine. In individualist societies the record might seem to show that public decay and psychic malaise spread as private aggrandisements and preoccupations accumulate. Efforts to depend on human sociability and civic responsibility, on the other hand, have ended in combinations of chaos, manipulation, and despotism because people remained irreducibly selfish, greedy, and short-sighted. Attempts at civic-mindedness have often resulted, as Patrick Moynihan has reminded us, in "maximum feasible misunderstanding," bickering and contentiousness. It seems absurdly naive to suppose that disinterested concern for the public good, by either leaders or citizens, might be a trustworthy basis for politics. But if both "realist debunkings" are accepted there remains very little prospect for a decent, humane, democratic, or civilized society of any kind. Perhaps it is useful to ask, then, which utopian faith, the individualist (*laissez-faire*) or the civic, is the least far-fetched or the more partially attainable. Obviously, there is no clear answer. Injustice, social disarray, tyranny, and stagnation seem as often the fruit of one idealism as the other, and each seems to suppose a dubious altruism or benignity in human nature and society.

There is a way, though, in which the individualist dynamic and assumptions are especially problematic in their impact on the practice of citizenship. In that model, citizens

> do not and cannot trust each other, because they understand themselves as self-interested individuals, so each must envy and secretly regard the other watchfully, eager for the chance to go one better than his neighbor. In such a situation, the mutual care from which civic culture grows is truncated and suffocated. The impersonal mechanism of the market is, for such *decayed citizens*, preferable to common deliberation about their common welfare.[19]

The individualist assumptions, then, amount to a self-fulfilling prophecy. The very positing of the individual as independent and self-actualizing creates a posture that decays and atrophies precisely the trust, sociability, and common deliberation that the individualist ideology says are not to be depended upon and are not even as valued as the more self-reliant qualities. In many ways, then, an idea of citizenship resting on an ideology of individualism (however genius-enhancing and morally admirable it might be in its own right), diminishes and trivializes the sense of citizenship as an office.

A form of government designed to cope with factions and special interests of all kinds – the basic rationale for a system of checks and balances – thus might encourage people and groups to think atomistically and selfishly (that, after all, is what the system assumes is the case) and perhaps even *require* them to so behave in order to survive. If it is so that "what is honored in a country will be cultivated there," then one should not be surprised to find, in a nation celebrating self-aggrandizement and faction, the flourishing of those characteristics beyond what might be the case under a system upholding other values. After a decade of government under the constitution of 1787, John Taylor of Caroline argued that its system of checks and balances encouraged an "unnatural" degree of faction and self-seeking in American society. Generalizing, he observed that "if a good form of government too often fails to make men good, a bad form of government will too often succeed in making good men bad."[20] He wondered, then, whether the whole tendency of the American system might not be pathological, and thus foreclose the encouragement of more admirable human qualities. Taylor, that is, saw a system designed to contain and balance factions as a self-fulfilling one, likely to encourage the development of the very parochial qualities it assumed were required for its operation. Is it possible that the whole growth of individualism (especially since the seventeenth century) has been so self-feeding that we now mistake a nourished and conditioned quality – autonomous individualism – for a fact of human nature? Is it possible further that the presumed benignity of competitive models, if it rests on conditioned and perhaps even uncommon human characteristics, is itself a dangerous illusion?

A JEFFERSONIAN MODEL OF CITIZENSHIP

On the other hand, the assumptions linked to the more deliberative, publicly responsible model of citizenship, though utopian and far-fetched at least within the perspective of modern, western society, can be thought of in a way that makes them seem more practical. Thomas Jefferson, for example, believed *both* that good government was possible only when those who governed were virtuous (a postulate emphasized in Greek-civic humanist political thought) and that, since government was a convenience originating in the individually defined needs of those in the society, government should rest on the consent of the governed (an argument implicit in individualist, liberal political thought). He was attracted, then, to some of the idealisms of both approaches to citizenship. He wanted government, deliberative and positive, to aspire to the distinction Aristotle had in mind when he asserted that "a state exists for the sake of the good life, and not for the sake of life only."[21] Yet, he also had a keen sense of the tyranny of most governments and of the wonderful liberation that limited, consent-oriented conceptions of the state could encourage. He often argued that the self-reliant individual needed only to be freed of the strictures of government, of bad laws, of stultifying customs, and of ancient, unjust privileges in order to gain happiness and rise to creative heights. He thus also accepted much of the liberal faith that unfettered, competing modes of life were individually and socially beneficent.

To sustain some parts of both idealisms, Jefferson gave careful, life-long attention to the *quality* of citizenship attainable in any given society. He did this partly because of his belief that it was essential for individuals to have the widest possible opportunity to fulfill their own potential – and he was confident that such fulfillment would be socially useful. He sought for all responsible members of a society (for Jefferson, as for most eighteenth-century Europeans and Americans, this did not include (initially) blacks, women, and others regarded as inferior or "uncivilized" and thus not (yet) part of the social compact) the freedom that would facilitate the Lockean *summum bonum*, fulfillment of diverse individuality. His concern that people have character-building occupations, enough land to give them economic independence, education in at least the rudiments, and practical participation in their own government, all in part rested on his exalted conception of the potential of individual life. In that way he shared the rising Enlightenment faith in a creative, open-ended, self-regulating human nature.

But none of Jefferson's individualist enthusiasms was detached from an Aristotelian sense of the *necessarily* social quality of human life: man was by nature a political animal. Human government was much more than a necessary evil; rather it was part and parcel of the very capacity to be a *human* being. Thus Jefferson's celebration, even idealization, of the yeoman farmer rested partly on his *political* virtue and usefulness. The yeoman farmer, through the daily need he had to care for land and animals, to accept responsibility for his own deeds and decisions, to plan ahead and husband resources, and to be in harmony with the cycles of nature, received steady training in the qualities essential to good citizenship. Practitioners of other livelihoods were not so lucky morally: the merchant's need to "buy cheap and sell dear" tempted him constantly to cheat and lie, the mindless monotony of factory work deadened creative energies, and lawyers were required to advocate what they did not believe. Though the inherent virtue of agriculture and the vast expanse of land in the United States led Jefferson to favor farming as an occupation, his reasoning was not basically economic, nor did it denigrate other jobs if they could be rendered virtue-sustaining. Thus, mechanics and tradesmen brought up on the character-building adages of Franklin's "Poor Richard's Almanac," or even factory workers schooled in "participatory" democracy through autonomous unions, or women practiced in family management, might be good citizens. Jefferson's ideal was a *moral* one, not bound to any particular time, place, or economic mode.

The critical foundation of civic virtue, then, was a predominance of occupation(s) that nourished, inherently, the essential qualities.

And this was especially crucial in a self-governing society where the people generally, even as they worked at their jobs, would also be active politically. The widespread ownership of land was essential not only to heighten the sense of responsibility but also to banish the dependence that went along with working on someone else's land or in someone else's shop. Such dependence, Jefferson asserted, "begets subservience and venality, suffocates the germ of virtue, and prepares fit tools for the designs of ambition."[22] The ideal was the independent, yeoman farmer – a model that Jefferson gleaned in part, of course, from antiquity in the writings of Aristotle, Virgil, Cicero, and many others.

To re-enforce humankind's inherent moral sensibility and the good effects of proper occupations, Jefferson believed some education was necessary for all those (potentially everybody) who would have some political role. Again there was a double purpose: education would enhance personal growth and achievement, but it would as well prepare individuals to be responsible citizens. Building in some way on Puritan arguments that clergy and laymen needed to be literate and educated, and reflecting a Lockean concern to properly furnish the "blank mind," Jefferson became the premier American advocate of *public* education; that is, support of schooling for all in order to better prepare citizens for the discharge of their critically important *public office*. Horace Mann, John Dewey, and many lesser champions of public education have simply elaborated and extended Jefferson's argument to suit later circumstances, and there is still widespread endorsement of Jefferson's basic equation: if self-government is to be good government, then the governors (ultimately the people) must be properly educated to the task. This parallels the Greek argument (well known to Jefferson) that freemen entitled to a public role had to be liberally educated to discharge that obligation wisely. Otherwise even government by the people would nonetheless likely be a *bad* government.

Finally, Jefferson thought some form of actual experience in government would be necessary to complete training in republican citizenship. Though by his time representation was well-established as part of the practice of self-government, and thus some dilution of the classical idea of direct participation seemed necessary and acceptable, Jefferson still believed that dutiful discharge of citizenship, as well as experiencing the individual fulfillment that came with a role in public affairs, required some direct, active involvement. Fortunately, Jefferson thought, American federalism, decentralized and resting on strong local governments, furnished a potentially ideal laboratory of direct participation for nearly all citizens. Town meetings, local boards of education, county court juries, militia duty, road improvement commissions, city ward political committees, and so on, kept close to local neighborhood needs, would be latter-day equivalents of the assemblage of all citizens, giving them vital "public space," in Hannah Arendt's phrase, in which to learn and conduct their public business. Jefferson supposed that the experience gained in these various participations would motivate and equip people to elect good representatives for higher levels of government, and build the self-confidence, community spirit, and enlarged understanding that were essential to the fulfillment of man's *political* nature. Vital local government, then, was more than a guard against the tyrannical tendencies of centralization and an efficient way to handle provincial concerns. It was also the indispensable nursery of citizenship.

These aspirations for occupation, economic independence, education, and local government are, of course, as utopian as the individualist assumption of self-regulating competitive energies. Indeed, it may seem utopian in the extreme to presume one's occupation might be morally uplifting, to suppose education will train people in responsible citizenship, or to expect local government to furnish constructive experience in affairs of state. Is it realistic, the skeptic asks, to believe that any combination of vocation, property ownership, education, and political practice will create a *public*, that is, a body of citizens able to think and act wisely and disinterestedly on behalf of the common good? In fact, the almost contemptuous denial of such a possibility undergirds much individualist ideology. If one starts with the self-centered model, assuming that diversity and individual needs and desires are the unchangeable foundation – the facts of human nature – then it would be foolish to expect any nurturing combinations to alter that dynamic. If human nature is conceived atomistically and if individual, idiosyncratic needs and ambitions are the inevitable, basic motivations, then no laws or environment will be able to call forth civic virtue. Indeed, the individualist paradigm doesn't even *aspire* to such sophisticated public consciousness because it supposes value and virtue and fulfillment are essentially private and require only a minimal public dimension for their realization.

But the Jeffersonian model suggests alluring, even compelling alternatives if one regards the individualist utopia as at least as far-fetched as the civic one, and, moreover, supposes that the individualist assumptions do less than justice to the full dimensions of human nature. Jefferson was enough of an Enlightenment man to celebrate the enhancement of individual life that came with liberation from ancient tyrannies, ignorance, superstitions, and inequities, but he also retained Aristotelian conceptions of man's political nature. His ideal person, then, was self-reliant and self-actualizing, but this person was also profoundly, irreducibly political; he was both a creature of his *polis* and an indispensable participant in its ennoblement. For Jefferson every element of individual growth had a public significance. The personally valuable self-reliance and responsibility learned while being a yeoman farmer were also essential qualities of good citizenship. Though personal benefits flowed from learning to read and write, there were also crucial public benefits: persons thus equipped would have the tools needed for intelligent self-government. And participation in politics would not only provide means to protect one's private interests, but would also strengthen one's sense of membership in society. The model citizen encouraged by this comprehensive nurturing process, then, had both personal and public "talent and virtue." But the personal and the public, often thought of as somehow antagonistic, were in Jefferson's understanding two sides of the same coin of human dignity. The public role, played with effectiveness and satisfaction, was as much a fulfillment, an enhancement of human life as any private creation or achievement.

Jefferson insisted, then, that individuality itself is in part social, that it reaches fruition not in isolation or detachment from society but in self-evoking relationship to it. The tension for him was not the often-noted one between private and public inclination (though, ritualistically, he pleaded frequently for release from public office in order to enjoy "farm and family"), but rather it was between the poverty and narrowness of the oppressed or merely private life and the enlarging opportunities, moral and social, of participation in self-government – that is, citizenship. Jefferson's sense of human nature was so deeply social (as contrasted, for example, with Thoreau) that he would simply not have entertained the notion that the avoidance of "publicness" might enhance individuality; such avoidance would to him have diminished or truncated one's potential.

The office of the citizen, then, as conceived by Aristotle and Jefferson (and in this century by Joseph Tussman)[23] is best understood as the part each person in a democracy plays in the government of the community. This requires, most fundamentally, the perspective of the good ruler, that is, a disinterested regard for the welfare of the whole, rather than a narrow attention to self or special interests. That is, it requires *civic virtue*. The need is not that citizens necessarily devote large amounts of time to public concerns (the key amendment the Jeffersonian model makes to the Greek one is to suppose that citizens – freemen – will also have full-time occupations wherein they support themselves and their families), or that they be experts in all the details of government. Rather, they must have a disinterested perspective, and must ask the proper *public* question, "What is good for the polity as a whole?," not the corrupt private one, "What public policy will suit personal, special, partial needs?" Citizens must bring an attitude formed by words like "obligation," "responsibility," and even "duty" to their public role, rather than a perspective formed by words like "desire," "drive," and "interest." The public and civic virtue required of the responsible citizen is, after all, a moral quality, a posture not quantifiable in terms of amount of time expended or amount of information accumulated.

The qualitative difference suggested here can be applied, of course, to any form of rule. It is the same as the one Aristotle makes in distinguishing between the good and bad forms of government by one, the few, and the many. Kings can be reckoned good when they rule wisely and in the interests of the nation as a whole (the Roman emperor Hadrian, or Elizabeth I of England, in commonly cited examples), or bad when they are corrupt, selfish, and oppressive (Nero or Richard III). The terms "aristocracy" and "oligarchy" represent the good and bad forms of rule by the few, while the phrase "tyranny of the majority" suggests even rule by the many can be bad government. Oppositely, the Enlightenment designation "benevolent despot" reveals an ideal for absolute rulers who could be seen as good if they acted in ways beneficial to the nation as a whole. Similarly, then, citizens in their role as rulers can be accounted good or bad depending on whether they try to think and act disinterestedly on behalf of the public good or self-interestedly for their own aggrandizement. Citizens can be small-scale Hadrians or small-scale Neros, good or bad "rulers," depending not so much on time spent or amount of knowledge as on perspective and intention.

Such an approach again seems wildly utopian in that it asks individual citizens to recognize and restrain self-interest and instead understand and seek the general welfare. The point is not, though, that people can entirely transcend their own particular (partial, narrow) perspective, or entirely overcome the tendency toward selfishness. Those inclinations are ancient, ineradicable facts of human nature; perhaps even properly thought of as the "original sin" of self-love. No one supposes that people can wholly escape this "sin," but there is a vast difference nonetheless between acknowledging self-interest as an indelible tendency we need to curb, and the celebration of it as a quality "to be encouraged and harnessed."[24]

The civic model of citizenship does not deny this fact of human self-interestedness, but rather proposes another way to handle it – and also posits a more complex or mixed view of human nature. In this model a person becomes a *responsible* citizen in so far as he or she, through education, moral instruction, occupational influence, political practice, and conscientious resolve, is able to curb selfish tendencies and instead achieve in some degree a public perspective. Relative terms are used because there is no expectation that the selfish drive can be entirely eradicated or that the public perspective can be completely attained. The utopian faith, though, is that the capacities both to curb and to transcend are in some degree present in human nature. Steady effort by human beings in society, through nourishment of institutions, laws, and habits, *can* yield enough public-spiritedness to make government by the people in some degree *good* government; that is, government according to what Jefferson in 1801 called "ideal right."[25]

The reconstruction of the idea of citizenship, then, suited to an understanding of human nature more social and more complex than that generally accepted by individualist thought since 1600 or so, and attuned to the multiple interdependences of the late twentieth century, would place less faith in the hope that competing self-interests are benign in their effects. More faith, however, would be placed in the possibility of people achieving a public perspective that allows them to be good rulers in some degree. It may be that the somber view of human nature that questions whether very many people can ever, under any circumstances or nurturing, achieve such a perspective will prove more realistic. Two factors, though, argue with some urgency and perhaps validity that the more social model of citizenship deserves a more earnest trial than it has sometimes been accorded.

First, the stage in human history when the more pressing need is to break free from clear and present tyrannies of all kinds, a need best abetted ideologically by arguments on behalf of individual autonomy, may have passed, at least in much of the western, developed world – though, as anti-authoritarians in Korea, for example, insist, in many places the primary need may still be for larger doses of liberal democratic ideology. In the West, though, that need must now share the stage with additional urgencies. Concern over resource and energy depletion, damage to the biosphere, communications in the "global village," economic interdependence, international terrorism, and the possible extinction of life on the earth in a nuclear holocaust, all dramatize the danger of individuals and nations supposing their fate is independent of the fate of other people or nations.

Second, and perhaps even more basic, it may be that in the West, and especially in the United States, we can now see certain flaws and inadequacies that demean our conceptions of human fulfillment and of public life. The counterpoint of East Asian cultures sets the matter in dramatic relief: are there modes of human relationship, and conceptions of wise and efficacious government, that open up enriched and deepened understanding of human nature and ways to diminish social and political pathology? The idea is not that people will soon or easily discard long-validated habits of self-centered citizenship and conflict of interest politics, but that a change in the posture of participation (begun with a change in validated attitudes as young people learn about citizenship) can gradually alter the quality of public life. Furthermore, we might encourage, by education and example, a latent sense of social obligation (Aristotle's political nature), rather than teach that self-seeking is necessary and proper in public life. That might break the self-fulfilling cycle of assumed selfishness leading to factions leading to checks-and-balances politics requiring special interest advocacies which exalt and nourish the very self-interest assumed in the first place.

INDIVIDUALISM, PLURALISM, AND THE LEADER AS BROKER

Revised understandings of human nature and of citizenship imply or suggest modes of leadership appropriate to them. The competitive, autonomous, liberal idea of human nature has tended to encourage what is often called a "brokering" mode of leadership. That is, the leader's role is seen as one of recognizing the diverse interests present in a society, sensing both conflicts and points of agreement among them, negotiating compromises, and finally, putting together policies that give each of the various factions something, but not all, of what it seeks. The assumption is that any interest or concern group has legitimacy, roughly in proportion to the size and intensity of its constituency. This is consistent with the conception of society as the sum of its individual parts, each important, creative, and to be protected and nourished above anything else.

Though this style of leadership is not very grand or dramatic, it nonetheless requires sterling qualities and high skills. Such a brokering leader must be open and undogmatic in outlook, reach out easily and effectively to diverse groups and individuals, have a keen intelligence for modes of accommodation, be a skilled negotiator, have an eye for the realistic and the practical, enjoy give-and-take, and, if at all possible, have a sense of humor. Gathering points of view, finding areas of agreement, hammering out compromises, and persuading people to accept and work to achieve the practical become the tasks of the leader. The leaders of the United States Senate in the 1980s – Robert Byrd, Robert Dole, and Howard Baker – have been of this type *par excellence*. Virtually without ideology of their own (except "moderate," "middle of the road"), they have cajoled, managed, and mobilized their colleagues to get legislation passed. The result has inevitably been compromise because the process of gathering a majority for any particular measure is always intricate – and to those on the outside not possessed of the knowledge, insights, and skills of the leader, nearly miraculous. Democrat Robert Strauss and Republican William Brock have functioned similarly in various administrative posts, while of modern presidents Lyndon Johnson has been the supreme practitioner of brokering politics. This is not to argue that these men had no purpose or vision of a good society (Johnson, at least, certainly had such), but rather to emphasize in their daily exercise of leadership the bargaining, compromising skills necessary to form majorities.

Abroad, virtually all Japanese prime ministers in the last 20 years, and the various heads of the Italian coalition governments since World War II, have exhibited brokering leadership. Two of the most successful British leaders since World War II, Harold Macmillan and

Harold Wilson, also gained sway as highly skilled managers and consensus seekers, each eschewing and warding off the ideologues and dogmatists of his party. Such leaders earn and deserve high praise for their ability to get things done amid the swirling interests and clashes of faction spawned by the politics of free societies.

Recalling that these leaders are all thought of as "good party people" reminds us that the brokering style has been linked closely to the rise of party politics in democratic nations. Though parties can and have had ideological and even dogmatic foundations, they also often survive and gain power by containing within themselves compromising factions and interest groups. The first British leader who deliberately, openly, and successfully practiced interest group politics, Sir Robert Walpole (in power 1721–42), was also the first prime minister in a parliamentary system and is often thought of as the first modern British leader. Walpole introduced in Britain, that is, a style of leadership dependent on response to commercial interests, manipulative of parliamentary factions, and skilled at court politics. He gathered and maintained power by his brilliant management of these sources of support. And it is not that he was the first such skilled *practitioner*; many of the ministers of the Tudor and Stuart monarchs had possessed such skill in high degree. Rather, Walpole candidly revealed what he was doing, and sought credit and honor for the virtuosity of his performance as a party leader-manager. He thus gave the western world its first model of the modern, brokering politician who held power and led not by divine right or because he embodied, or even claimed to embody, the good of the realm as whole, but because he accepted and managed the interplay of interests arising from the increasing openness, prosperity, and expansiveness of British society. For this ability and point of view he has enjoyed a high reputation among modern students and practitioners of brokering politics.

This style of leadership received further impetus in Britain and the United States in the 1820s and 1830s as the first modern political parties emerged in each country. In the United States, the leading spokesman and practitioner of the new-style party leadership was Martin Van Buren. Political parties, contending with "candor, fairness, and moderation," he observed, could by "the very discord which is thus produced...be conducive to the public good."[26] He built the coalition of interests that elected Andrew Jackson to the presidency in 1829, and became the basis for the Democratic Party. When he became president himself, Van Buren denied that it was the function of government "to create systems of agriculture, manufactures, and trade." He urged instead "a system founded on private interest, enterprise, and competition" where, without legislative or executive plans or regulations (positive leadership), prosperity and the public good would be insured.[27]

Rising to prominence in American politics at the same time as Tocqueville coined the term "individualism," Van Buren articulated both a new style of party politics and a new conception of leadership to go with it. Scoring the "amalgamating" and above-party intentions of James Monroe, John Quincy Adams, and their predecessors in office, Van Buren endorsed the notion that individuals and groups seeking their own interests could at the same time serve the public good. He also argued that political parties, containing these various interests, could fashion programs, organize support, and direct campaigns that would embody principles just as honorable and patriotic as those articulated by supposedly above-party leaders. The competitive party system, moreover, would more *effectively* work toward the public good because it accepted and made use of the diverse, self-oriented energies of a free people. It validated, that is, the more modern view of human nature and molded a style of leadership appropriate to it.

Other leaders of Anglo-American politics in the nineteenth and twentieth centuries have endorsed the same assumptions and style. John Kennedy declared that for a president to suppose he was above politics and refuse to be a party leader "blurred the issues" and came close to dealing "a death blow to the democratic process."[28] Like Van Buren, Kennedy was endorsing the political version of Mandeville's aphorism "private vice: public virtue." The very "discord produced by contending parties and interests" could "be conducive to the public good," just as in economics competing self-interests resulted in the wealth of the nations. In the intellectual version of the same dynamic, truth emerges in "the marketplace of ideas." The two-party, or the multiparty, system of politics, depending on contending forces for the prevention of tyranny and even the definition of policy, increasingly became orthodox in modern democratic politics.

This model of politics encourages two styles of leadership. The first, following Edmund Burke's famous definition of a party as "a body of men united, for promoting by their joint endeavors the national interest, upon some particular principle in which they are all agreed," sees the leader as one who gathers support for "right principle" in order to carry the day against those organized for evil purposes. The style accepts the diversified nature of public life in a free society, and assumes that contending political forces are thus inevitable, but it also retains a strong sense of right and of purpose. The admired leader is one who keeps an eye on some "particular principle" he conceives to be in the national interest, and then articulates and builds support for that position. The purpose of party politics becomes to achieve certain public policies, and the role of the leader is to mobilize effectively to that end. In this view, "innocuous and ineffectual" opposition to evil or corruption, as Burke put it, "falls miserably short of the mark of public duty. That duty demands and requires that what is right should not only be made known, but made prevalent; that what is evil should not only be detected, but defeated." The leader, then, Burke insisted, had to "find out the proper means. . . [and] pursue every just method" to enable right-minded people "to carry their common plans into execution, with all the power and authority of the state."[29] Woodrow Wilson and William E. Gladstone exemplify this model of party leadership. In an extension of this view (though Burke did not accept it), the best foundation for good government becomes open, ongoing clash between two parties of principle, each standing for different ideologies reflecting different ideas about what good government requires.

Vigorous, purposeful party leaders from Jefferson and Disraeli to the Roosevelts and Churchill have had such principled intentions in mind. And, as the powerful opposition aroused by each of those leaders attests, such a style of leadership is inherently "dissensual" in that it seeks "to expand the field of combat, to reach out for more followers, to search for allies." Such "meaningful conflict. . . produces engaged leaders who in turn generate more conflict among the people."[30] Thus, though this mode of leadership welcomes diversity and conflict in politics, it also pursues "right" policy. Even this incessant struggle, though, requires agreement on the *limits* of party conflict. Moderation, fair play, and good judgment become crucial in the political process. In effect, then, even the "battling parties of principle" model of democratic politics rests on vital agreements which constitute a sort of philosophy of the public good (pages 187–95).

The demands of finding proper means and just methods for gaining political power, of gathering more followers and allies, and of thriving in the midst of conflict, though, all have a way of accentuating the clever management of diverse groups and the adroit manipulation of political forces and processes. The prototype for this mode of leadership in American political history is Franklin Roosevelt, one of the most ideologically partisan presidents as well as one of the most dexterously political. In the end, though, the enduring image of FDR is that of the supreme politico, maneuvering among his co-workers, tending his coalition supporters, cajoling Congress, and building and staffing a federal bureaucracy responsive to his intentions. His leadership was at once remarkably principled, remarkably partisan, remarkably manipulative, and remarkably effective.

Yet, the tendency is for this to become a second mode of leadership more and more emphasizing merely the brokering demands on the party chief become president. And it is not just that such an emphasis is a necessary evil in order in some degree to retain and expand power (the perennial need of any political leader), but that the implicit conception of public life celebrates and exalts the style itself. If one conceives of politics as an arena of contending forces, some good and some bad and many in between, forever changing and adjusting, then the skillful manager and adroit coalition builder becomes the most effective leader. Preoccupation with the diversity of interests in the political arena (all more or less legitimate) and with processes, formal and informal, for reaching compromised but nonetheless constructive policy resolutions, focuses attention on negotiating and bargaining skills and more and more downplays ideology.

The distinctive institution of this style of public life, the large but often amorphous political party, is also shaped by the demands of diversity and compromise. Though the two large American political parties have more or less stood for something at various times in their long history, it is also true that their main purpose is often to gather enough support, to seem all things to all people, and to clarify some issues and obscure others, in order to win elections. Thus party leaders, though generally asserting principled positions, are also most admired for their pragmatism, their ability to gain a little here by giving a little there, and, if necessary, to subordinate conviction to what works. Leaders skilled at that process are rightly admired as useful functionaries in democratic societies, and even achieve a certain heroism in so far as they mollify otherwise irreconcilable differences and manage occasionally to take two steps forward for every one or one and one-half taken backward. Such leaders, moreover, seem entirely in tune with the individualized conception of human nature and the dynamic of competitive diversities that undergird modern pluralistic societies.

But useful and effectively pragmatic as this style of leadership is in some ways (distributing half-loaves, preventing bloodshed, etc.), it often becomes merely clever and manipulative. Though the exceptional leader, like Gladstone or Woodrow Wilson, will succeed occasionally in inspiring the party system with large, idealistic purposes, on the whole the tendency, in a climate of opinion steeped in individualism, pluralism, and competitiveness, is to empower the adroit broker. The ceaseless need for his abilities, the congenital weakness of the counter-argument in favor of adherence to principle, and the apparent inevitability that politics in a free society be an arena of clashing interests, all work to exalt the (merely?) skilled negotiator.

Though there is a kind of virtue in this style of leadership, especially when its practice seems to be the only way to get things done and still be open to the bewildering diversity of a free society, there is also, at least in the long run, a debilitating lowering of sights and even cynicism that goes along with it. In a "Gresham's law of politics," the tenacious operative, incessantly cajoling and compromising, commands day-to-day politics, displacing high-minded leadership. He thus wears down or pushes aside long-range, larger, enlightened views that are made to seem impractical, elitist, and compulsive. Why not, the predictable argument goes, respond to the current pressure, the immediately visible, the politically expedient, rather than to someone else's (self-serving) argument for a wiser or more long-range policy? As this "law" operates, moreover, it becomes self-fulfilling as more and more people and groups with special interests turn to the broker, who welcomes them, validates their partial perspective, and usually manages to get for them part of what they want. Both leaders and followers, then, have a sense of being effective, of getting something, and of participating in a public life that has a certain openness, fairness, and practicality. They have insured as well, however, that the process or "game" they have been at will sustain self-oriented habits, and that other approaches to public life will seem less attuned to the immediate, tangible needs and concerns of many people.

As a sense of what is happening becomes more apparent, of politics becoming more and more a rather crass, even cynical, horse-trading business, of course people less respect and admire its practitioners and processes. This evolution, moreover, is seen not only as an inevitable tendency in free, democratic government, but it comes increasingly to define the only acceptable (or at least only successful) mode of leadership. Conception of leader, then, comes to be not one who, in Jefferson's phase, aspires to "ideal right," but rather a skilled broker. It should not be surprising, under such circumstances, if no very noble or value-laden relationships grow up between leaders and the general populace, and, more ominously, if people come to accept appeals and styles of leadership more or less overtly crass and cynical. (One thinks at once of Richard Nixon's striking electoral success in appealing to the less worthy impulses in American public life; his strident clamor that the United States not become a "helpless, pitiful giant," in the 1972 presidential campaign, for example.) The word "politician" becomes freighted with all the pejorative connotations it now has to many Americans. But if there is something in human nature that feels sullied by such incessant brokering and pandering, and yearns instead for a public life more evocative of shared social values and of a community or nationhood possibly larger than the sum of the parts, then a disgust with brokering politics and a desire for something less demeaning might be latent in a people.

Indeed, as the history of the Weimar Republic underscores emphatically (and the course of many other foundered experiments with democratic government also demonstrates: the Philippines in 1972, Nigeria in 1966, Pakistan in 1958, Argentina in 1944, Italy in 1923, etc.), disillusionment with, even a kind of revulsion at, the bickering, horse-trading, corrupt character of democratic government at its least edifying often causes a people to hearken to stronger, more stirring leadership. (Plato had seen the same phenomenon in Athens.) Thus, though it would be inaccurate, probably, to see a too inevitable cause-and-effect relationship between the lowered sights of a mundane, brokering democracy and the rise of totalitarian movements, there does seem to be a way in which the one is conducive to the other, not only as a matter of political progression, but also as a plausible cycle in human moral history: as people experience the unsatisfying, often dismal maneuvering and manipulating of clash of interest politics, they feel alienated, revulsed, angry. A turn at that stage to a more uplifting, even more demanding leadership would not be surprising.

Hitler's idea of *der Führer*, for example, as a style of leadership, rested on a conviction that people wanted, craved firm direction since they were psychologically incapable of enduring any longer the strains of freedom, choice, ennui, and indeterminateness that characterized Weimar government. Furthermore, since people often respond most deeply to stirring ceremony, to emotional speeches, to the camaraderie of the camp, and to the exertions and sacrifices of battle, it made little sense to cultivate reason and give-and-take between leaders and the masses. Rather, *der Führer* was to guide and direct not only the public life of the nation, but much of private life as well. The principle, or more precisely, the spirit of the polity, moreover, came not from some consulting of the various interests and concerns of the members of the society, or even from some rational concept of the public good, but from the mystique of the race and nation. The people were *die Volk*, the beings embodying the spirit and mores of the nation as a whole, and were thought of politically as the bearers and instruments of the national will. *Der Führer* evoked, mobilized, and led *die Volk* in a grand quest of racial supremacy and "the state marching through history" to fulfill their destiny. The leadership, that is, received its character and purpose from the ideas of human nature and of polity embedded in the mystical conception of race and nation.

In an odd way, though, this totalitarian style of public life is both deeply apolitical in an Aristotelian sense and intensely political in that it emphasizes common, general, national purposes. The division of society into masses, "undifferentiated, amorphous, banal, and purposeless. . . globs of humanity," and an elite, sharply defined, purposeful, and brilliantly manipulative (the party of Lenin as well as of Hitler comes to mind), eliminates at both ends the idea of meaningful, participatory *politics*. Consent – meaning informed, public-spirited attention to common problems resulting in willing agreement to political decisions – becomes instead a sort of commitment, a basically psychic phenomenon where the masses, bleak, isolated, and desperate, accept almost frantically the direction of the elite. Gone is the idea of *polity* where effective, disinterested citizens take part and thus intentionally and wisely empower leaders who then carry out truly public policies.

In another sense, though, modern totalitarian governments have "re-asserted the political with a vengeance. They have destroyed the autonomy of groups and replaced it with a highly coordinated policy; they have oriented every major human activity towards political goals;

through propaganda and controlled education they have instilled among the citizens a strong sense of the political order;...through plebiscites and mass elections they mobilized a general form of support and approval."[31] This cures the disintegration and anomie engendered by emphasis on the parts and by conflict of interest politics, but it does so by nourishing the bleakest notions of individuality and the most cynical precepts of leadership.

There are, then, not only styles of leadership appropriate to various ideas of human nature and of the purpose and dynamic of public life, but also a certain self-sustaining aspect to each linked conception of human nature, political dynamic, and leadership. The individualist assumptions of the primacy and rights of each separate person call forth a politics keyed to the convenience and well-being of the parts, which in turn require that leaders be both responsive to the separate (special) interests in the polity and skilled at brokering among them to produce, quantitatively, "the greatest good of the greatest number [of individuals]." Freedom, responsiveness, equality, and democratic access become the cherished ideals of such a society. In the totalitarian model, the presumed "*Volk* mystique," the yearning for immersion in a cause, and the psychic hazards of freedom call forth a nationalism or communism that embodies and transcends the individual parts and requires a leader who inspires, manipulates, and compels the people in the pursuit of a common destiny he (and/or his party) defines and evokes. Each style, too, elicits a sense of the preferability of the other, often resulting in a cyclical pattern, or at least yearning, caused mainly by the manifest flaws in each. Brokering flux and bargains, that is, call forth longings for firm, spirited leadership, while totalitarian tyranny and conformity highlight the blessings of openness and compromise. Neither mode, though, seems able to sustain the consenting, positive, disinterested precepts embodied in good leaders from the Duke of Chou and Pericles to Lincoln and Gandhi. It is this fundamentally ennobling, perhaps utopian, yet much-needed alternative to both brokering politics and its monstrous but in some ways legitimate offspring, modern totalitarianism, that may be needed in the nuclear age.

LEADERSHIP AND IDEAL RIGHT

Instead of these flawed brokering and totalitarian styles of leadership asking little of ordinary people, let us suppose, as the civic concept does, that the office of the citizen requires people to be in some degree disinterested, to have some capacity to seek the common good, and to find in willing participation in public life an important fulfillment of their own lives. Then it would be important for the political system to encourage deliberation and quest for the public good, and the leader would be obliged to explore, initiate, and guide with that goal in view. The goal, moreover, the understanding of the good society, would be substantial and objective in its own right, ideally arising from reason, goodwill, and a sense of community. And since this goal would have an inherent validity apart from the conflicting interests in the society, the role of the leader would not begin with the parts, but would have an eye to discerning and articulating an objective, transcending common good. A leader in this model, for example, would not fashion a national energy policy by gathering the concerns of the various special interests in the nation in order to arrange compromises among them. Instead, he would seek first to understand the problem whole (knowing about particular concerns, of course), then prepare solutions as consistent as possible with that large view, and finally seek support on the basis of general good rather than utility for segments of society. Theodore Roosevelt's articulation of a national conservation program and Woodrow Wilson's campaign for the League of Nations embodied such leadership. Roosevelt said shortly after his retirement from the presidency, "I simply made up my mind what the people ought to think, and then did my best to get them to think it."[32]

This perspective emphasizes not the way a leader is chosen or his ability to sense and accommodate diverse interests, but rather a moral and intellectual capacity to discern what is wise and fair and good in the long run. Within such a standard, much of the pattern of good leadership in human history becomes intelligible. The wise and patriotic leader has in almost any time and in any place been admired for the same qualities. Solomon, the Duke of Chou, Lycurgus, Nehemiah, Pericles, Ashoka, Hadrian, Prince Shotoku, Charlemagne, Elizabeth I, Lincoln, and Gandhi are acknowledged as good and great leaders most fundamentally because each ruled effectively and wisely and judiciously in the interests of the people as a whole – that is, they were not notably corrupt or cruel or selfish or partial or power-mad or short-sighted. Each, furthermore, left his or her nation and people ennobled and edified, with ideas of the public good and the national purpose enlarged and uplifted. Each was also, being human, flawed, but not in ways that undermined the basic conception of each as devoted to the commonwealth, working wisely for the benefit of all. All leaders, of course, are prone to employ rhetoric to that effect, but only the genuinely good ones can evoke the public response that enables them to exercise *authority*, rightful power. The most esteemed leaders, that is, all govern by a kind of consent among the people that itself rests on a "general will," a sense of the good of the whole. Good leadership, according to these widely admired models, requires many sterling qualities, though not any particular mode of selection. Most essentially it requires a generous posture, an understanding of self and society that substantially aligns one's personal talents with pursuit of the public good, and which thus often elicits public support. "He who rules by moral forces is like the pole star. . . . If a ruler himself is upright, all will go well even though he does not give orders. But if he himself is not upright, even though he gives orders, they will not be obeyed," were Confucius's precepts.[33]

The necessary qualities of good leadership within the civic model of polity are clarified further when they are contrasted with inadmissible traits. Outright pathologies such as bribery, greed, treason, squandering public monies, and willful negligence are proscribed. Most particularly denigrated, though, are any partiality toward one interest or segment of the nation above others, and any favoring of person, family, or dynastic interests at the expense of the general welfare. Shunning such qualities is surely the source of the veneration Elizabeth I has always been accorded in English history and of the standing Washington has as "the father of his country." Each, moreover, had an acute self-consciousness of the need to protect that standing as an essential part of a continuing ability to lead the nation effectively and authoritatively. Any perception to the contrary (in Washington's case, for example, that during his second term as president he was an instrument of Federalist party purposes) undermines seriously if not fatally an ability to continue as a trusted leader of the whole nation. Again, the supposition or claim is not that Elizabeth I or Washington or any other alleged good ruler could be entirely selfless and patriotic, but rather that both the people at the time and the judgment of history subsequently concede and acclaim exceptional success in those directions. Oppositely, those seen to be greedy, partisan, corrupt, power-mad, or negligent – Nero, Richard III, Talleyrand, Nixon, Idi Amin, Somoza, etc. – are scorned precisely because they exalted partial and self-indulgent intentions over the public good – and were hence bad leaders.

Most performances and even conceptions of leadership, of course, fall in between the diabolical Nero and the deified Gandhi, but the critical point of judgment is often nonetheless the *degree* to which the devilish or edifying qualities are manifest. Thus, to take two recent American presidents, Gerald Ford is generally accorded high marks for his earnest intention to transcend the horror of Watergate ("our long national nightmare," as he put it in his first speech as president), to heal wounds in the body politic, and to reintroduce a fundamental decency into the nation's public life. He is criticized, though, for his limited vision and inability to rise above the partisan, interest group approach of his long career in Congress. Jimmy Carter, on the other hand, while widely admired for his intelligence, concern for human rights, and serious effort to deal far-sightedly with energy, arms control, and protection of the environment, is faulted for his inability to infuse his administration with any large sense of public purpose, and for his continuing, debilitating preoccupation with election politics. Each man thus possessed *some* of the qualities of admired leadership – but is perceived as seriously flawed by limited vision or excessive partisanship.

In a larger perspective Ford and Carter were flawed precisely because they accepted willingly in themselves many of the characteristics celebrated in the brokering style: their loyalty to party, their savvy about political process, their willingness to build coalition support, and so on. And it is not that those characteristics are in themselves "bad" – on the contrary, they are in many ways highly valuable – but rather that their too incessant and uncritical application proved compromising or demeaning in an office designed to give leadership to the nation as a whole. We can imagine that the Ford and Carter presidencies might have been more able to pursue the public good had the two men been less absorbed, in their own minds and in the institutions of government they had to manage, in a style of politics inherently partisan and oriented to special interest. One could say, then, that each was in some measure a victim of a pervasive attitude and a political system that not only allowed but encouraged distraction from disinterested attention to the common good.

But the victimizing itself, though, arose in some measure from a desire to be open, democratic, and responsive. When Mr Ford, a veteran of a quarter-century in the Congress, consulted with and even deferred to his former colleagues there his intentions were laudable – to be in touch with the desires and interests of the people through their elected representatives and to test the practicality of proposals in the real world of Congressional clash of interest politics. In some way fidelity to government by the people, responsiveness to the diversities in a nation of 230 million people, would seem to require such consulting. Indeed *not* to do so would seem a dereliction by a leader in a democracy.

Mr Carter's "populism," his repeated efforts to reach beyond the government to the people and to "make the government as good as the people," also seems laudable. More problematic but also apparently populist was Mr Reagan's conception of the presidency as an office where he could be the people's advocate "against the government." If government by the people is to be taken seriously, then the postures of these presidents would seem to be constructive efforts to give reality to that precept. Reagan's stance, for example, seemed at least to get the priorities straight: if the people are one thing and "the government" another, then concern for the well-being of the people would seem to be the first order of business. In all these instances, however, the deeply planted assumptions are that one properly begins thinking about government by considering the diverse energies and interests of the parts, and that the basic role of the leader is to respond to and negotiate among these parts – special interests. Except in discerning the viable compromise, the leader has no role to urge or suggest policies that might transcend particular concerns, or to seek something other than a calculus of them. Indeed, according to one theory of democratic politics, it would be elitist, arrogant, imposing, for a leader to suppose *he* was to supply the initiative and wisdom rather than deriving or gathering it from the people. And though this view of leadership is preferable to a dictatorial one, there is a troubling tendency, as suggested above, for the brokering mode to provoke a reaction where the dictator becomes a welcome relief.

But is another style possible that retains in a democratic context some of the benefits of the good leader evident in such figures as Pericles and Elizabeth I? Is there some way the Confucian ideal of the wise law giver-administrator, cognizant of Heaven's Way, could be adapted to the politics of government by consent? Is it possible, as Abigail Adams hoped in 1783, that the leader in a republic might be a "Solomon in wisdom"[34] and thus guide the nation in paths of justice and virtue? Is it possible that Ford and Carter and Reagan, each personally upright and even idealistic, are flawed as leaders because, in contrast to this private goodness, their *public* philosophies are pathetically, dangerously infantile? Is there some way an elected executive faithful to his constituents could assume the same posture of disinterestedness we have seen is the essence of good citizenship properly understood?

In fact, to retain in a republic ancient ideals of vigorous, virtuous leadership was precisely the long-range goal sought by Thomas Jefferson. Steeped in Aristotle and Plutarch, in Cicero and Tacitus, Jefferson had a keen sense of the Classical qualities of good (and bad) leadership. But he was also committed to the ideas of natural rights and government by consent he had learned from Locke, Hutcheson, and other Enlightenment political theorists. Before the eighteenth century, though, virtually all models of good leadership had been monarchs or other non-elected officials. Jefferson sought for the United States a mode of leadership guided more by the precepts of Aristotle and of Plutarch's Pericles than by the practices of the quarrelsome, small-minded, anarchic democracies so scorned by virtually all eighteenth-century historians and political thinkers. The crucial question for Jefferson was: how could one be a wise yet faithfully republican leader?

Jefferson offered luminous clues to his conception of republican leadership when he noted during his first month as president that since it was "impossible to advance the notions of a whole people suddenly to ideal right," it was well to heed "Solon's remark that no more good must be attempted than the nation could bear." He displayed the same perspective when he wrote a year after his retirement that in a republican government "it is the duty of the chief magistrate . . . to do all the good which his station requires, . . . and to unite in himself the confidence of the whole people." Only then, he insisted, could "the energy of the [whole] nation . . . [be] pointed in a single direction" when circumstances required.[35] Jefferson thus began his thinking about the role of the executive with "notions of . . . ideal right" toward which it was his duty to advance the nation. There were, that is, objective standards, "ideal right," that were the basis of the good society, as he had learned from Aristotle. The leader, furthermore, had to act purposefully and positively, at the head of the *whole* people, if the energies of the nation were to be called forth in anything like their full potential. And the willing support of the people for faithfully republican leadership, Jefferson observed in his first inaugural address (1801), would create "the strongest government on earth," with all the "energy" it needed to "preserve itself" and pursue the public good. Though Jefferson wanted the executive to work faithfully within the Constitution, and reserved vital roles for Congress and for state and local governments, he also saw the presidency as a powerful, indispensable force for the achievement of "ideal right" in the nation as a whole.

Within this conception it was impossible for Jefferson to think of the president primarily as a *party* leader – or even as a party leader at all. Although he reluctantly accepted political organization and campaigning as necessary evils in his zeal to offer *effective* opposition to the Federalists during the 1790s, he did not think of political parties as permanently useful organizations for generating popular participation and for providing a constant challenge to the party in power. He hoped political parties would disappear when the animosities of the 1790s faded and Americans realized they were "all republicans and all federalists." The idea of government as ceaseless party warfare, or as a brokerage for arranging compromises among competing groups, would have been anathema to him. He realized, as did Madison and his other close colleagues, that in a free country differences of opinion and conflicts of interest (factions, in the common eighteenty-century pejorative) were inevitable and perhaps even of some practical use in preventing tyranny. But political parties and the clash of interests had at best a counterbalancing usefulness as leaders and the people worked toward the higher purpose of the polity, the achievement, in harmony, of "ideal right."

As we saw in Jefferson's continuing concern for the improvement of the individual "citizen parts" in republican government, he believed it was possible to bring most people to some awareness of higher public purposes – and he believed that an effective leader could tap and guide that awareness. He envisioned, then, a mutually encouraging relationship wherein the people, nourished by proper occupations, education, and practice in local government, and the national leader, supported by this steadily improving quality of citizenship, would work together to implant "ideal right" at the center of the national polity.

Another way Jefferson believed the president might accomplish "all the good which his station requires" was to lead Congress toward a legislative program consistent with the general welfare. He recognized, however, the dilemmas of democratic leadership: if the president too openly led and pressured Congress, people could rightly complain that he perverted the representative's role to that of mere endorsement of "the edicts of a sovereign." On the other hand, if the president sought to lead indirectly, there would be charges of "back-door counselors." If he said nothing it would seem he had "no opinions, no plans," really no program at all. Jefferson's resolution was to stay in close touch with friendly members of Congress (at famous White House dinners where he exerted his considerable magnetism and persuasiveness), asking them to bring forward measures, if they agreed with them, that he and his cabinet proposed. He also paid close attention to the business of government (and required the same of his able cabinet) so that he was well-informed on all issues, and thus often was able to make wise and attractive proposals. He intended as much as possible, he said, to see that the government under his leadership was one not of "accident, but of design."[36]

Though Jefferson worked largely with members of Congress who thought of themselves as of the Jeffersonian-Republican party and thus in a way operated through a majority party leadership on Capitol Hill, he was not really a "head of party" president as Theodore and Franklin Roosevelt would be a century or more later. Jefferson resisted putting party discipline pressure on members who disagreed with him on particular measures (in such cases he switched to other leaders), used patronage sparingly, and never appealed either to members of Congress or to the public to act for the good of the party. Instead he sought always to gather such broad support on all sides for measures so clearly in the public interest that the opposition would seem foolishly or selfishly on the fringe. Both the intention and tactics, then, of his republican-style leadership shunned the "sharpening of conflict" dynamic cherished in nineteenth- and twentieth-century party politics in Britain and America, and sought rather to capitalize on the perennial attraction of harmony and common purpose in public affairs. The difference with such effective leaders of Congress as Lyndon Johnson and Ronald Reagan is that while they also sought wide support, they did so in the posture of *party* leaders and coalition builders – that is, as assemblers of parts and as perpetuators of party.

Jefferson attempted, then, to bring the acknowledged benefits of leadership above party and for the common good to the government of a republic. It is as if he thought it possible that an elected executive, committed to working with the representatives of the people, could as well exhibit the leadership qualities and carry out the good works of a Nehemiah or a Hadrian. Jefferson made some accommodation to the inevitable pluralism of a free society, and he was an earnest advocate of opportunity for the individual, but neither in his view required an abandonment of the idea of a public "ideal right" or of active leadership in its formulation and pursuit. Like Washington, the Adamses, Madison, and Monroe, Jefferson believed not only that there *was* a mode of leadership neither tyrannical nor brokering, but that its identification and use were vital if self-government was also to be *good* government.[37]

Confucian concepts of government suggest further guidelines for fashioning a model of leadership keyed to some version of "ideal right," yet not merely autocratic. Within a society according highest value to orderliness, benevolence, and the cultivation of morally correct relationships, leaders would have the responsibility and authority to publicly encourage those virtues. Indeed, Confucian societies exalt the state as "the highest embodiment of civilization" because it encompasses the elaborate, virtue-engendering patterns of relationship. Historically, for the same reason they enshrined the emperor as the enduring symbol of the benevolence and order that sustained the whole. Anarchy, a society of mere commercial convenience, and military dictatorship are alike anathema to the Confucian world-view. (Examples of such episodes in far eastern history, though abundant, are unsanctioned by that view.)

But order and insistence on the formalities of hierarchical relationships alone were not enough. Practical wisdom, moral knowledge, and disinterested, long-range understanding also had to infuse the polity. To accomplish this Confucians exalted the scholar-administrator who would serve and guide the emperor. A thorough education in the Confucian classics, and then entrance into state service on the basis of the rigorous examinations, were the devices used to assure that wise and virtuous people would sit in the councils of government. From local administrators to the very right hand of the throne itself the virtuous scholar would fill the key offices of government, discerning the "Mandate of Heaven" (a Chinese version of natural or higher law) according to which human affairs were to be conducted. The first kings of the Yi dynasty in Korea (AD 1392–1494) implanted neo-Confucianism as the official state philosophy by instituting daily "royal lectures" where scholars expounded the principles of Confucian thought to the monarch, and then discussed with the king and his counselors the implications for public policy. Theoretically at least, these sessions were decisive forums for the guidance of government, and assured its conduct according to proper morality; ideal right.[38]

Within this system, neither the people at large nor the head of state ex officio were supposed to have anything substantial to do with the achievement of good government. The people were to be loyal and obedient to the policies of the state, and the monarch was obliged to heed his sage advisors. But the obligation of the people to obey and of the head of state to accept counsel were both grounded on the presumed wise, disinterested quality of the guidance provided by the scholar-administrators. Their moral education in the classics, their training to discern the common good, and their long experience in public affairs qualified them to know and to seek the "ideal right" that alone could be the foundation of a virtuous society. Ideally, this resulted in the good of the polity as a whole as the people experienced the peace, order, prosperity, and benevolence that wise government could provide.

As the Confucian counselor to the Meiji emperor of Japan advised in 1877 (see pages 130–3), it was necessary for the good ruler to "throw open all the doors" of communication with the people, and to know and sympathize with their needs and desires, but it was also his responsibility to make public decisions *himself*, guided by his scholar-advisors. For Confucians, there is no relationship at all between numerically overwhelming sentiment by the people or pressure from interests groups, and wise, correct opinion. Similarly the greed or power-lust or depravity of any ruler, hereditary or otherwise, could not be legitimate ground for government action because there was no "Mandate of Heaven" for such deeds. (Confucian political thought, hence, justifies revolution – 革命, *ke min*, in Chinese, and 革命, *kakumei*, in Japanese; literally "Heaven changes its mind" – against rulers who thus violate the "Mandate of Heaven.") Thus though the needs and interests of the people must be always in mind, and the injustices of any would-be tyrant exposed and resisted, the foundation of the polity had to be the wisdom and virtue of the administrator-sages.

Something, then, begins to emerge of a model of leadership suited to a polity at once faithful to the principle of government by consent and to the existence of an "ideal right" according to which public life should be guided. As in the model of citizenship suited to these precepts, the key is a posture of disinterestedness, learning and practicing the habit of seeking as much as possible the public good rather than partial or selfish ends. Indeed, the leader's responsibility in this regard is heavier than for citizens because the official is committed full-time to active planning and administration – all requiring, ideally, that he be uncorrupt, that is, impartial, unselfish, wise, and devoted to the commonwealth.

The model is Platonic, too, of course, in that it extols a leader akin to a philosopher-king; wise, well-educated, disciplined, and guarded in every possible way from temptations to subordinate public to private ends. Two key Jeffersonian amendments in the Platonic conception, though, make it more useful, and less dangerous, in a modern context. First, the idea of only a very few people attaining the public-mindedness of Plato's philosopher-king ideal, and those few achieving it fully, is set aside. Rather, all human beings, officials as well as citizens, are presumed to be limited in some degree, to be incapable of entirely transcending partial and selfish perspectives. No education, no isolation from distracting property or family ties, no exaltation in power or authority, will succeed in making even a few human beings, however talented, into perfect rulers, philosopher-kings. The aspiration, then, is not to find and train such people, but rather to encourage and evoke, especially in leaders, enough disinterestedness and wisdom to make possible solid progress toward discerning and fulfilling the public good. That all leaders will fail in some degree, and that others will fail egregiously, is accepted as a given, but this still leaves a potentially wide range of more or less good leaders. And the political need then becomes to find and empower those who most of the time in most ways will be faithful and disinterested servants of the common good. Unless this quest is held up as the goal, and unless there is some supposition of progress toward it, then there is not much hope of any system of government serving the public good.

The second necessary addendum in a democratic polity, as Jefferson saw, is that there be some assumption or aspiration that some political virtue, some capacity to understand and take an interest in the public good, is possible in almost all citizens. Since the requirement is *not* one of expertise or intellectual capacity, but rather one of perspective and moral stance, there is a possibility of the necessary qualities existing in all elements of the population – and of it also being possible, with proper social institutions, occupations, political experience, and so on, to *educe* higher and higher levels of those qualities. If these qualities can be found and enlarged broadly in the population, then, the leader's role in part is to encourage that process. He can also, ideally at least, depend on a certain good sense and interest in the public welfare among the citizenry, and thus attune his administration to that resource.

This by no means suggests that wise and far-sighted public policy can somehow very often well up from the people themselves. They *can*, however, be supposed capable of contributing actively to the improvement and judging of it, in ways that neither the Platonic nor the Confucian conceptions, for example, make much room for. The relationship in a republic, then, between leader and citizen is mutually supportive and united by a common posture: disinterested concern for the public good. And this does not require that the United States be, as some cynics have said in scorning the unrealism of the civic model, a nation of 230 million Aristotles; nor does it even require, as Oscar Wilde observed in criticizing socialism, "too many evenings." The vital quality, that is, is not amount or intensity of investment in public affairs, but the moral stance brought to them, whether for one hundred hours, or ten hours, or even ten minutes a week.

The difference between this rather classical mode of good leadership and the totalitarian one, where everything depends on *der Führer* and where the qualities required in the citizenry are not notably edifying or virtuous, is clear enough, especially when democracy is also justified and insisted upon. The distinction from the brokering model seems less clear, though, especially when the democratic aspect is valued highly. The leader as broker easily regards himself as seeking the public good (in so far as the phrase can have any meaning in a pluralistic society) by listening to various groups, discerning common denominators, and arranging compromises that allow public business to be done. His role is important and his skills are readily admired. Furthermore, he seems to be the quintessential democrat in that he is in touch with and responsive to the people, and he then fashions public policy in the light of their needs and interests. Indeed, his democraticness seems heightened partly because he harbors no (elitist?) notion of "ideal right" and thus sets up no objective alternative to the resultant of the interplay of the people and interest groups in the society. This process, at its best, is visibly fair, and thus is justly accorded some moral approval.

There is also, in addition to the fairness motif, a bond of self-interestedness that draws together leader and people and supplies the dynamic of the polity: all assume that bond as individuals and interest groups assert themselves and as leaders arrange accommodataions in order to keep jobs and power. All also can sustain a sense of enlarged and fulfilled individuality as each, in part at least, achieves personal goals. Such mingled motives rest congenially in a pluralist society. The widely felt give-and-take fairness this can evoke is thus tempered by what Thorstein Veblen called "the pennywise spirit of self-help and cupidity," characteristic of the frontier and other places of strong individualism and commercial ethos.[39] But it may be that the *validated* "cupidity" has an inherent tendency to be more potent in molding character and habits than the less personally rewarding component of fairness.

In the civic model, though, different bonds and assumptions link leaders and citizens. To begin with, the public interest is thought of as more than the sum or resultant of the parts. It is rather an objective that leaders and citizens seek together, basically no more accessible or important to one than to the other. Indeed, understood as a configuration of habits, values, and common purposes that improve the quality of life available to all people in the polity, the cultivation of the public interest might even be more important (and easier) for those whose personal resources are least able to create the private world of their heart's desire. A perception of the value of such a public good, furthermore, is a vital step in an understanding of its nature. One can say that the public interest in part consists in being interested in the public. Leaders thus have an important responsibility to articulate for the populace at large attractive, enlightened conceptions of the public good, and then to evoke in them an active attention to that good. Without such deliberation and common concern, rhetoric about the public interest tends to be either self-serving, elitist cant about "what is good for the people," or mindless insistence on the immediate needs or desires of whatever majority faction can control the power of the state. Since neither of these approaches would likely result in good government, leaders are obligated to encourage and elicit the disinterested attention of the citizenry to the common good.

Such guidance is not anti-democratic, but may actually be the only way democratic government can participate in the benefits of a shared and elevating public life that in turn fulfills the otherwise incomplete individuality of the merely private person. This, at least, was Jefferson's thinking when he sought as president not to oppress, dominate, or even dazzle the people, but rather to call forth in them a fulfilling, enlarging sense of competent participation in their own government.

There could be such leadership, of course, in a party of principle where the party becomes an instrument to assure that "what is right [is] not only made known, but made prevalent, and that what is evil [is] not only detected, but defeated." The tendency remains strong, though, for such a party as time passes to exist for its own sake, and to utilize a "transactional leadership [where] leader and follower exchange gratifications in a political marketplace. They are bargainers seeking to maximize their political and psychic profits," and tend to deal mainly in "calculable, tangible, measurable properties," a mode well-suited to the individualist ethos. But Jefferson's idea of leadership was more "transforming" than transacting in that he sought not brokering exchange but guidance toward "ideal right."[40] He was a *democratic* leader as well, moreover, because he insisted that the people could, with proper environment, institutions, and practice, share in understanding that right, or the public good. Some such linking of leadership and people and ideal right, perhaps imbedded in political parties but transcending them if necessary, might help revive the health of the American polity in the last part of the twentieth century. If this seems an impossibly idealistic notion, that may be a measure not of the unreality or obsolescence of the idea, but of the distance our conceptions of polity have moved from what their good health requires.

CONFLICT OF INTEREST POLITICS

For a half-century or so basic college courses in American government have often begun with an explication of certain phrases and arguments from Madison's tenth and fifty-first *Federalist Papers*. Factions, combinations motivated by passions or selfishness "adverse to the rights of other citizens, or to the permanent and aggregate interests of the community," Madison asserted, are "sown in the nature of man." They are thus sure to exert political influence under any free government. "Diversity in the faculties of men," the protection of private property, and the strong connection between human reason and human self-love, all operated to insure "a division of society into different interests and parties." Since these motivations and divisions were inevitable (resting as they do in human nature itself), Madison reasoned that tyranny and oppression would actually be deterred by the inclusion in a nation of enough factions (special interests) to prevent any one from gaining too much power. "Ambition must be made to counteract ambition," he generalized. The constitutional principles implicit in this dynamic have been hallowed as "separation of powers" and "checks and balances." Not only would various interests among the people jostle and counteract each other, but within the government itself each department would be given "the necessary constitutional means, and personal motives, to resist the encroachments of the others." A system of checks and balances would thus "oblige [the government] to control itself," that is, be prevented overall from oppressing the people. Though one might argue that the *ad hoc* clash of factions in any free, democratic government makes formal checks and balances in a constitution unnecessary, Madison foresaw factions, in various intricate and ingenious ways, using the formal devices (bicameralism, executive veto, etc.) as ways and means of exerting influence on decisions – getting something of what they wanted.

This argument becomes stronger the more completely and effectively the various groups and interests in a society are able to participate in the political process. Each faction must have the means to defend itself not only for its own sake but also for the sake of the public. Without effective advocacy for itself some other faction in the society might too much (unfairly and tyrannically) get its own way. In Reinhold Niebuhr's neat characterization, "man's inclination to injustice makes democracy necessary." Though Niebuhr himself emphasized as well that "man's capacity for justice makes democracy possible," this side of the argument has generally received less attention and been accorded less importance than the realistic justification for democratic decision-making derived from the "counteracting factions" dynamic. The paradox is the same, moreover, as in the argument that an invisible hand guides competitive economics toward the wealth of nations: in politics no one need *seek* the public good because some sort of surrogate for it, the best that can be attained, realistically, emerges from the free and full interplay of factions. This view of politics also welcomes the ideology of liberal individualism into the nation's public life: individuals need only to know and then assert the political dimension of their own wants and interests in order to participate responsibly in self-government.

This hard-headed (though one could also argue *narrow*) view of human interests and motivation has become the foundation for a widely accepted model of democracy in the United States, said to be consistent with the open, non-ideological, pragmatic "genius of American politics." The model is thus more than a mere recognition that when interests clash or people disagree, some sort of compromise is often necessary. It also supposes that self-advocacy, negotiation, compromise, horse-trading, voting, majority rule, and ongoing opposition are the *best*, perhaps the *only*, ways to make decisions in a free, democratic, pluralistic society. If politics is a matter of "who gets how much of what when," and if the public interest is conceived as simply the resultant sum of the pressures of the individual and group parts in the society, then the "preponderance-aggregate" way of making decisions seems proper as well as inevitable. It reflects the individualist assumptions of modern liberalism, it embodies a mode of intercourse analogous to that of competitive economics, it accepts the axiom that "truth" is best defined by the clash of ideas, it validates the notion of a "pluralistic universe," it requires democratic institutions, and it sees progress itself (or at least change) as the essential goal of human society. In fact, this process seems so obvious, realistic, and practical that its validity is taken for granted in many modern, western democracies. Its existence in some form is even used to test whether a polity can indeed be regarded as free or democratic.

The definition of democracy as "whatever can be done democratically" encapsulates the argument. That is, if there is freedom of expression and association to allow interests to be articulated and organized, a multitude of "mediating institutions" to assure countervailing sources of power, voting mechanisms open to all, and representative legislatures for making laws – then a nation is considered democratic. It possesses the essential devices to make decisions according to the fairly weighted will of the people. The particular decisions made by the process – even major ones such as whether to have a capitalist or socialist economy, the extent of the social welfare system, and whether to have local or national control of education – are not regarded as necessarily better one way or the other as long as they are made *democratically*. All is thought to be free, fair, and just when there is open and equal access to "the process" by all people, when decisions are made according to it, and when "the process" remains in existence so further changes can be made using it. Something of the mindlessness of this view, though, can be seen in the parallel argument by pornography publishers that they do no more than provide the public with what it wants. The public, that is, has settled the matter by deciding to purchase the magazines; no other standard or concern is necessary or even admissible.

Even so, process itself can be seen as a sort of objective standard, or natural law, or essence of the public good. Furthermore, liberal, pluralist politics can be said to rest on a consensus of values and aspirations that provide a framework within which the apparently ceaseless conflict of interests takes place. Finally, two (or perhaps more) faithfully democratic parties, each upholding principles and policies plausibly good for the whole, might, by perpetual contention, not fracture and demean public life but actually enrich and edify it. Arthur Balfour, once prime minister and a force in British public life for nearly half a century, wrote in 1928 that "our alternating cabinets, though belonging to different parties, have never differed about the foundations of society. And it is evident that our whole political machinery presupposes *a people so fundamentally at one* that they can safely afford to bicker, and so sure of their own moderation that they are not dangerously disturbed by the never-ending din of political conflict."[41] There are, then, perhaps within even the most elaborately adversarial political systems, both objective standards and faithfulness to principle latent amid the "bickering" and "never-ending din of political conflict."

In two ways, though, this sense of guiding principle within the conflict model needs clarification. First, the notion that process by itself can be a kind of natural law is at some point contradictory: if the process allows *any* change to be made (democratically) then on what grounds can that process itself be exempted from the "law of change?" Cannot the process be allowed to change itself? If not, then what more transcendent principle forbids such a change? What, for example, forbids the repeal of the First Amendment to the United States Constitution? Nothing, technically (if the amendment process is used). But if some principle excludes such a move, then it, not the process, would seem to be the higher law.

Even the model, most fully developed in Great Britain, of large "parties of principle, each standing for different ideologies reflecting different views of what good government means," though rising above conflict of interest notions, is freighted with limiting assumptions. It does insist that parties be more than interest group coalitions, and it does grasp that people of principle can and ought to unite (form parties) in order to defeat evil-doers – as Burke and Jefferson, for example, had urged in the eighteenth century. Thus parties, and partisan activity, can be viewed as contributing to the public good by exposing and opposing interests "adverse. . . to the permanent and aggregate interests of the community," and by articulating instead more enlarged, principled views. Even the ceaseless rivalry of such parties can advance ideas of the common good rather than be mere exercises in self-advocacy.

In fact, much of the most admirable party activity – stimulating principled discussion, clarifying issues, collecting and disseminating information, enlisting citizen support, identifying and supporting good leaders, and so on – can be justified as sustaining the search for ideal public right. One can even envision a sort of grand combining of the best of Plato, Rousseau, Madison, and J. S. Mill in a polity where increasingly enlightened discussion among all people hones and fashions a "general will" not qualitatively different from what philosopher-kings might discern. But even so, the debate and party rivalry takes place among, in Balfour's phrase, "a people. . . fundamentally at one." How "at one?" About what? Within what limits? Is it merely the process that is accepted by all? The answers to these questions must open up, or assume, areas of basic agreement, and at that point even the most determined partisans accept the reality of a common good. As Burke put it, ideally "Parliament is a deliberative assembly of *one* nation, with *one* interest, that of the whole – where not local purposes, not local prejudices, ought to guide, but the general good, resulting from the general reason of the whole."[42]

Second, if there are "foundations of society" that keep "a people . . . fundamentally at one" amid the "never-ending" conflict, then those "fundamentals" need to be acknowledged and understood more than they are in conflict theory taken by itself. If there are principles or higher law that do limit and guide what the clash of interests can decide (as conflict theory would seem to deny), then the polity does possess a substantive "law," however unarticulated or taken for granted. If these "foundations" exist but are not acknowledged, and the conflict of interests is asserted to have full sway in making decisions, then the system is simply not what it purports to be. Likewise, the persistence of principle in political parties, and reasonable discourse among them, would also seem to assume "fundamentals" not acknowledged in opposition party ideology standing by itself. Arguments and practices that limit conflict of interest politics, then (probably more widespread in Britain than in the United States), do indeed soften some of its fragmenting, amoral aspects. At the same time, though, this softening restores concepts of objective standards that bring the argument back toward public philosophies frankly attentive to ideas of higher law and common good.

The principled aspect of political party rivalry, though, tends to get lost as citizens, interest groups, and party leaders alike find themselves preoccupied with the process itself. So second nature becomes the idea of reaching decisions by encouraging conflict of interest, moreover, that it is used everywhere in western (and especially American) society – and it is soon taken to be "first" or basic human nature itself. Private clubs, school classes, fraternal organizations, political parties, business boards, churches, committees, and children's groups pride themselves on their operating mode – to discuss (advocate), vote, and decide by majority. Indeed, to proceed in any other way requires earnest reasons for making exceptions. The practice of discussing and voting to make decisions, ingrained in a people, is of course, a powerful barrier to dictatorships of any kind as well as a useful means for giving people a measure of control over their lives. Indeed, a free, open democratic society would seem impossible without widespread, habitual use of such a mode of decision-making.

The assumptions about human nature implicit in such decision-making match those in the interest-advocacy concept of citizenship and in the brokering style of leadership. It is not just that self-interest is the assumed motive, but also that interaction of parts is assumed to be the way things work. None of the three modes, that is, has any conception of the purpose or even the existence of "the whole."

At a number of stages in the process individualism is emphasized and encouraged. By speaking up, asserting themselves, and representing their own interests, individuals in the polity assure justice to themselves, and, in a marvelously invisible way, to others as well, by participating in the vigilance and variegated pressure that prevents undue domination. To properly discharge this "duty" to themselves and to the "public good," individuals need to be well-informed and alert, aware rationally of their own best interests, skilled at advocacy and negotiation with others, and sophisticated about the realities of the political process. Freedom of expression and association, public debate and openness at all levels of government, and vigorous institutions of education and dissemination of information are vital if the process is to be fair and effective. These useful public devices, moreover, also enhance the capacities of individuals. Leaders do not so much need to provide wisdom and guidance for the society as a whole as to sense the needs of diverse segments within it so they can transact the nation's business. They thus require, to properly do their job, clear, vigorous, advocacy by groups and individuals of their particular concerns. Even the leaders themselves have as a primary motivation the preservation of their own power by the adroit manipulation and compromise of the diverse interests within their scope. They too benefit and serve by self-seeking.

As the mechanisms of government reach the point of decision-making, whether in legislatures or in executive offices, the need remains to be fully responsive to interests present in the society. Representatives must have their ear to the ground, alert to shifting concerns, emergent minorities, and newly-organized pressure groups. Executive officers (including bureaucrats) are supposed to be yet further points at which diverse individuals and segments can exert influence. Elaborate bureaucracies empowered to provide services for the public are simply so many more places (offices, agencies, commissions, etc.) where citizens and groups can state their cases. Even courts, in this view, are thought of as properly made accountable to the public. Their decisions and personnel should be voted on, subjected to majority decision-making – thus increasing the points at which individuals and groups can exert pressure on government. If the process is open and responsive enough, that is, all "servants of the public" will see their function as providing as much access and service to the people as possible. Thus "big government" can be "better government" because it affords more means for satisfying individual needs in some degree. Society has freedom to choose, unlimited by pre-existing dogma or principle, how much government it wants, and what its functions should be, all in service to the needs and interests of the parts. As John Dewey put it in defining the "new liberalism" of the

New Deal era, "liberals today are committed to the principle that organized society must use its powers to establish the conditions under which the mass of individuals can possess actual as distinct from merely legal liberty."[43]

This undogmatic notion of public decision-making has become so pervasive and so widely accepted as the ideal for democratic government that even theoretical discussions of democracy have often merely elaborated versions of decision-making. Analyses speak of "Madisonian" attempts to use checks and balances to prevent "tyranny of the majority," yet remain faithful to the principle of government by consent. "Populist democracy," straightforward majority rule, is examined both to discern its "ethical foundations" (usually found to be non-existent) and to see if it is ever actually adhered to (seldom, if ever, studies conclude). "Polyarchy" is offered as a description of all the various systems of government and decision-making that at least "divide up" power and provide some kind of access for diverse groups. Finally, after noting the diversifying tendency of modern democracies, a "hybrid democracy" is discerned where "elections and political competition do not make for government by majorities in any very significant way, but they vastly increase the size, number, and variety of minorities whose preferences must be taken into account by leaders in making policy choices."[44] Democracy, that is, becomes a variety of processes more or less providing individuals access to influence in government.

In Great Britain, for example, since 1832 attention has been on expanding the franchise toward the one person, one vote ideal, on limiting the power of the unelected House of Lords, and on strengthening the democratic process within the great political parties, all to improve access, participation, and responsiveness. Justice, fairness, equality, and widened opportunity are generally assumed to follow from the improved process. In the United States the democratization of state constitutions during the first half of the nineteenth century and the movements for direct election of senators, direct primaries, initiative, referendum, and recall during the Progressive era had the same intention. Campaigns to insure full voting rights for women, blacks, and young people have been similarly motivated, as have efforts to make processes within political parties (for example, the "McGovern reforms" of the Democratic Party in the early 1970s) more open and representative of more interest groups. Even attempts to restrict the undue importance of money in political campaigns usually seeks not so much to limit the influence of special interests as to give them *all*, rich and poor, a fair share of "clout."

By making elaborate, sophisticated studies of the effect of these reforms on the decisions of government, and by often using the degree to which the reforms seem actually to distribute power more equally to all groups in the society as the gauge of their "success," political scientists accept and validate the process as the key mark of good democratic government. Even critics of pluralist theory tend to concentrate on its failure to fulfill its own claims, rather than on its assumptions and intentions. They point out "oligarchical tendencies" in its working, the preponderant influence of "the power elite," the undue responsiveness to "groups in existence as against those in process of formation," and so on. Though these critics sometimes call for a stronger sense of political community, or other ways to resist the fragmentation implicit in most pluralist theory, in general they accept the liberal individualist starting points.[45] Yet, well-intended as these studies are, and useful as they might be in improving the process, their implicit neglect of vitally important aspects of public life gives poignant force to Leo Strauss's observation about "the new political science:" "it would be false to call it 'diabolic'; it has no attributes peculiar to fallen angels. . . . Nor is it Neronian. Nevertheless one may say that it fiddles while Rome burns. It is excused by two facts: it does not know it fiddles and it does not know that Rome burns."[46]

DECISION-MAKING AND HUMAN NATURE

All this is not to say we should in any way neglect the need for full and fair access to the political process. The opposites, exclusion of women and blacks from the voting booth, decisions made by political parties in smoke-filled rooms, the domination of politics by money, and so on, are hardly laudable. The removal of procedural bars and inequities may even be a prerequisite for valid democratic government. And certainly the notorious elimination or perversion of democratic devices by totalitarian governments is a further gauge of their necessity.

Yet, nagging, serious questions remain. Polities that seem most fully to embody the decision-making process in its (self-defined) ideal form are not notable either for their own (self-evaluated) sense of happiness, creativity, and general well-being, or for seeming to rank high in the admiration and esteem of others. The phrases "lowest common denominator" and "tyranny of the majority" make further grave and scornful accusations. Both the British and American constitutions, furthermore, contain important reservations about things *not* to be done, no matter how democratically. "Certain subjects, . . . fundamental rights," Justice Robert Jackson declared for the Supreme Court in 1943, are in the American system of government "placed beyond the reach of majorities and officials. . . . [They] may not be submitted to vote; they depend on the outcome of no elections."[47] Neither experience nor constitutional law, it seems, validate unreservedly the idea that all decisions made according to the democratic process are desirable or even acceptable.

If we ask *why* these reservations seem so crucial, the first and most notable answer is that only with them can "unalienable" individual rights be protected. The first amendment declares that *Congress* (chosen by the people) shall make no law abridging freedom of speech, press, and religion, and other clauses in the Bill of Rights state other fundamental restraints on the powers of even duly elected legislatures. The fourteenth amendment extends the restrictions to (democratic) state governments. Thus the rights of *individuals* are granted primacy; they are beyond the legitimate infringement of any government. There are some things, that is, that *cannot* be done, even democratically, in the interest of preserving individual rights. The fact that the amending process, though theoretically making any change possible, is so seldom used and is itself so at odds with majority rule reveals profound reservations about democracy as a process.

Yet the contradiction or tension remains, irresolvable in governments affirming, as the American Declaration of Independence does, both that certain rights are "unalienable," that is, not to be denied by any government, and that the "just powers" of government derive from "the consent of the governed." What principle is primary when a government of consent invades an unalienable right? The conflicting rights, to freedom of expression and to make laws by majority consent, cannot each be given full scope under the doctrine of individualism that gives sanction to them both.

But a more subtle and profound difficulty is also implicit: the process-preoccupied mode of government seems as well to leave unaccounted for deep aspirations of human nature and society. Is there no substantial goal, no objective good, no qualitative sense, no ideal right toward which human life ought or might aspire, and for which government might be an agency? Failure to attend explicitly to ends generally results in a "pragmatic acquiescence," that is, an acceptance of the basic propositions and structure already existing in a society. This acquiescence then inhibits *fundamental* criticism and *creative* search for *radical* alternatives. Interests and groups already established, and skilled at using the existing political process, tend both to dominate decision-making and to resist effective access to power by new or previously unarticulated or unorganized interests.[48] Society, moreover, loses the habit of raising basic questions and of looking for distant new horizons. Visionaries are not honored in the land, and "blah" politicians like George Bush and Walter Mondale run for high office.

Finally, the very mode of decision-making itself, emphasizing self-advocacy, attention only to the parts, a tendency toward settlement according to mathematical percentages, and a habit of compromise seldom cognizant of the *quality* of the resulting decision (which might "fall between two stools"), has a way of accentuating some of the less admirable human characteristics. Though egocentrism, partiality, quantification, and short-run compromising are not qualities likely to be eradicated from human life (nor is it even desirable that they be), there is something perverse and ill-advised about a mode of politics that encourages and even celebrates them. The result is the slow but steady movement of public life away from large aspirations, wise conceptions, and thoughtful concern for the general welfare toward stridency, attention to power-brokering, and a demeaned idea of the nation's common life. There is, of course, no *intention* that this happen, or any explicit repudiation of the public interest. The idea is just gradually impoverished. And in fact, the notion of "mechanical aggregation of conflicting desires...verges on moral bankruptcy. It accepts and makes no attempt to change the foundations of selfish desire." One might even say that such "adversarial" democracy is the democracy of a cynical society.[49]

Such a public philosophy, furthermore, often has the pathological effect, as John Taylor of Caroline notices, of "making good men bad." That is, it atrophies such virtue as might exist in a polity for seeking the public good by requiring and eventually exalting instead the selfish, quarrelsome, factious tendencies that also exist in human nature.

Though one could doubt realistically whether *good* government could make men *good*, it seems clear that bad government would certainly as time went by heighten pathological inclinations. A disinterested concern for the public good put down by realists as unlikely, slowly becomes unnecessary, and finally is regarded as hypocritical and even dangerous. The system of checks and balances, resting on an assumed foundation of the interaction of factions, become a classic self-fulfilling prophecy: by requiring only the self-interested striving of its citizens, it nourishes the very factions and self-orientation it assumes.

The problem of republican government, then, is both intricate and challenging. Since such government requires that people be free, it would, as Madison argued, permit and even call forth a diversity of private interests. At the same time, though, since the people were also the governors, ultimately, they had to fulfill their "office as citizen" according to the time-honored tenets of good rulers. They had in some degree to be virtuous, wise, and disinterested. The political system had both to manage and cope with the factions and special interests born of human freedom *and* to nourish the virtues required if self-government was to result in good government. The first task "makes democracy necessary" because only when all groups in a society have access to power can the tyranny or unfair dominance of one or a few be prevented (the logic of *Federalist* no. 10). The openness of the process and intricate, sophisticated study of how it really works become legitimate preoccupations. But the second task, nourishment of civic virtue and disinterestedness in the people, is in tension with the first task, in so far as preoccupation with it encourages habits of individual isolation or special interest advocacy antithetical to good citizenship. The goodness, that is, needs cultivation in its own right and protection against the corrosive effects of conflict of factions habits. Only then is there much prospect for *good* democratic government.

THE WHOLE: MORE THAN THE SUM OF THE PARTS?

The assumptions and practice of the self-advocating, brokering, compromising, majority-voting mode of decision-making are tied closely to the whole ethos of individualism. The values throughout are much the same, and in many respects embody important moral axioms. As Locke and others have argued, for example, legitimately diverse "parts" can, morally, only be regarded as both equal and free. In the eyes of God and of just law, each individual, given his or her unique and self-fulfilling nature, has an equal right to pursue her own ends, and needs freedom to become his own, idiosyncratic "self." Abridgements of these moral axioms are unjust and tyrannical. Thus slavery and conquest are wrong because each violates a condition essential to human nature. So too, in a more sophisticated society, are denial of full civil rights to any citizen and even limitation on equal opportunity for any individual on any grounds whatever. Vital principles of justice seem to derive from the individualistic conception of human nature and the brokering style of decision-making that, ideally, provides full access and voice for the diverse parts.

If one questions, though, whether individualistic ideas of freedom and equality, and ways of making social decisions, are part of human nature, complications arise. Suppose one begins not with Tocqueville's "novel idea" of individualism or even with some of the less autonomous ideas of individuality that have coursed through western history. What modes of decision-making, for example, go with, seem appropriate to, the Confucian-derived emphasis on relationships and on the place of the individual in the group? Since the good life is not considered to be one of (separate) individual fulfillment, but is rather one of proper and enriching relationships with others, then the "parts" in all their unique diversity are not thought of as the starting place, the point at which ultimate value is focused. Furthermore, since the enriching web of relationships creates hierarchical family, group, and social life with an encompassing intensity less characteristic in individualistic cultures, the tendency is for decisions to be made according to the informal authoritarian or consensual modes of family and clan life. At least the notions of each autonomous individual having one vote, of decisions being made legalistically by majority vote, and of an ongoing opposition-advocacy being a normal and useful part of social life, would seem bizarre and pathological. They affront the very basis of society. The ideas, that is, that each person should have and assert his or her own opinion, or that a counting of equal, discrete parts is a valid way to make decisions, or that continued insistence on one's own position, however principled, is socially useful, would be simply unheard of.

Two other modes of deciding would be far more congenial to the relationship-based society. First the authoritarian, or perhaps more to the point, the patriarchal (or matriarchal) way would often seem fitting because the relationships themselves are hierarchical, calling for loyalty, obligations, and obedience. Thus younger siblings defer to elder ones, children obey parents, servants are loyal to masters, and subjects accept the rule of sovereigns, all in dutiful fulfillment of relationships. In the other direction parents care for children, sovereigns rule wisely in the interest of all, and so on. And, since the *quality* of the relationship, its moral and emotional fullness, is of the essence, there is little room for contract or quantitative calculation. Indeed, in so far as such ideas come into play, the relationship would be regarded as defaulted or betrayed. Though there is nothing of what the West calls democratic in this system, and abundant opportunity for unfairness and oppression (though those words have vastly different manifestations in different cultures), there is also, ideally, a rich and complex sense of responsibility and devotion to the welfare of the whole. The ideal, in fact, is not far from the concepts of wisdom, fairness, and concern for the whole that characterize the best western models of leadership, where decisions are admired for their quality or *goodness* rather than, as democratic theory often requires, for the *way* they are made.

On the other hand, the emphasis on group life, and denial of individual autonomy, in many different ways requires a great deal of discussion to reach widespread if not complete consensus. If a person's orientation, his sense of identity and purpose, derives from *inclusion* in family and social groups (up to and including the nation), then there is a strong need to feel empathy, harmony, at-one-ness with those groups. Not to do so is psychologically, morally, and socially devastating. Even in situations where making the decision is the responsibility of an elder or leader, the obligation to consult and act in concert with the views and interests of the group often requires long sessions of talk and exchange of ideas. Furthermore, since all concerned know a majority vote will *not* be decisive (or even in the picture), there is much less motivation to insist on one's own opinion, to maneuver for a narrow victory in the vote, or to prepare to win in a subsequent vote if not in the most immediate one. Rather, the approved and admired conduct (violated by some, of course) for all involved will be to contribute unegotistically to discussion of the problem, to sense points of convergence, and to acquiesce willingly in the decision of the group (even when formally made by a leader).

There is also an underlying sense of objective good, timeless wisdom, "Heaven's Mandate," which the group as a whole, or at least its leader, tries to discern and seeks to make the basis of the decision. There is, that is, not only the internal relationships of the group motivating toward consensus, but also an outside standard or sense of fitness that should guide the path a group takes. The point of honoring the leader or the wiser person is to benefit from their supposed better understanding of what the Chinese call *li* (理), basic principles. With this assumption firmly in place, group dynamics are undergirded not by transient or shifting individual desires but by a sense of common, persisting values. If something approaching full consensus is not reached, a sense of moral failure as well as a psychic discomfort pervades the group – and the desire to transcend that disarray, so painful in a culture valuing above everything the bonding of the group, is strong enough to more or less overcome individual insistences.

The point is not that individuals in such a culture would not have personal desires or needs or principles – they certainly do, and often very powerful ones – but rather that the habits and values of the society militate against them rather than condoning and celebrating them. People in group-oriented societies are not, one supposes, less selfish inherently than those in individualist ones, but cultural and moral pressures are exerted in different directions. And this difference, resulting in markedly different habits and values as their effect works its way over long periods, has a large influence on *how* people interact, how they make decisions, and how the polity works; what has been said in chapter 3 (see pages 121–2) about law in China and about political parties in Japan illustrates the point. Human beings *can*, at least, make public decisions with different assumptions and in different ways from those now often regarded as axiomatic in western democracies.

A similar distinction is evident if one compares a public philosophy where the qualities associated with friendship are dominant with one where "adversarial values" dominate. Among friends, intentions are shared or at least complementary, bonds of affection exist, time spent on common concerns is pleasurable, and decisions are on the whole consensual. Adversaries, or even unassociated individuals, on the other hand, take opposed interests for granted, debate rather than deliberate, prefer precise contractual relationships, and accept majority decision-making as both just and inevitable. One can take either set of values into public life, but, depending on which is assumed or encouraged, very different qualities and potential can infuse the political culture.[50]

Modes of decision-making resting on values and habits long nourished in a culture, though, are not easily transferred to a different one. Before 1853, for example, important practices often assumed to be essential to western-style democracy – public speech and debate, adversarial political parties, voting by the people, interest group advocacy, and aggregate-sum methods of calculating utility – simply didn't exist or fit in Japanese society. Could Japan, then, become democratic? Many thoughtful, public-spirited Japanese believed not only that was Japan unsuited for democracy, but also that it was an undesirable, even repulsive and immoral form of government. How could one admire a system validating open advocacy of one's own interest, making decisions by requiring people to stand up and be counted in opposition, and denying that the whole was any more than the sum of the parts? Each of those propositions, indispensable parts of modern democratic process it seemed, affronted deeply-held Japanese values. Yet, over the course of a century or more Japan has evolved a form of government fairly described as democratic, even though the way it works is strange and often baffling by western standards. The Japanese, that is, have managed to take some western ideas and practices, adapt them to their own purposes, and emerge with a kind of hybrid polity perhaps "better" than either their ancient imperial institutions or what might have resulted had they more completely adopted western ways (see pages 127–30).

Even within western culture different modes of decision-making have sometimes held sway. Among Quakers, for example, decisions are made according to "the sense of the meeting." Self-interested pleas are reproved, and even personal statements are discouraged unless prompted by "inner light." Indeed, the quest for the sense of the meeting is hindered by mere statements of personal interest because they distract from the element (inner light) shared by all. Special pleading, mechanical compromising, and voting are thus all out of place. The sense of the meeting is not only more than the sum of the parts, but is damaged by partiality. The idea, then, is not to call forth the individual needs of the people present, but rather to tap that part of the ideal right (God's will) within every person. In practice, of course, the human beings present at a Quaker meeting sometimes speak partially and even self-seekingly, and the sense of the meeting is often unclear, or even manipulated or falsely articulated. These manifestations, though, are neither welcome nor appreciated, and their presence is readily "sensed" in the meeting.

But, because there is serious, sustained effort, shared and nourished by those present, to see and respond to an inner, yet transcending light, a sense of the meeting can be reached that is very little akin either to the view of any individual or to an aggregate sum of the views of those present. The ideal is to share insights (literally), and silence, until truth emerges. The possibility of achieving any success, though, depends on the ability of those present to set aside selfish perspectives and respond instead to something beyond their own egos. The intention, carefully instructed and practiced, to "center" oneself, to set aside selfish and trivial concerns in order to be open to inner light and to the spirit of the meeting, is thought capable of eliciting determinations qualitatively different from those reached without that intention. The process does not claim perfection or deny human weakness, but does affirm that deliberate intention, silence, and thoughtful reflection can in some degree overcome self-orientation and that that in turn can yield insights beyond the sum of the parts. In contrast, much political talk is "the babble of raucous interests and insistent rights vying for the deaf ears of impatient adversaries." Even in public discussion, there might be use for more silence, "a precious medium in which reflection is nourished and empathy can grow."[51]

The fact that before the 1640s the English Parliament did not ordinarily make decisions by majority vote is a more political example of the same process. Parliament had arisen in English history as a council for the monarch, designed "to offer counsel and reason to bolster that provided by" the king and his permanent advisors. It was to discuss and amplify the king's measures and to confirm his justice. Thus it debated and made suggestions, and came in time to exercise veto powers, but it was not supposed to *oppose* the king, nor was it to be an arena for the clash of interests or the exercise of adversarial energies. Under James I, MPs were instructed to speak "their consciences in matters proposed in the House but with all due respect for your majesty." Honest discussion was allowed, that is, but the intention was *agreement* on the business of the realm, not endless opposition and partisan dispute. After debates "designed to convince, not to conquer," bills were ordinarily referred to committee with the expectation that its report would receive unanimous consent. Committees unable to agree were ordinarily reduced in number, sometimes to only one member, until agreement was reached. When the House did "divide" (rare before the Long Parliament, 1640–60), those who sought innovation had to leave the chamber, thus receiving the onus of being "outsiders." English parliamentary procedures, that is, until the bitter controversies of the seventeenth century, disdained adversarial stances, factional maneuvers, and majority voting in the conviction that an atmosphere valuing and seeking accord could contribute to the wise government of the nation.[52]

One wonders, then, whether the modern, political West, and especially the United States, might benefit from some perspective on the pathologies in its own decision-making. Is it really necessary and healthy, for example, to suppose a majority vote is the only or even the best way to decide matters? Is there something about the whole culture and process of conflict of interest politics that "makes good people bad," or that frustrates intentions to act in the public interest? Is it possible, on the other hand, that the Confucian and Quaker and early parliamentary modes (very different from each other, of course) might suggest approaches to decision-making that would improve some of the unsatisfactory and demeaning aspects of American public life?

Jimmy Carter, for example, entered office with high hopes for an administration that would be good for all the people – and the public perceived him as a new-style politician who might transcend interest-group-oriented government. But his efforts to devise a long-range national energy policy were first mangled and then overwhelmed by advocacies for different kinds of energy, regional disputes, bureaucratic rivalries, and party differences. None of these contending advocates had in mind or even sought to discern in any serious, profound way an overall public good. As a result, a widely recognized national need, to have long-range, assured access to an adequate supply of energy, was simply impossible to achieve. Efforts to restrain the arms race, to improve relations with Latin America, to rescue the social security system, and to revive the productivity of the national economy also were caught in cross-fires of competing forces. Other presidents of both parties have experienced similar frustration. Students of the Congress, noticing this, emphasize the astonishing influence political action committees (PACs) are able to exert with their money and their assiduous cultivation of representatives and senators. The effect, they point out, is to make the Congress a place where grass-roots, unorganized, local concerns are not much attended to, to say nothing of more general public needs. Rather, the arena is left to vociferous local groups, those with money, and possessors of computerized mailing lists who can at least "get a hearing," and often, in the virtual absence of wider perspectives, have a decisive impact on legislation.

The Carter presidency, though, was vitiated not only by the seething snakepit of contending forces around it, but also by serious flaws in its own self-conception. It had gained power in an adroit campaign that used the most sophisticated techniques of polling, fund-raising, and interest group manipulation. Carter's closest associates, moreover, were, more than anything else, skilled political operatives (Jody Powell, Hamilton Jordan, Bert Lance, and indeed Rosalynn Carter, too, as her autobiography so graphically reveals). These were people of intelligence and goodwill, but utterly preoccupied with the process of elective politics. As presidential advisors they lacked wisdom and grasp of substantial issues, a deficiency that seemed constantly to turn their attention back to something more congenial: planning and managing political campaigns. The triumph over the vulnerable Senator Kennedy in the 1980 primary presented a startling contrast as the president and his aides succeeded in politics but failed repeatedly to either sense or attain worthy public goals. The disarray, air of purposelessness, and too-frequent fits of pique resulted in a chastening picture of a bright, decent, earnest president intensely disappointing to himself and to his followers – and ripe to be turned out of office by an even more faction-dominated and short-sighted challenger.

Carter, then, was "a good man made worse by a bad government." That is, he in some degree possessed the aspirations and qualities to be a wise, far-sighted national leader. But his own political experience, the preoccupations of his closest advisors, his failure to find better ones, the power pathways in Congress and the bureaucracy, and, most basically perhaps, the special interest orientation of so much of the effective political atention in the country at large, made it virtually impossible for him to lead in the public interest. And if one were to look closely at American politics, one could find many other instances where what Joseph Tussman has called "the schoolboy logic of *Federalist* no. 10," upheld as the ideal political dynamic of an individualist, pluralist nation, has frustrated wiser and larger perspectives. To a tragic degree, we might even say, the United States has had a form of government and a mode of political decision-making suited to its habits and values. The problem has been not that the country has failed to achieve an open, responsive polity, but rather that such a polity has not resulted in very good or edifying government.

In an argument that might have had poignant force for Jimmy Carter, Rousseau observed that when

> not encumbered with confused or conflicting interest, . . . the common good is everywhere plainly in evidence and needs only good sense to be perceived.

> When the social bond begins to grow slack, when the interests of individuals begin to make themselves felt, and lesser groups within the State to influence the State as a whole, then the common interest suffers a change for the worse and breeds opposition. Opinion is no longer unanimous. . . . Contradictions appear and debates arise.

Then, in a final stage of degeneracy, Rousseau sees the state "near ruin," living on in

> a vain, illusory, and formal existence, when its very heart, the social bond, is broken, and the meanest interest brazenly lays hold to the sacred name of "public good." Then does the general will fall dumb. All, moved by motives unavowed, no more give their views as citizens than if the State had never been, and iniquitous decrees directed solely to private interest get passed under the name of laws.

The cause of this disaster, Rousseau asserts, is that the citizen has

> changed the form of the question, and [sought] to answer something he has not been asked. Thus, instead of saying, through the medium of his vote, "this is to the advantage of the State," he says, "it is to the advantage of this or that individual [or lesser group] that such and such a proposition become law."[53]

Throughout Rousseau's language assaults the dynamic of "sum of the parts decision-making:" the influence of "lesser groups . . . breeds opposition;" the state becomes "illusory and formal;" selfishness "brazenly" proclaims itself "public good;" the general will becomes mute; private interest becomes law; and citizens become anti-citizens by asking themselves wrong (private interest) questions.

So again the question arises: might it now be possible in the light of what we see are flaws in the concept of individualism, in view of alternatives visible elsewhere, and in response to the growing interdependence of modern society, to conceive and work toward different ways of reaching public decisions? It is neither desirable nor necessary, of course, to discard elections or majority rule. It might be worth while, though, to soften, amend, and supplement that process in order to achieve better results. To revitalize citizenship, for example, Benjamin Barber suggests a nationwide network of neighborhood assemblies, at first having only deliberative functions, but eventually having legislative power as well. A national initiative and referendum process, tied to sophisticated, publicly sponsored electronic media information systems, might stimulate informed and responsible participation on a national scale. A "multichoice format," letting citizens express reasons and nuances of choice rather than just "yes" or "no" preferences, and a requirement of two votes before an initiative could become law, might further encourage thoughtful, increasingly enlightened judgment, rather than acting on impulse.[54] Thus modern technology might help prevent the "intemperate and pernicious resolutions, . . . monuments to deficient wisdom," that Madison thought often characterized the hasty acts of faction-ridden legislatures.[55] The need, in any case, is to move toward a politics tending less to "make good men bad" and to encourage citizens to betray their calling. Is it necessary, that is, to continue the self-perpetuating cycle of individualist assumptions leading to conflict of interest politics which in turn emphasizes factional groups that themselves nourish and validate a self-seeking individualism? Can citizens learn to ask the proper question, "is this to the advantage of the public as a whole?" Simply understanding what it means to phrase and put such a question, in fact, would require, at least in the long run, very different ways of approaching and making public decisions. Again it seems clear that at the outset the public interest consists of interest in the public.

DECIDING ON A LAW OF THE SEA

On an international scale, the negotiation over a span of nearly two decades of a Law of the Sea Treaty furnishes remarkable evidence of what is possible when wise and effective statesmen work together, seeking consensus on complex problems of common interest. Meeting under United Nations auspices and thus without a sovereignty to settle either process or substance, the negotiating conference had to devise its own rules and was free to find its own solutions. Dozens of nations, hundreds of interests, and thousands of delegates created a scene initially baffling and chaotic. No one nation, group, or person was in a position to dictate to the others, yet all stood to benefit from sensible decisions about transit of straits, limits on territorial and resource exploitation waters, pollution, depletion of sea life, access to deep sea metals, and so on. There was both a common agenda and wide latitude for seeking paths to its completion. Those with knowledge, goodwill, wisdom, integrity, and negotiating skill were in positions to make crucial contributions. They could be statesmen possibly able to discern policies in the public interest that, until thoughtful and serious people deliberated about them, had likely not been thought of beforehand by any nation or individual. The solution, that is, might indeed be more than the sum (or difference) of the parts.[56]

Yet, the conference was also rife with special interests: nations with long coastlines and those without, developed and developing economies, metal ore producers and consumers, capitalist and socialist systems, straits controllers and users, creators and experiencers of pollution, rich and poor, weak and powerful, fish- and non-fish-eating people, and so on. Throughout the conference nations and interests within nations lobbied vigorously for their particular concerns, and in the fashion of veteran negotiators, formed intricate networks of coalition and support-swapping on a multitude of issues. Since there was no way to exclude any of these interests, they spoke and operated freely, creating an atmosphere of openness and assured access. All the parts, that is, were present, visible, and able to assert themselves.

A rather surprising trust developed gradually, moreover, partly because all of the special interests knew that they could not only be heard but could not even lose in a majority vote. Out of order, then, were the adroit maneuvering, horse-trading, threats, and whipsawing characteristic of bodies approaching a close, majority-decides vote on a crucial issue. Knowing defeat could not be forced upon any particular interest in such a vote, the pressure to be insistent and manipulative, to engineer a majority, so prevalent in voting bodies, was largely absent. Freedom from and security against majority rule, then, fostered both openness and a need to achieve broader insights and consensual understandings. The result was a surprisingly open and creative search both for the accommodation of interests all knew could not be steamrollered, and for the transcendence of the particular to recognize the common good.

In the absence of both dictate and majority rule, then, there was increased motivation for candid and creative statesmanship. Big powers (especially the US and the USSR) soon learned that heavy-handed, arm-twisting representatives did more harm than good. Elliot Richardson, head of the American delegation for crucial years of the conference, for example, earned a high reputation (and influence) for his soft-spoken, flexible, yet often ingenious suggestions on major treaty stumbling blocks. The Soviet delegation was shuffled quietly to bring more genial, less threatening diplomats to the fore. Another crucial bonus to the conference came from delegates from "unimportant" nations who, partly because they operated from no power base, had a trust and presumption of disinterest not easily granted to weightier representatives. Delegates from Sri Lanka, Bulgaria, Peru, Fiji, East Germany, Tanzania, and Singapore made stunning contributions by bringing off tough negotiations and chairing difficult meetings. These wise and skilled statesmen again and again brought disparate interests together, *made* them deliberate honestly, and often themselves formulated solutions that were beyond anything put on the table initially by any of the more partial delegates. The conference thus developed a pool of creative leaders who were able to guide the once factional but increasingly open-minded other delegates toward propositions truly in the public, this time world, interest.

In a way, then, the Law of the Sea Conference, denied the majority-vote habit second nature to democratic politicians, had to come to new modes of citizenship (i.e. ways of participating in the political process) and of leadership as well as of decision-making. The fact that many of the delegates came from cultures less tied to majority vote methods doubtless helped the conference devise often unique ways of deliberating and of deciding. The conference thus gained some of the peculiar benefits of conversational as opposed to contractual talk. Responding to the wide experience of the delegates and respecting the legitimacy of every human perspective, the conference worked toward "rich ambiguity rather than narrow clarity." Conversation gradually evoked a sense of commonality not reducible to contractual precision but still productive of important shared understandings. Exactly because majority voting and legalistic clarity were de-emphasized, conversation, colleagial deliberation, had a surprising (at least to delegates used to western legislative process) effectiveness.[57] In any case, the conference achieved an atmosphere and mode of proceeding that penalized the strident and the narrow-viewed and instead encouraged patience, goodwill, trust, and fair-mindedness. It even seemed that new ground rules and new postures toward public questions could gradually alter the style and even the character of the participants.

Another key factor in the success of the conference was the "higher law of interdependence" that again and again imposed itself. All knew that there were needs and opportunities that simply could not be dealt with without the participation, the disinterestedness (in part, at least), and, eventually, the consent of all. Pollution, conservation of sea life, off-shore and deep sea resources, and navigation of straits affected everybody. Even though some nations were in positions to block far-sighted proposals and others had crucial conflicting interests, it was also true that on many issues the disadvantages of no agreement were sufficient to prod nations into grudging consent. There was a reservoir, that is, of transcending value and opportunity, recognized in some degree by everyone, that acted as a sort of common purpose or ideal for all. To put it yet another way, a "natural law," an objective good valuable to and valued by all, existed that acted as a touchstone for the conference.

The upshot, then, was that a sense of "world purpose" or "higher law" enabled the fahioning of new postures of participation, new modes of leadership, and new processes of decision-making. These novel aspects of public policy formation, together with a continuing abundance of special interest trading and compromise, combined to allow the completion of a comprehensive Law of the Sea Treaty that virtually no one had thought possible when negotiations began in 1968. Though some nations (notably the United States) have declared their dissatisfaction with the result (despite the approval of the treaty by the

American delegation), this recalcitrance itself is almost universally condemned as an affront to the clear mandate of international purpose and as a betrayal of the deliberative process through which the treaty had been achieved. It seemed poignant, even tragic, that the United States, with (perhaps *because of*) its strong liberal tradition and despite its keen interest in resolving law of the sea issues, was notably unable to honor and accept a treaty fashioned, as it were, by a body without such a disabling history. There does exist, on a virtually world wide scale, it seems, an objective notion of the common good the repudiation of which provokes widespread scorn. Those perceived to be acting contrary to this common good lose standing and support.

Perhaps the most remarkable thing of all about the conference, though, was the immense resource the delegates discovered among themselves as they realized that neither dictate nor majority rule would be decisive. Nor, furthermore, would the preconceptions and non-negotiable positions brought to the conference by the various nations, however added, subtracted, or compromised, furnish the material for wise solutions. The process of honest exchange of views, of effort to understand opposing needs, of patient deliberation, of offering novel proposals, and finally of finding fair agreements in which all could see wisdom – or at least see the foolishness and futility of *not* agreeing – yielded a substance akin to higher law. Though there was a good bit of the familiar search for a "package deal" that gives something to everyone, the total result of the treaty process was also much more than that. The final treaty, complex and embodying many ingenious modes of settling international affairs, was far beyond the beginning conceptions or intentions of any of the participating nations. It demonstrated, that is, that the whole can be much more than the sum of the parts when "the parts" tap the resources of reason and concern for the whole that are in some degree present in human nature and perhaps even in human affairs.

A POLITICS OF THE PUBLIC INTEREST

The law of the sea negotiations suggest, as do the enlarged conceptions of citizenship, leadership, and decision-making, that the individualist-based political axioms so customary and so celebrated in the United States are not the only ones available. Furthermore, they are not necessarily the best and wisest ways to conduct public life, nor are they the only modes that can fairly be designated as democratic. Even more to the point, the disproportionate idealization of individualistic, conflict of interest values in the United States, especially since 1945, has imposed a problematic orthodoxy on American habits and ways of thinking about public life. It is this orthodoxy, encompassing the assumption of the self-seeking individual, the brokering political leader, and the majority rule process, all operating as pluralistic, conflict of interest politics, that, whatever its virtues (and it has many), also has many harmful side effects.

We must ask whether a movement toward a concept of citizenship, a style for leaders, and ways of making decisions that take more seriously the idea of a public good and that seek more directly to encourage disinterestedness and deliberation might not improve our political health. No one supposes that our public life might (or even *should*) be transformed overnight along, let us say, Aristotelian or even Jeffersonian lines. But it is worth pondering (perhaps even critically so) whether, if we decided to try, we might not gradually be able to nudge our politics in less atomistically individualist, less conflict-advocacy-oriented, and therefore, probably, less self-defeating directions.

The magnitude of the reorientation required in one way makes the task seem exceedingly difficult (what is harder to change than people's attitudes and assumptions about themselves and about society?), but in another way makes significant change possible virtually at once. The opportunity is something like the change that can take place in a classroom when the attitude and approach and manner of the teacher alters. If the teacher sheds an authoritarian, rigid, punitive attitude requiring only silence and obedience from the children, and instead encourages openness, creativity, and mutual respect, the room, and, surprisingly soon, the children themselves, can become very different. And this can happen without startling change in the system, the bureaucracy, salaries, the building, or equipment. The key is attitude, human relationships, and a new sense of purpose. Gradually, of course, if such a new approach becomes widespread, institutions, methods of leadership and support, and physical surroundings would change, but that would, for the most part, be effect rather than cause. One could envision a similar process in churches and other private organizations, and even in business, labor unions, and government bureaucracies. Imagine the altered scene at labor contract negotiations, in the social welfare department, and even in corporate boardrooms, for example, if deeply-ingrained adversarial, turf-defending, quarterly-profit-focusing habits and assumptions were somehow softened or set aside. The "if" is a big one, and one would not expect immediate, radical changes. Simply to contemplate the *possible* changes, though, reveals the potential for profound new directions with different attitudes and self-conceptions.

If one asks how the attitudes become widespread, it is soon apparent that one thing leads to another. Institutional and leadership changes can be powerful aids in stimulating the more basic alterations in practice, attitude, and preconception. The familiar circle exists where change anywhere impacts on all other parts of the circle. But this very dynamic means that *some* impact is possible at any point, and that one can expect any change to alter gradually all the other parts. Thus, there is reason to "start anywhere" and to suppose that such beginnings have a potential to cause large-scale, even momentous change in human affairs. Martin Luther King's civil rights campaign, for example, undertook to change laws, attitudes, educational practices, and social conditions, recognizing that progress in any area would lead to improvement in the others. The crucial point is to *know* what is wanted and to begin affecting the values and postures that will encourage movement in the desired direction.

This suggests that beginnings made in altering attitudes toward citizenship would be significant, and perhaps even important. Suppose from their earliest acquaintance with public affairs children were taught that the crux of their education to become "part-rulers" in a self-governing society (which each would be) was a posture of disinterestedness, a habit of thinking that one's participation in democratic government must as much as possible pay attention to the good of the public as a whole. And suppose, even more fundamentally, that the classroom itself became a laboratory where children practiced learning cooperatively, where the teacher kept "common good" perspectives constantly in view, and where the experience of finding the whole greater than the sum of the parts became commonplace. Surely such an approach, built into all instruction, would have some effect on the attitudes young people would bring to their roles as citizens. To accomplish this, classes in the workings of government and in the realities of politics would have to point beyond merely teaching children methods of analysis and how to use political processes for their own benefit – often the implicit message in instruction about political behavior and about the facts of government administration, political parties, and policy analysis.

One sees at this point, too, how completely the individualist ideology undergirds the American political system. The assumption that the individual will (Hobbesian or Lockean) is at the center of existence readily validates conflict of interest politics. If it is so, as Locke argues, that people consent to live under government for "the great and chief end...of the preservation of their...lives, liberties, and estates,"[58] then "the game" will be the use of the public arena to gain personal advantage or ends. Within such a system it makes sense to teach children both how it works and how to calculate their own participation in it. And the system of checks and balances, put in place to contain the struggle of wills, in turn encourages and even requires strenuous, clever efforts by individuals and groups to seek their own interests. Without conceptions of public good, what else can one do but learn the techniques of self-advancement? Leadership becomes the art of managing and manipulating these forces. All this, taught as fact, as self-evident, and as fitting and proper, creates a self-perpetuating system where each generation supposes its political obligation is simply to take part effectively in the conflict of interest political system.

But suppose one begins teaching a different axiom: that disinterestedness and a sense of the reality of the public good are at least potentially significant parts not only of one's posture of citizenship but also of one's own self-fulfillment. This would require first a different approach to citizenship education and a different mode of participation in public life. Self-interest or special interest, of course, would not disappear from politics. Indeed, that would not even be desirable in a pluralistic society since people and groups speaking up for their particular needs and concerns often provide information and point of view useful to the political process. What is possible, though, is the cultivation of a degree of concern for the public good, and then the development throughout public life of processes, modes of leadership, and institutions that sustain and honor such concern. Hundreds of hearings conducted throughout New York State by the Department of Environmental Protection, for example, have evoked a remarkable quantity and quality of citizen participation in important public questions. The building of effective, ongoing institutions to sustain this public interest, and to buttress that perspective rather than special interest domination, could gradually invigorate and edify democratic citizenship.

To recast Reinhold Niebuhr's aphorism, if counteracting selfish tendencies makes a system of checks and balances necessary in a democracy, then the restraint thus achieved may make possible (create opportunity for) an active, disinterested concern for the public welfare which is indispensable to *good* democratic government. (This was precisely Madison's argument in *Federalist* no. 10.) Preoccupation with the premise for dealing with selfish tendencies and neglect of the conclusion about the possibilities of good government may result in a form of government fairly termed democratic. At the same time, though, such disproportion is reasonably certain to atrophy disinterestedness, make "good men worse," demean the public life of the nation, and assure that democratic government will be bad government. Such a system, that is, is likely to be preoccupied with fiddling (unrecognized as such), and be unaware that Rome is burning.

It seems clear that in western culture generally, especially in the last three or four centuries, and even more especially in the United States since 1945, there has been a disproportionate and often (increasingly?) pathological emphasis on what Tocqueville called "the novel idea of individualism." The paradoxes and flaws of post-war American public life, moreover, reveal a degenerative, self-sustaining, cycle of self-interest, checks-and-balances government, and public infantilism. Another model, though, might discard the atomistic assumptions and instead set more socially responsible guidelines for public life. The experience of East Asia and the wisdom of many western sages from Aristotle to Jefferson shows that such a reorientation is possible and might yield approaches to public life better suited to the modern, interdependent world.

Walter Lippmann observed in 1955 that, so far as governing was concerned, most of the century before 1914 was in the western world "a brief spell of exceptionally fine weather." This allowed governments to "dream...that in the rivalry of diverse interests all would somehow come out for the best." They thus could "normally be neutral and for the most part avoid making positive judgments of good and bad and of right and wrong. ... The public interest could be equated with that which was revealed in election returns, in sales reports, balance sheets, circulation figures, and statistics of expansion." Altogether, in the classic liberal faith, government could be praised for its weakness, and "the public good could be thought of as being immanent in the aggregate of private transactions." There was relatively little need to "tax, conscript, command, prohibit," or to face the hard decisions that in most places and times have made it the duty of governments to "swim against the tide of private feeling."[59]

The surprising thing, in a way, is not that this alluring moment in political history should have been so quickly overwhelmed by world wars, depression, ecological threat, and nuclear peril, but that it should have occurred at all. The romanticism, the *laissez-faire* utopianism, and the reinless sense of public life embodied in nineteenth-century individualism can be viewed not so much as an inexorable triumph as a notable aberration in human affairs. Understandable as the culmination of patterns of thought long building in western culture (see chapter 2), and extraordinarily useful in upsetting countless primordial prescriptions and tyrannies, individualism, psychically and morally, also unanchored and disconnected humankind in truly novel ways, as Tocqueville saw. And the "brief spell of exceptionally fine weather" was especially beguiling in its capacity to make people unmindful both of normally cloudy skies and of the bracing opportunities for responsible citizenship and public obligation.

The pattern in all its attraction as well as its danger is evident if one sees American history from 1815 to 1940 as an unusual era of "free security" (see pages 7–8). *Pax Britannica* began in the New World with the secure demilitarization of the US–Canadian boundary (1818), and the announcement in the Monroe Doctrine (1823) of a common US–British interest in the demise of European colonialism in Latin America. American energies were thus released for the expansion of the frontier, the development of a complex industrial economy, and the absorption of millions of new immigrants, all phenomena congenial to the burgeoning ideology of individualism and to a government little needing to "tax, conscript, command, prohibit." The return of more normal "weather" came, however, first gradually with the international expansionism of 1898, World War I, and the Great Depression, and then dramatically with the end of free security in 1940. The consequent end of isolationism (geopolitical individualism, if you will), the acceptance of the corporate state by both political parties, and the burdens of cold war and worldwide responsibilities, signalled a new era for Americans – and the need for a public philosophy attuned to it.

That both the historical "moment...of fine weather" and the heightened individualist ideology suited to it are aberrant in a larger picture of things, though, highlights the growing paradoxes of the post-war era (chapter 1). The 125 years preceding the era of free security, 1690–1815, was, in the first place, a time of intense, dangerous, and responsible American involvement in world affairs. Between 1689 and 1763 four increasingly global wars between England and France were fought in part in North America and had traumatic, life-and-death significance for the British colonies there. The American Revolution took place within that rivalry and was affected critically by it. The ideology of the Revolution, moreover, was an influential part of "the Age of Democratic Revolution" that swept over Europe between 1760 and 1800.[60] This immersed Americans in worldwide currents of thought. Then, until the end of the Napoleonic era the new nation's survival depended on skill in diplomacy, war, and international trade. All American presidents before 1829, except Washington, had long experience either as minister abroad or as secretary of state. (In the following century, none, through Coolidge, had more than fleeting experience with foreign affairs, at least until taking office; the technical exception of Buchanan seems somehow only to prove the rule.) The founding of American government and the forging of its public philosophy, then, took place amid a perilous, enlarging international context much different from the inward-turning, "free security" of the following century or so.[61]

Perhaps even more significant, the founding took place in a climate of political ideas still partly Classical. This implanted in American institutions and in the nation's "first" public philosophy an ideology only partially imbued with "the novel idea of individualism" that became dominant in the age of Jackson and afterwards. Jefferson, Madison, Hamilton, and the other founders were in part enthusiastic Lockeans eager to attune the nation's politics to the burgeoning bourgeois liberalism they saw as the wave of the future. But they also remained profoundly Classical and each lived within the British neo-classical world-view of the age of Addison, Swift, Pope, Bolingbroke, and Hume. Their political understanding, therefore, rested partly on the precepts of Aristotle, Cicero, and Plutarch. They assumed that a polity was to be honored *only* if it cultivated the public good, that such a good could be discerned through reason and public discourse, that leadership to that end was an essential mark of good government, that nurturing institutions (schools, local government, etc.) were needed to undergird responsible citizenship, and that republican (or democratic) government was admirable only in so far as it embodied these precepts.

There is, then, in American experience, and even in the founding institutions and public philosophy themselves, a political resource richer and more profound than the "novel" ideology of individualism perhaps only suited to the "exceptionally fine weather" enjoyed by the nation during Tocqueville's visit. There is a further resource in the precepts and practices of the Far East, where Americans can find ancient lessons in the social dimensions of human life. The richly bonded character of daily life there rests on an understanding of personality in some ways more profound, less " irretrievably absurd," than that imbedded in post-seventeenth-century, self-centered western individualism (chapter 3). This is not to suggest that we should or could return to some mythic "golden age of the founders," or should or could take to ourselves the ways of another culture, or that there are not unenviable and unjust aspects of the politics both of eighteenth-century America and of East Asia present or past. It does reveal to us, though, that American political practice and the accompanying liberal ideology may be peculiarly, and in the last decades of the twentieth century, cripplingly time-bound. If our experience since 1945 has been notably paradoxical in the persistent, enlarging gap we find between the requisites of "the good life" and the axioms of our political thought and practice (chapter 1), then it might be prudent to reconsider them in the light of the wisdom of other times and places – especially when one part of that wisdom looms large in America's past and another part of it stands as an enduring counterpoint to the whole (disporportionate?) individualist emphasis in western culture (chapter 3).

There are, then, good grounds for transcending the illusions of the "exceptionally fine weather" of large parts of American history, and for finding a public philosophy suited both to more normal weather, and to an understanding of self and society more enduringly fulfilling than that encompassed by the "novel idea of individualism." The paradoxes and enlarging incongruities of American society evident since 1945, in many ways caused by projection of nineteenth-century values and habits, are evidence that those values and habits may not be ultimate wisdom. Even the growing, millennia-long preoccupation with individualism in western history, set beside more socially-oriented cultures and the thought of Aristotle, Confucius, and Jefferson, can be seen as a neither dominant nor inevitable nor even satisfactory conception of human nature. Rather, reconceptions of basic features of democratic government – citizenship, leadership, and decision-making – impelled by a sense of the inadequacy (even pathology) of unrestrained individualism and impressed with the value of more substantial ideas of public life, may be both necessary and possible in the last decades of the twentieth century.

Notes

CHAPTER 1   PARADOXES, 1945–85

1 Luce editorial reprinted in J. A. Garraty and R. A. Divine (eds), *Twentieth-Century America* (Boston, 1968), pp. 472, 475–6.
2 H. A. Wallace, speech before Free World Association, May 8, 1942; reprinted in ibid., pp. 477–81.
3 Wendell Willkie, *One World* (New York, 1943), pp. 202–6, 188, 192–5.
4 Ibid., pp. 74, 86.
5 Arthur Vandenberg, speech in the US Senate, January 10, 1945; reprinted in Garraty and Divine, *Twentieth-Century America*, p. 497.
6 Clark Kerr, *The Uses of the University* (New York, 1964), pp. 88, 118.
7 F. J. Turner, *The Frontier in American History* (New York, 1962), p. 259; reprinting an essay originally published in 1903.
8 David Potter, *People of Plenty* (Chicago, 1954), pp. 165, 139.
9 Benjamin Barber, *Strong Democracy* (Berkeley, 1984), p. 136.
10 John Dewey, *Liberalism and Social Action* (New York, 1935), pp. 44–5.
11 Chie Nakane, *Japanese Society* (Berkeley, 1970), p. 152.
12 Christopher Lasch, *The Culture of Narcissism* (New York, 1979), p. 27.
13 Gail Sheehy, *Passages: Predictable Crises of Adult Life* (New York, 1977), p. 364; quoted in Robert Bellah and others, *Habits of the Heart: Individualism and commitment in American life* (Berkeley, 1985), p. 79.
14 Reinhold Niebuhr, *The Children of Light and the Children of Darkness* (New York, 1944), pp. 56–7.
15 Bellah, *Habits of the Heart*, p. 120.
16 Niebuhr, *Children of Light and Darkness*, p. 19.
17 Matthew 10:39.
18 Bellah, *Habits of the Heart*, pp. 134–5.
19 Max Lerner, *America as a Civilization* (New York, 1957), pp. 48, 629.
20 Ibid., pp. 729–30.

CHAPTER 2 INDIVIDUALISM IN WESTERN CULTURE

1 Alasdair MacIntyre, *After Virtue* (Notre Dame, 1981), p. 122.
2 Herbert Muller, *The Individual in a Revolutionary World* (Toronto, 1964), p. 8.
3 Gilbert Murray, "The meaning of freedom" (1949), in E. K. Bramsted and K. J. Melhuish (eds), *Western Liberalism: A history in documents from Locke to Croce* (London, 1978), pp. 738–9.
4 Pericles, "Funeral oration," in Thucydides, *The Peloponnesian War*, book II.
5 Sheldon Wolin, *Politics and Vision* (Boston, 1960), pp. 78–9.
6 Mark Roelofs, *The Tension of Citizenship* (New York, 1957), p. 59.
7 Luke 9:25.
8 Matthew 22:21.
9 John 3:3.
10 Marguerite Yourcenar, *Memoirs of Hadrian* (New York, 1954), p. 191.
11 St Augustine, *City of God*, pp. 193–5; quoted in Quentin Skinner, *Foundations of Modern Political Thought* (2 vols, Cambridge, 1978), II, p. 349; Radaslav Tsanoff, *The Great Philosophers* (New York, 1953), p. 168.
12 St Augustine, *Soliloquies*, I:7, in W. J. Oates (ed.), *Basic Writings of St Augustine* (New York, 1948), p. 262.
13 Quoted in J. H. Randall, *The Making of the Modern Mind* (Boston, 1926), p. 35.
14 Burke, *Reflections on the Revolution in France* (1790) (Chicago, 1955), pp. 125–6.
15 J. B. Ross and M. McLaughlin (eds), *The Portable Renaissance Reader* (New York, 1968), pp. 476–9.
16 Reinhold Niebuhr, *The Nature and Destiny of Man* (2 vols, New York, 1941, 1964), I, p. 61.
17 Machiavelli, *The Discourses* (Harmondsworth, 1970), p. 278; quoted in Skinner, *Foundations*, I, p. 167.
18 Skinner, *Foundations*, II, p. 349.
19 J. G. A. Pocock, *The Machiavellian Moment: Florentine political thought and the Atlantic republican tradition* (Princeton, 1975), p. 462.
20 Benjamin Barber, *Strong Democracy* (Berkeley, 1984), p. 195.
21 Wolin, *Politics and Vision*, pp. 191–4.
22 John Winthrop, *Journal*, May 1645; and "Christian charitie. A modell hereof" (1630); reprinted in E. S. Morgan (ed.), *Puritan Political Ideas* (Indianapolis, 1965), pp. 137–40, 90–2.
23 Niebuhr, *Nature and Destiny of Man*, I, pp. 65–6.
24 Pope, *Epilogue to the Satires*, dialogue I, lines 161–2, in W. K. Wimsatt (ed.),

Alexander Pope: Selected poetry and prose (New York, 1972), p. 364; and John Dryden, *The Medal*, lines 172–4, in G. R. Noyes (ed.), *The Poetical Works of Dryden* (Boston, 1929), p. 130.

25 Pocock, *Machiavellian Moment*, p. 483.

26 Jane Mansbridge, *Beyond Adversarial Democracy* (New York, 1980), p. 5.

27 Charles Schultz, *The Public Use of Private Interest* (Washington, DC, AEI, 1977), p. 18.

28 H. Mark Roelofs, *Ideology and Myth in American Politics* (Boston, 1976), pp. 47–9.

29 William Breitenbach, "Unregenerate doings, selflessness and selfishness in New Divinity theology," *American Quarterly*, vol. 34, winter 1982, pp. 494–502.

30 Ibid.

31 Kenneth Lockridge, *A New England Town: The first hundred years* (New York, 1970), p. 174.

32 A. N. Whitehead, *Science and the Modern World* (1925) (New York, 1948), p. 2.

33 Descartes, *Discourse on Method* (1637), parts 1 and 6; *Rules for the Direction of the Mind*, rule 4; quoted in Randall, *Making of the Modern Mind*, pp. 222–4.

34 Daniel Boorstin, *The Americans: the colonial experience* (New York, 1958), p. 1.

35 Pope, *Essay on Man* (1733), lines 267–8, 289–92.

36 Hobbes quoted in Wolin, *Politics and Vision*, p. 247.

37 Joyce Appleby, *Capitalism and a New Social Order: The republican vision of the 1790s* (New York, 1984), pp. 31–5.

38 Goethe, *Dichtung und Wahrheit* (1770), book XI, Oxford translation; quoted in Randall, *Making of the Modern Mind*, p. 394.

39 Emerson, "The American scholar" (1837); and Parker, "Theodore Parker's experiences as a minister" (1859).

40 Emerson, "Politics" (1844), in W. H. Gilman (ed.), *Selected Writings of Ralph Waldo Emerson* (New York, 1965), pp. 353–7.

41 Jeremy Bentham's Economic Writings (3 vols, London, 1952–4), III, p. 340; quoted in Wolin, *Politics and Vision*, p. 342.

42 J. S. Mill, *On Liberty* (1859), chapter III, "Of individuality."

43 J. S. Mill, *Logic*, Book IV, chapters 7 and 9; quoted in John Dewey, *Liberalism and Social Action* (New York, 1935), p. 40.

44 Isaiah Berlin, *Four Essays on Liberty* (London, 1969), p. 8.

45 *Abrams* v. *US*, 250 US, 616, 624 (1919).

46 Holmes, "Speech to the Massachusetts Bar" (1900), in Max Lerner (ed.), *The Mind and Faith of Justice Holmes* (Boston, 1951), p. 43.

47 J. R. McCulloch, *The Principles of Political Economy* (Edinburgh, 1825), p. 23; quoted in Wolin, *Politics and Vision*, p. 303.

48 Archibald MacLeish, "We have purpose... we all know it," in *The National Purpose* (New York, 1960), p. 40.

49 I am using "liberal" here and throughout in the very broad sense of meaning all that espouses and sustains freedom, release from restraint, opportunity, government by consent, toleration, and the open society. It thus includes, for the most part, federalists as well as Jeffersonians, Democrats as well as Republicans, "liberals" as well as "conservatives," and all but narrow fringes of both left and right; in 1980s politics, everyone at least inclusive of Ronald Reagan and William Buckley as well as George McGovern and Michael Harrington. This may seem like an almost meaninglessly broad category, but if one considers the wide basic agreement within the spectrum, and the large amount left out, especially if ideologies popular in other parts of the world are kept in mind, there clearly is a "liberal consensus" in the United States.

50 Reagan speech in Dallas, Texas, August 23, 1984; reported in the *New York Times*, August 24, 1984, p. A11.

51 Samuel P. Huntington, *American Politics: The promise of disharmony* (Cambridge, Mass., 1981), pp. 42–51, 64–78.

52 A. O. Hirschman, *Exit, Voice, and Loyalty* (Cambridge, Mass., 1970), pp. 1–20, 106–19.

53 *On the Prospect of Planting Arts and Learning in America* (1725).

54 J. K. Galbraith, *The Affluent Society* (New York, 1958), p. 240.

CHAPTER 3   EAST ASIAN COUNTERPOINT:
THE SHADOW OF CONFUCIUS

1 Huston Smith, *The Religions of Man* (New York, 1958); Liang Chi-chao, *History of Chinese Political Thought* (1922), trans. L. T. Chen (New York, 1930, 1960), p. 6.

2 Hwang Byung-tai, "Confucianism in modernization: a comparative study of China, Japan, and Korea," PhD dissertation, University of California (Berkeley), 1979, pp. 307–47, 481–97.

3 Martin Shapiro, *Courts: A comparative and political analysis* (Chicago, 1981), p. 157.

4 Smith, *Religions of Man*, pp. 214–15.

5 Hajime Nakamura, *Ways of Thinking of Eastern Peoples: India-China-Tibet-Japan* (Honolulu, 1964).

6 See, for example, Sidney L. Gulick, *The East and the West: A study of their psychic and cultural characteristics* (Tokyo, 1962), and F. S. C. Northrup, *The Meeting of East and West* (New York, 1949).

7 E. O. Reischauer, *The Japanese* (Tokyo, 1977), pp. 44–5.

8 Arthur Waley (trans.), *The Analects of Confucius* (London, 1938), pp. 187, 83, 84, 88, 204.

9 H. G. Creel, *Chinese Thought from Confucius to Mao Tse-tung* (Chicago, 1953), pp. 29–32.

10 Mencius (3A: 4), in Wing-tsit Chan, *A Source Book in Chinese Philosophy* (Princeton, 1963), pp. 69–70; David M. Earl, *Emperor and Nation in Japan* (Seattle, 1964), p. 4; W. M. Tu, "On neo-Confucianism and human-relatedness," *Senri Ethnological Studies* (Osaka, Japan), no. 11, 1981, pp. 111–24.

11 Waley, *Analects of Confucius*, p. 37.

12 Gore Vidal, *Creation* (New York, 1981), pp. 467–8, 492.

13 Smith, *Religions of Man*, p. 183.

14 *New York Times*, editorial page, April 4, 1978.

15 Ahn Byung-joon, "Korea family system," in *News Review* (Seoul, Korea), January 13, 1979, p. 25.

16 Ivan Morris, *The Nobility of Failure: Tragic heroes in the history of Japan* (New York, 1975).

17 Tu, "On neo-Confucianism," p. 113.

18 Tae Hung-ha, *Korea – Forty-Three Centuries* (Yonsei University Press, 1982), p. 15.

19 Aristotle, *Politics*, book III, chapter 9.

20 Confucius, *The Book of History*, in James Legge, *The Chinese Classics* (Hong Kong, 1861–72), III, p. 41; Liang, *Chinese Political Thought*, p. 10.

21 G. W. F. Hegel, *Philosophy of History* (1832–40), introduction; quoted in J. H. Randall, *The Making of the Modern Mind* (Boston, 1926), p. 431.

22 Nishi Amane, *Hya Kuichi Shinron* (1874); quoted in Thomas R. H. Havens, *Nishi Amane and Modern Japanese Thought* (Princeton, 1970), p. 121.

23 Liang, *Chinese Political Thought*, pp. 7, 43–4, 56–7. Jonathan Spence, *The Gate of Heavenly Peace: The Chinese and their revolution, 1895–1980* (New York, 1981), details Liang's place in Chinese political and intellectual life, and Philip C. Huang, *Liang Ch'i-Ch'ao and Modern Chinese Liberalism* (Seattle, 1972), explains the development of Liang's thought.

24 *The Autobiography of Fukuzawa Yukichi*, trans. Eiichi Kiyooka (Tokyo, 1960), pp. 215–16.

25 Ibid., p. 91.

26 Ibid., pp. 190–1.

27 Ibid., pp. 223–4; Earl H. Kinmouth, "Fukuzawa reconsidered: *Gakumon no susume* and its audience," *Journal of Asian Studies*, vol. 37, 1978, pp. 677–96, emphasizes Fukuzawa's traditionalism.

28 Earl H. Kinmouth, *The Self-Made Man in Meiji Japanese Thought* (Berkeley, 1981), especially pp. 9–43, points out differences in the

"message" of these western writers, and of similarities between them and Japanese thinkers of the late Tokugawa era, but without upsetting the profound sense of contrast between western and Confucian-based thought.

29 Janet Walker, *The Japanese Novel of the Meiji Period and the Ideal of Individualism* (Princeton, 1979), pp. 30–61; M. G. Ryan, *Japan's First Modern Novel: "Ukigumo" of Futabatei Shimei* (New York, 1967).

30 Walker, *Japanese Novel*, pp. 106–20.

31 Ibid., p. 176. *Haikai* was translated into English as *The Broken Commandment*, and published in Tokyo, 1974.

32 Chie Nakane, *Japanese Society* (Berkeley, 1970), pp. 23–86.

33 Ibid., pp. 69, 75, 77.

34 Ibid., pp. 144–6.

35 Takeo Doi, *The Anatomy of Dependence* (Tokyo and New York, 1973, 1977), pp. 12–13.

36 Ibid., pp. 33–9.

37 Ibid., p. 39.

38 Ibid., p. 141.

39 Ibid., p. 43.

40 Quoted in Gerald Stourzh, *Alexander Hamilton and the Idea of Republican Government* (Stanford, California, 1970), p. 18.

41 F. J. Turner, *The Frontier in American History* (New York, 1920, 1967), pp. 259, 37, 307.

42 J. S. Mill, *On Liberty*, pp. 85–8.

43 *New York Times*, March 10, 1982, p. 1.

44 Shapiro, *Courts*, pp. 157–93.

45 C. S. Wren, "The Chinese legal system," *New York Times*, December 5, 1982, pp. 1, 22.

46 Ezra F. Vogel, *Japan as Number One: Lessons for America* (New York, 1979), pp. 204–22; David Bayley, *Forces of Order: Police behavior in Japan and the United States* (Berkeley, 1976).

47 Barbara Crossette, "The opulence of Singapore," *New York Times Magazine*, December 16, 1984, pp. 122–4, 142–8.

48 Roy Hofheinz and Kent E. Calder, *The East Asia Edge* (New York, 1982).

49 Nakane, *Japanese Society*, pp. 144–7.

50 Reischauer, *The Japanese*, p. 237.

51 Yukio Mishima, *After the Banquet* (Tokyo, 1960).

52 Wayne H. Oxford, *The Speeches of Fukuzawa* (Tokyo, 1973), p. 105.

53 Benjamin Barber, *Strong Democracy* (Berkeley, 1984), p. 175.

54 Reischauer, *The Japanese*, pp. 290–5.

55 Donald Shively, "Motoda Eifu: Confucian lecturer to the Meiji emperor," in D. S. Nivison and A. P. Wright (eds), *Confucianism in Action* (Stanford, 1959), pp. 303–33; quotes on pp. 322 and 325.

56 Ralph Ketcham, "Aristotle, Confucius, and Jefferson and the problem of good government," *Journal of East and West Studies* (Yonsei University, Seoul, Korea), vol. XIV, no. 2, fall/winter 1985, pp. 127–42.

CHAPTER 4   INDIVIDUALISM AND
THE PUBLIC INTEREST IN THE 1980s

1 William Lucy, *Observations...of Notorious Errours in Mr Hobbes' His Leviathan* (London, 1663); quoted in Joyce Appleby, *Capitalism and a New Social Order* (New York, 1984), p. 20.
2 Pope, *Dunciad*, book IV, lines 455–6, 477–80.
3 Tocqueville, *Democracy in America* (1835–40), vol. II, part II, chapter 24 (Reeves trans.); pp. 310–11, H. S. Commager (ed.), New York, 1946.
4 C. F. Adams (ed.), *The Works of John Adams*, I (Boston, 1856), p. 319.
5 Tocqueville, *Democracy in America*, pp. 311–18.
6 Solzhenitsyn, interview, *New York Times Book Review*, October 28, 1984, p. 1.
7 Solzhenitsyn, "Address to Harvard graduates," June 8, 1978; as reported in *The Wall Street Journal*, June 9, 1978.
8 David Kolb, "American individualism: does it exist?" in *Nanzan Review of American Studies* (Nagoya, Japan), vol. VI, 1984, pp. 21–3.
9 Aristotle, *Politics*, book VII, chapter 13, 1332a.
10 Jefferson to W. C. Jarvis, September 28, 1820, in Edward Dumbauld (ed.), *The Political Writings of Thomas Jefferson* (Indianapolis, 1955), p. 93.
11 Carter, "Farewell address," *New York Times*, January 15, 1981, II, 10:1.
12 William Sullivan, *Reconstructing Public Philosophy* (Berkeley, 1982), pp. 157–8.
13 Isaac Kramnick, "Republican revisionism revisited," *American Historical Review*, vol. 87, 1982, p. 630.
14 Quoted in Robert Bellah, "Religion and legitimation in the American republic," in T. Robbins and D. Anthony (eds), *In Gods We Trust* (New Brunswick, NJ, 1981), p. 36.
15 Adam Smith, *Theory of Moral Sentiments* (*Works*, I), p. 138, and *Oeuvres politiques de Benjamin Constant* (Paris, 1874), p. 281; quoted in Sheldon Wolin, *Politics and Vision* (New York, 1959), pp. 280–1.
16 Emerson, *Ode Inscribed to W. H. Channing* (1847).
17 Bellah, "Religion and legitimation," p. 40.
18 Reinhold Niebuhr, *Moral Man and Immoral Society* (New York, 1932), p. 263; Sullivan, *Public Philosophy*, p. 218.
19 Ibid., p. 213; emphasis added.

20 Taylor to Jefferson, June 25, 1798; *John P. Branch Historical Papers of Randolph-Macon College*, II (1908), pp. 271–6.

21 Aristotle, *Politics*, book III, chapter 9.

22 Jefferson, *Notes on Virginia* (1784); in A. Koch and W. Peden (eds), *The Life and Selected Writings of Thomas Jefferson* (Modern Library, 1944), p. 280.

23 Joseph Tussman, *Obligation and the Body Politic* (New York, 1960).

24 Ibid., p. 112.

25 Jefferson to Walter Jones, March 31, 1801; H. A. Washington (ed.), *The Works of Thomas Jefferson* (New York, 1884), IV, pp. 392–3.

26 Quoted in Michael Wallace, "Changing conceptions of party in the United States: New York, 1815–28," *American Historical Review*, vol. 74, 1968, p. 489.

27 Message to Congress, September 4, 1837; J. D. Richardson (ed.), *Messages and Papers of the Presidents, 1789–1897* (Washington, DC, 1897), IV, p. 1561.

28 Quoted in S. G. Brown, *The American Presidency. Leadership, partisanship, and popularity* (New York, 1966), p. ii.

29 Edmund Burke, *Thoughts on the Cause of the Present Discontents* (1770), in *The Writings and Speeches of Edmund Burke* (Boston, 1901), I, pp. 482–4.

30 James M. Burns, *Leadership* (New York, 1978), p. 453.

31 Wolin, *Vision and Politics*, pp. 420, 428, 434.

32 Quoted in E. J. Hughes, *The Living Presidency* (New York, 1973), p. 166.

33 Confucius, *Analects*, 2:1, 13:6.

34 Abigail to John Adams, June 20, 1783; L. H. Butterfield (ed.), *The Book of Abigail and John* (Cambridge, Mass., 1975), p. 353.

35 Jefferson to Walter Jones, March 31, 1801, in Washington, *Works of Jefferson*, IV, pp. 392–3; and to Garland Jefferson, January 25, 1810, in P. L. Ford (ed.), *The Writings of Thomas Jefferson* (New York, 1897), IX, p. 270.

36 Jefferson to William Duane, March 22, 1806, and M. Barnabas, July 5, 1806, in Noble Cunningham, *The Process of Government under Jefferson* (Princeton, 1978), pp. 193, 189.

37 R. Ketcham, *Presidents above Party: The first American presidency, 1789–1829* (Chapel Hill, 1984), especially part II.

38 Yonung Kwŏn, "The Royal Lecture and Confucian Politics in Early Yi Korea," *Korean Studies* (East-West Center, Honolulu), VI (1982), 41–62.

39 Thorstein Veblen, "The independent farmer" (1923), in Max Lerner (ed.), *The Portable Veblen* (New York, 1950), p. 400.

40 J. M. Burns, *Leadership*, pp. 257–8.

41 Balfour, introduction to Walter Bagehot, *The English Constitution* (Oxford University Press reprint, 1982), p. xxiv; emphasis added.

42 Letter from P. M. Williams, May 22, 1984; Edmund Burke, "Speech

to the Electors of Bristol...," November 3, 1774; in *Writings of Burke*, II, p. 96.

43 John Dewey, *Liberalism and Social Action* (New York, 1935), p. 27.

44 Robert Dahl, *A Preface to Democratic Theory* (Chicago, 1956), p. 132.

45 William E. Connolly (ed.), *The Bias of Pluralism* (New York, 1969); R. P. Wolff, "Beyond tolerance," in *A Critique of Pure Tolerance* (Boston, 1965); Theodore Lowi, *The End of Liberalism* (New York, 1969); Henry Kariel, *The Decline of American Pluralism* (Stanford, 1961); and Benjamin Barber, *Strong Democracy* (Berkeley, 1984) provide a fair sampling of the huge critical literature.

46 H. J. Storing (ed.), *Essays on the Scientific Study of Politics* (New York, 1961), p. 327.

47 *W. Va. Board of Education* v. *Barnette*, 319 US, 638 (1943).

48 Wolff, "Beyond tolerance," pp. 46–51.

49 Jane Mansbridge, *Beyond Adversarial Democracy* (New York, 1980), p. 18.

50 Ibid., pp. 8–10.

51 Barber, *Strong Democracy*, p. 175.

52 Mark Kishlansky, "The emergence of adversarial politics in the Long Parliament," *Journal of Modern History*, vol. 49, 1977, pp. 617–40.

53 Rousseau, *Social Contract* (1762), book IV, part I, using both Barker (New York, 1960) and G. D. H. Cole (New York, 1950) translations.

54 Barber, *Strong Democracy*, pp. 267–73, 281–9.

55 *Federalist Paper* no. 62.

56 The account of the Law of the Sea Conferences is based largely on William Wertenbaker, "The Law of the Sea Treaty," *The New Yorker*, August 7 and 14, 1983.

57 Barber, *Strong Democracy*, pp. 184–5.

58 Locke, *Second Treatise on Civil Government*, chapter IX, paragraphs 123–4.

59 Walter Lippmann, *The Public Philosophy* (New York, 1955), pp. 15–16.

60 R. R. Palmer, *The Age of Democratic Revolution: The challenge* (Princeton, 1959), especially pp. 239–468.

61 R. Ketcham, *From Independence to Interdependence* (Aspen Institute, 1975).

Index

Index by Moira Greenhalgh